SOM journal 7

HATJE CANTZ

In memory of
Detlef Mertins

Contents

7	Size, Scale, and Atmosphere Juhani Pallasmaa	117	Hundred-Year Vision for the Great Lakes and St. Lawrence River Region
11	SOM Journal 7 Jury Report Luis Fernández-Galiano	127	SOM Research
15	Juror Essays Rita McBride Peter MacKeith Erik Olsen Joan Ockman	141	Beyond Tall: Issues of Scale and the Evolution of Tall Buildings at SOM William F. Baker
		149	The Integration of Emergence and Flow: Combining Forces from the Ground Up Mark Sarkisian
30	SOM Journal 7 Submissions		
33	The Chongqing River Tower Chongqing, China	153	Notes on the Articulation of Highrise Form, 1896–2003 Kenneth Frampton
47	John Jay College of Criminal Justice New York, New York	169	The Skyscraper Problem Thomas A. P. van Leeuwen
61	Lotte World 2 Seoul, South Korea	177	How the Leopard Got Its Spots: Lever House as a Skyscraper Nicholas Adams
77	Project Floyd Geneva, Switzerland	191	The Seagram Building: Thoughts on Context Nicholas Adams
93	PSAC II The Bronx, New York	196	Biographies
105	High Performance Building Enclosures A Cross Section of Curtain Walls	202	Project Credits

Size, Scale, and Atmosphere
Juhani Pallasmaa

The worldwide reputation of SOM is based on the more than ten thousand buildings designed by the firm around the world since 1936, when it was founded. The image of SOM in professional circles focuses on a number of experimental and pioneering buildings of various functions and scale. Many of these buildings are an indisputable part of the established history of modern architecture. The list of SOM projects seems to contain all imaginable design tasks: headquarters of banks, insurance companies, and international corporations; art galleries and libraries; military academies, airports, and airplane hangars; stadia and industrial plants; bridges and other special structures, such as a solar telescope. The list of projects also includes numerous residential developments and large-scale planning schemes.

Yet, SOM is publicly best known for its groundbreaking highrise buildings, built around the globe, some of them among the highest buildings ever constructed. Regardless of the significance of the tall building as an architectural type in the SOM oeuvre, as well as for the public and professional reputation of the firm, the juries of the SOM *Journal* have not often accepted tall buildings among the selected projects. This fact, no doubt, reflects the preference of the individual juries for projects in smaller scale and of less domineering role, but also the inherent problems in the design of this specific building type.

The current Editorial Board discussed this evident disproportion and decided to dedicate *Journal* 7 to the special issues, functional and technical requirements, challenges, and expressive potentials of the tall building. The ongoing competition for the tallest structures ever conceived or built undoubtedly reveals a desire for fame, visibility, and dominance among the clients.

The essays in this edition of the *Journal* are engaged in aspects of the design of the tall building. Excerpts from Thomas van Leeuwen's book *The Skyward Trend of Thought: The Metaphysics of the American Skyscraper* reveal the metaphysical and mythical aspects behind the story of the skyscraper. Kenneth Frampton surveys the architectural and aesthetic evolution of this building type, which originated in America, and—regardless of their geography—skyscrapers still carry echoes of their American origins. His essay analyzes the evolution of the characteristic architectural themes of tall buildings which are still often associated with symbolic, mythical, and heroic connotations.

Nicholas Adams continues his series of surveys of historical SOM masterpieces. In this issue, he presents the story of the legendary Lever House as seen from a somewhat unexpected viewpoint: the forceful and skillful public relations and marketing operations that accompanied the visionary design and construction of this landmark building.

Adams also introduces Mies van der Rohe's Seagram Building—regarded by many as the apex of modern highrise buildings—and the surprisingly successful contexual dialogue with its neighbor across Park Avenue, the Racquet and Tennis Club.

William F. Baker and Mark Sarkisian explore the structural, functional, technical, and economic logic of tall buildings. Baker introduces the structural thinking of Myron Goldsmith and Fazlur Khan in the SOM practice, and points out the internal criteria and limits arising from the various realities of construction and the essence of constructional scale. He even suggests that Frank Lloyd Wright's legendary 1956 proposal for a Mile High Tower in Chicago would not have been realistic due to its conflicting aspects regarding the internal logic of super-high towers.

Sarkisian's short and somewhat polemical piece introduces theoretical structural ideas arising from emergence theory as applied to the highrise structures of today. Novel theoretical concepts of structures, augmented by today's computerized technologies of simulating, modeling, and calculating complex structural behaviors will produce unforeseen highrise structures in the near future. The ever-rising demands for the sustainability of the construction and use of structures will undoubtedly speed up development even in this specific category of architecture. Today's sculptural and dynamically shaped towers, often seeking an eye-catching visual above structural advantage, suggest new typologies for tall buildings. Inclusion of energy production by means of sun and/or wind forces, as well as protection from excessive heat and solar radiation, provide additional parameters for novel forms beyond mere aesthetics.

Tall buildings tend to evoke our awe but they have rarely the capacity to convey experiences of sensuality, nearness, and intimacy. Highrise towers are designed as singular objects rather than settings or milieus, and we remain external observers rather than participants in relation to them. As objects of distant visual observation, they most often fail to address our sense of the body and other senses but vision, and rarely create an atmosphere, or emotive presence. True enough, today's grand towers are often entire vertical cities, internalized worlds, but they fail to represent the complexities and serendipities of human interaction and collective life within.

As William Baker shows, tall buildings have their internal logic of use, structure, and economy, but regardless of their sheer size they also have to deal with the human experiential scale. We measure our surroundings through the unconscious projection of our bodies, and this automatic embodied dialogue either finds a resonance in the setting, or it does not; and we either feel rejected or welcomed. Meaningful architectural entities always mediate between the intimate and the monumental, the huge and the minute, near and the distant, through a sequence of scaling devices that facilitates the understanding of sizes and scales in relation to our own body and its factual or imaginary realms of action. This perceptual fact applies to the Pyramids of Giza, the Temple of Karnak, Gothic cathedrals, as well as other gigantic structures being constructed today, from bridges to power plants and skyscrapers. Buildings are also unavoidably in a dialogue with their settings; profound buildings always collaborate with their contexts, and they make even disorder or incompatible existing elements appear as meaningful parts of the overall landscape. To give new meaning and dignity to the setting is the ethical task of buildings.

As architects, we tend to think of our design work and its results in rational and conscious terms, and architectural projects are usually conceived and assessed in terms of form, space, structure, proportion, materiality, color, and light, i.e. their conceptual, cognitive, and perceptual aspects. Yet, it seems that the emotional impact of landscapes, cityscapes, settings, buildings, and interior spaces arises predominantly from unspecified and immaterial characteristics that create an atmosphere, ambience, or mood of the place. This architectural atmosphere arises more from unconscious and peripheral perceptions than a conscious and focused encounter. Gabriele d'Annunzio (1863–1938), the Italian poet, makes a thought-provoking suggestion: "The richest experiences happen long before the soul takes notice. And when we begin to open our eyes to the visible, we have already been supporters of the invisible for a long time."[1] The poet points out the importance of our unconscious, comprehensive, and multi-sensory grasp of complex entities. Yet, as designers we are rarely consciously aware of, or concerned about, the atmospheric characteristics of our work. In the case of the tall building, the unavoidable consequences about superhuman scale, distance, and implied outsideness, impoverish the encounter, and eliminate the possibility of creating an engaging overall atmosphere beyond the sublime experience of awe. This experience of outsideness promotes a sense of loneliness and alienation rather than of belonging.

Yet, many of the early skyscrapers manage to evoke an atmospheric experience through engaging materiality, surface relief, abundant detailing and ornamentation, and, most importantly, the articulation of scale and proportion allows us to project ourselves on the immense volume and, consequently, assimilate it. The sensation of human insignificance in relation to the Karnak Temple is eventually positively humbling and life enhancing. No wonder Louis Kahn found inspiration for the Parliament Building in Dhaka, Bangladesh, in the structures of this superhumanly scaled temple.

The projects published in *SOM Journal* 7 were again selected by an outside jury appointed by the Editorial Board. The jury, which met in the Four Seasons Restaurant in the Seagram Building, in New York, made its decisions and choices completely independently. The jury consisted of five members: Luis Fernández-Galiano, who acted as the chairman, and Joan Ockman, Rita McBride, Peter MacKeith, and Erik Olsen as members. Two members of the Editorial Board, Kenneth Frampton and Juhani Pallasmaa, participated in the jury discussions but did not actively participate in the final selection of projects.

As previously in *Journals* 5 and 6, the jury members were invited to write their personal reports of the evaluation and selection process or the submitted and/or selected projects. They were instructed to choose their points of view, as well as their scholarly approach, freely. It has become evident that the jury process needs to be somewhat developed in the future. The reviewed projects are often the collective work of many architects and other professionals, sometimes over the course of several years, whereas the jury encounters the projects through drawings and photographs only for a very limited time. The essence of large and complex projects and planning schemes is in the danger of being bypassed or aestheticized in the limited time available for jury conversations regardless of a preceding personal familiarization with the submitted material.

SOM Journal 8 will be conceived and edited by a new editorial team, and the work selected by a new jury. Theirs will be a new conception of the *Journal*'s contents, as well as the methods of its production.

1 Gabriele d'Annunzio, *Contemplazioni della morte* (Milan, 1912), pp. 17–18. As quoted in Gaston Bachelard, *Water and Dreams: An Essay on the Imagination of Matter* (Dallas, 1983), p. 16.

 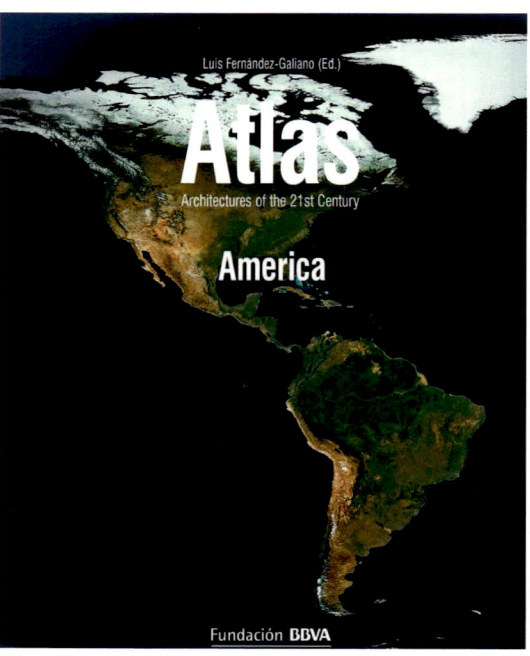

AV Monographs, no. 144; *Atlas on Architecture in America,* for the Fundación BBVA

SOM Journal 7 Jury Report
The Wisdom of Crowds
Luis Fernández-Galiano

Architects love and hate crowds. They love crowds because architecture belongs to the public realm, is enjoyed or suffered by many, and is designed and built by large teams of professionals. But they also hate crowds because great buildings are attributed to individual authors and supported by visionary clients, often struggling against the mainstream to change the rules of the game. If you live in a democracy, to believe in the wisdom of crowds is *de rigeur,* however many architectural masterworks were the product of despotism, and however bland the result of architectural competitions judged by a popular vote may be. Pace the worn alibi of Rockefeller Center, the old joke that describes a camel as a horse designed by a committee expresses well the uneasiness of the relationship between the individual and the collective in the field of design.

In the juries assembled by SOM to assess the work of the office, a small crowd is asked to select a group of projects among the many carried out by a larger crowd, the workforce of the partnership. Although projects have indeed design architects, and although the selection is later honed by an editor, the fact remains that a committee rather than a single curator is expected to deliver a meaningful choice of projects—with no names attached, and therefore considered as a product of the work of teams. This haphazard method is bound to deliver more camels than horses, but I am happy to say the 2010 jury was lucky enough to concoct a selection of projects that reveals the strengths of the firm while throwing light on the state of the world, and therefore invites us to believe in the wisdom of crowds.

Starting in Europe, a trip that is both geographical and typological, Project Floyd in Geneva shows the excellence that can be reached dealing with the conventional. A corporate headquarters in a prime site of a cosmopolitan European city, the design manages to join the urbanity required in this genteel town with a subdued iconic character, while providing very efficient and comfortable office space, threaded by an internal promenade—from the atrium lobby to the roof terrace—that facilitates horizontal and vertical connection between departments, blurring physical barriers to promote social interaction. In the same spirit, the gently folded shape of the building opens up the internal garden to the nearby parks, softening its crisp geometry with careful landscaping that is extended to the green and brown roof—one of the many environmentally-conscious features. Supported by an elegant structure of tubular box frames, and clad with a quilted façade that provides some shading while allowing panoramic views, the building sits lightly on the ground, showing the persistent ability of modernity to give shape to predictable programs with geometry and construction, and also the resilient capacity of its language to reconcile urban awareness and corporate values.

Crossing the Atlantic, the Public Safety Answering Center II in New York is both a haunting portrait of our time and a very professional response to an unusual program. Sparked by the attacks of 9/11, the new 911 Call Center is a cubic fortress located in stark isolation in a large green site in The Bronx, a hermetic volume rested among parkways that hopes to relieve public anxieties in the face of emergencies, and bolster a badly shattered collective confidence. Serving the five boroughs, and staffed by the police and fire departments, this defensible, blast-secure office building is clad in aluminum, with a serrated façade that only leaves very narrow slits to liven up the interior spaces with natural light—an inevitable result of its security demands, and partly compensated by SOM-designed interior green columns that bring the relief of plants to what can be a stressful workplace. Fascinating in the complexity of its services—many of which are duplicated for safety—this "dumb box" avoids the connotations of the predictable underground bunker and raises its anonymous grey volume in an open landscaped site, mildly reassuring in its oblique, elusive, trivial presence.

Always in New York, Manhattan's John Jay College of Criminal Justice is an extremely urban project for an

Jury assembled at the Four Seasons Restaurant in the Seagram Building: Juhani Pallasmaa, Peter MacKeith, Luis Fernández-Galiano, Rita McBride, Joan Ockman, Kenneth Frampton, Erik Olsen

institution whose very growth is perhaps a dismal sign of the troubled state of cities, where social crisis has fuelled the demand for the legal professions. With the purpose of more than doubling the size of its current facilities, the college proposed an extension in two phases to complete a campus that will occupy a whole city block, and the strategic intelligence of the architects suggested starting with the far end of the block, "taking it" with a vertical volume and leaving a low horizontal podium in between, thereby framing an outdoor commons that will be "interiorized" in a later stage. The academic complex is bifurcated by an internal street that cascades through the plinth connecting classrooms, social facilities, and gathering spaces, and offering students and faculty a space for interaction that also reinforces the identity of the institution. Sober and restrained in its civic presence, clearly articulated in its uses, and crisply argued in its strategy, the project is a show piece on how the right program can inject urbanity and sociability in the most compact metropolitan site.

Leaving America for Asia, the Lotte Tower in Seoul has been designed to be the second tallest building in the world, and what is more, a proud member of a SOM family of structurally innovative highrises that holds Chicago's John Hancock Building and Willis (formerly Sears) Tower as revered icons. Rather than a symbol of the economic might of the Pacific Rim, and deliberately devoid of conventional figuration—Eastern or otherwise—the tower is a fine exercise in structural and functional optimization, tapering to accommodate the different surface demands of the usual retail-office-hotel stack, and transforming the square base into a circular top to enhance the views from the observation deck. The diagrid structure allows a faceted, all-flat curtain wall system that simplifies construction and collaborates with the tapered shape to reduce wind loads, while the cleverly designed core reconciles structural efficiency and functional flexibility to service the different stacked uses. Although located in South Korea, this is a truly generic highrise that shows the stubborn persistence of type, structure, and geometry as tools for architectural design.

Our itinerary ends in China with another mixed-use highrise, but one in which structure defers to module as an organizing principle. The Chongqing River Tower is not as tall as the Lotte—three-hundred meters versus five-hundred-fifty-five—and this circumstance allows structure to play a subordinate role, giving all protagonism to a modular framework that accommodates the different programs—offices, hotel, and residential—stacked on top of a retail podium. A six-meter module is employed to undertake a regular but random eroding of the forty-eight-meter-square-plan tower as it goes up, giving it an iconic, memorable character while diminishing the floor plate to adapt to the uses, while an open void in the structural core brings light and air into the footprint in the residential part of the tower and permits a dramatic skylight in this hotel lobby. The subtle combination of elementary geometry and choreographed variety makes the highrise a very refined urban landmark, where the dialogue between structure and façade—with details like a column-free perimeter in the residential section to maximize views, and perimeter columns in the offices to ensure flexibility—accommodates the needs of the diverse uses and at the same time respects the formal integrity of this fascinating object, a pierced crystalline prism.

Last but not least, the jury highlighted three outstanding examples of the research work of SOM: the structural and topological investigation into Michell frames and surface or shape optimization using genetic algorithms, following a distinguished in-house tradition; the applied research and development of high-performance building enclosures, pedagogically explained with a very revealing sequence of five examples in China, the US, the Gulf, and the Great Lakes and St. Lawrence River Region. This latter is a comprehensive plan launched by SOM, which—one-hundred years after the Plan of Chicago—identifies the eight main issues facing the region and proposes eight pieces of policy to shape a consistent vision that may guide the next one-hundred years, showing the civic leadership and environmental awareness fitting for a firm that is part of the history of Chicago, and hopes to also be part of its future. If the wisdom of crowds is able to detect the forces that shape the world we live in, this is probably the direction we should look toward.

Rita McBride, *Mae West*, Munich

Imaginary Transcript Excerpt
SOM Journal Jury, November 12, 2010
Rita McBride

Ada Louise Huxtable impersonated by Rita McBride
Herbert Muschamp channeled by Rita McBride

Project 23: The New School University Center

ALH I am surprised by the brass-clad façade proposed for this building. It is unexpected and not entirely unpleasant, but rather not really in a vocabulary I can muster some support for. It could be beautiful, but for me brass carries more the vernacular of India than Ladies Mile.

HM Maybe it has something to do with the fire stairs. You know fireman and brass poles. Up and down. In and out. Vertical campuses need chance encounters . . . and not only on elevators.

ALH Smooth sliding circulation where Harry can meet Sally and *Love Story* begins . . .

HM Or where Clive transcends class and embraces Maurice.

ALH No seriously, how does this work? Is this really new stair topology?

HM It's egress meeting communication with added access points. And the egress stair is not alarmed in the classrooms!

ALH What, no bells and whistles? No fire drills through rare routes? Revolutionary!

HM I don't know if it is revolutionary, but it is reinvention. There is an efficiency that I admire about it. And also that the façade truss becomes a support for the stairs, but I don't know if I am ready for the geometry of the exterior façades to be determined from code structures for fire stairs.

ALH Can we really start predicating design decisions on fire codes? I guess so, why not? Codes do to a large extent define how buildings look so why not expose that? But it is hard to celebrate. Maybe that is just some prejudice we have, something architects have struggled with and prefer to ignore as a necessary evil. Not really something to embrace.

HM I don't know if that is what is happening, in fact. It isn't exactly embracing the codes just using them. The proposal is so fragmented it's hard to really get the whole. I mean, the fragments, the attention to all these features, is impressive and I am sure capable decision making, but how does this project find the terminology to excite. It isn't exactly a beauty even in the burlesque sense. The proposal is lacking a story line. It needs a hot story line. I would have died to be a fly on the wall at all those consensus building meetings between SOM, fire engineers, and the New York City Department of Buildings! Bet that was fiery!

ALH So this really isn't just another big gross building in Manhattan! I can get behind this thinking. Bucking the efficiencies of a program finding another way through the muck of huge footprints and dollar bottom lines.

HM But is it just another feature or is it really more?

ALH It is leveling to have the proposal cover so many bases—like the green campus feature. I am dubious about what claims are being made here but I am no expert—just that we have seen every project proclaim its greenness today and I have a hard time believing that a big gross building can be green.

HM This proposal would do better not trying to be such a good student. It should take some lessons from Lady Gaga. Play hooky and get an "F" for once!

ALH Story first then the brass tacks? I mean the daily fires architects have to put out can really leave them panting, asking Where do I begin? again and again? It's like the Stockholm syndrome, identifying with the captor—the captor here being process. But actually this project has a strong arm somewhere, but it isn't visible in the proposal.

Project 24: PSAC II—Public Safety Answering Center II

HM Look at this drawing!

ALH Yes, it is frightening isn't it?

HM What am I looking at?

ALH It's a "modern castle." And down here it says "the pure cube form offers flexibility and efficient planning for the functional demands of the workplace within. Internal spatial qualities of the free section and multi-story spaces reflect the cube design work of Le Corbusier and W. Gropius."

HM [Speechless]

ALH Somebody, call 911!

HM With all due respect for those who have given their lives in the line of duty at Ground Zero, I must really ask if this is the monument we want to make in their name. This is a project for Ground Zero, not the Bronx. I find it hard to believe that this is not purely cynical.

ALH Next year it will be an empty monument when the police and fire departments get their hands on the latest and greatest technology. Can this cube be retrofited? Or will it just hunker down on the Hudson for an eternity. I find it hard to believe as an office, a place where individuals go to work. Why not bury this building? There is no life in that 50,000-square-foot of core anyway.

HM Exactly my point! It is a monument to all that we have lost in our society. There isn't even any fantasy here. Gropius and Corbu are turning in their graves! No vision!

ALH If I accept the function for this building—the fact that it "looks the way it does" because of its function to provide "reliable continuous service" by top brass in the case of complete mayhem—I still cannot believe that this kind of design will serve that function. It is not flexible and, like a bunker, it will not protect us because we cannot see our enemy. If we can make this kind of building then we really do not see anything.

HM We see a portrait of society. This drawing is a portrait of fear.

ALH That's depressing. I refuse this line of thinking. Architecture is ultimate power.

HM I think this is the first example of architecture-designed-by-TV-miniseries, it's the fourth season of *24*, except the plan shows no special rooms for interrogation, what if some of the employees suspect other employees of treason? Where will they interrogate?

ALH My word, you are right! It is the architectural embodiment of the Jack Bauer credo "ends justify the means."

HM Also, no parking facilities for the fleet of black SUVs, no helipad, and no bathroom or break rooms for the rooftop snipers. Snipers are people too, you know! They have needs.

ALH The architects have clearly not done enough research about fortification design. I notice they have also completely forgotten to include any secret passageways. Secret passageways have always been a vital part of castle design.

HM I heard that a company in California is developing a hummingbird-sized surveillance drone for the US Army. It looks like a cute little hummingbird and has the same wing movement that allows it to remain stationary in the air while it videotapes potential miscreants and reprobates.

ALH Interesting! a perfect example of how shortsighted this actually is. Where will the little hummingbird drones rest between missions? At least they could have incorporated some fake trees with little recharging plugs into the site plan.

HM Did you know that the Fox network is starting their own architecture firm? And did you hear that this year the Emmy Awards will initiate a special Emmy for best TV architectural urban plan?

ALH Typical scenario: architects racing against the clock to thwart multiple terrorist plots, including presidential assassination attempts, nuclear, biological, and chemical threats, cyber attacks, as well as conspiracies dealing with massive corporate corruption.

HM Is that it?

Rita McBride, *Mae West*, Munich

 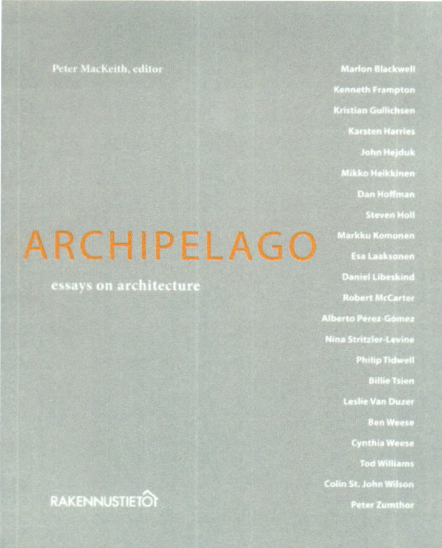

The Finland Pavilions: Finland at the Universal Expositions 1900–1992 (Helsinki, 1992) *Archipelago, Essays of Architecture* (Helsinki, 2006)

The Educational Moment
Two Generational Parables
Peter MacKeith

During the 1980s—a generation and two recessions ago, a succession of tragedies endured—a parable in common circulation in certain American schools of architecture concerned the number of well-educated (insert Harvard, Yale, Princeton, Columbia—or simply thirty-thousand-dollars-per-year-tuition) intern-architects in (insert New York City, Chicago, Philadelphia, San Francisco) devoting their days to compressing their newly-gained architectural intelligence, aesthetic judgment, and technical expertise into the outermost twelve of developer-commissioned commercial tower designs—center-city speculative ventures in optimum FARs and permutations of tinted, striated curtain walls, culminating in a charismatic crown. With any spare moments, the parable held, these same intern-architects conceptualized and detailed urban kitchens, bathrooms, and walk-in closets with the same intensity of "architecture or revolution" ambition as Le Corbusier, and the same intensity of focus as Swiss watchmakers. Expensive educations in history, principles, form, space, light, and materials were being collapsed into miniature interior monuments, or laminated into curtain walls of passing distinction. The moral of the story: this was the future; careers and reputations would be made, if not student loans repaid, by virtue of these miniature indulgences. The knowing student-architect should prepare accordingly.

A generation later, architecture students arriving into the profession may live in more interesting times, to paraphrase the all-too-appropriate, but only purportedly, Chinese proverb. To judge by the spectrum of the twenty-nine SOM projects submitted for review and possible inclusion in *SOM Journal* 7, the scale, locales, calibrations, and character of professional work emphasized in the contemporary parable have changed dramatically. Where once master-planning considered New York's Battery Park and London's Docklands, now the young professional must acclimate (geographically and linguistically) to Beijing's Central Business District—but also to that of Tianjin and Hongqiao, as well. The center-city sixty-story commercial highrises of a generation ago have been succeeded by the (on average) eighty stories proposed for the Al Hamra Firdous, the Digital Media Seoul Light Tower, the Lotte World 2, the Chongqing River Tower. In fact, the utter emphasis on urban design and master-planning dominates the spectrum reviewed: new city districts to be overlaid onto two-thousand-year-old urban centers, thirty-story cities rising from the demolition of eight-story cities, wholly new cities emerging from deserts, lakefronts, harbors.

Dreamlike, as if from another era entirely and certainly against the run of education, the urban housing commission has returned to the drawing boards . . . er, monitors—only now in a multitude of guises and cultural patterns: luxury, vertical, mixed-use, lowrise; in London, India, Singapore. The public building—be it library, courthouse, school, city hall, theater, museum—that locus of civic stability, the object of architectural education's desire—is most present by its near absence in the design work presented, save for an athletic arena, a college of criminal justice, and a university center. Indeed, the idea of the "public" is found most clearly (and most gravely) in the well-executed designs for a Public Safety Answering Center, a building for the protection of the people, but secured against the intrusions of the people, all too finely delineating the confines of civic engagement in a post-9/11 world. That world, too, by this survey, appears to be one of fading postwar monuments in need of renovation, even rejuvenation: the UN Headquarters, the Jefferson National Expansion Memorial (also known as The Gateway Arch), the Air Force Academy. In this context, the moral of the story is even clearer: the knowing student now prepares for the realities of immense number and need, for scale and security, alongside of necessary cultural diversity and sustainability, possessed as much by trepidation as by thrill in the face of such sublime commissions.

A Landscape of More

This altered professional landscape of design can only reposition the perspectives afforded by the academic design studio—a shift altogether to a landscape of "more": a larger, more international world, a more urbanized world, more densely populated, a more resource-challenged world shrouded in an expanding information cloud, a politicized world of deepened economic austerity.

To be sure, in the survey of these SOM projects, both the digital and the environmental paradigm shifts in education and practice are notably visible; skillful, compelling presentations of work *and* conscientious attention to environmental responsiveness and responsibility are present in equal measure. These are very much on the agenda of architectural education; any accredited program must by definition provide resources and instruction to these ends—indeed, in an unholy arms race of technology, many schools define their very identity by the number, size, and speed of their processors, laser cutters, and 3D printers; others will just as proudly, even evangelistically, proclaim their allegiance to the one true faith of sustainability. On both counts, the "landscape of more" is at least being surveyed from within education, in introductory preparation for the demands of practice. Interestingly, the growing convergence of the digital and the environmental approaches in education only highlights the central relevance of lived experience to both practices: successful REVIT-based design relies upon a thorough knowledge of materials and construction, productive ECOTEK-based design relies just as much upon a thorough appreciation of sun, wind, and rain.

To SOM's credit, the emphasis on, and support of, independent research initiatives—structural innovation, building enclosures and energy-efficient façade systems in this survey—continues an admirable tradition with new purposefulness. As well, these initiatives continue to indicate that directed research from within professional practice continues to outstrip research in architecture undertaken from within the university. This imbalance may yet shift, as university administrations press their schools of architecture to develop funded research programs, and as support arrives (up until recently) from the United States government stimulus funds, but practice-based research—as denoted in the SOM submissions, and focused mainly on building technologies—is still largely responsible for mapping the current landscape of design research. The SOM research initiatives suggest that significant partnerships between practice and the academy could yield greater benefits to both parties; this would be a productive, collaborative shift.

Notable, too, is the prioritization of analysis-driven design decisions: the ruthlessly pursued logics of program and site, in particular, definitively characterize the front-end of the SOM project presentations; in a post-theory world, it seems, pragmatism, allied with a cool-headed rationalism, clearly holds sway—or perhaps the methodology of analysis has become its own theory of design, a process assumed to lead inexorably to a more perfect and unique resultant monotype. This method has its antecedents in the quantitative rationalism of early modernist architectural thought, as well as in the emphasis on diagram and program that characterized the nineteen-sixties and nineteen-seventies, but the current default to the graphing of activities through time and the diagramming of program functions, reflexively followed by the awkward stacking of colored and labeled program blocks, interwoven with a counter-intuitive movement pattern, owes its tooling to a more contemporary Dutch method, transmitted through oversize books and provocative competition entries. These approaches, while aimed at the issues of scale, size and number (think: L, XL, BIG) are due for critique, both within education and within practice.

Immediate Responsibilities

But the evident shift is not in the design tools, fluid though the resulting forms may be, nor in the evidence of environmental concerns, responsible and consoling as those ambitions might be, nor in the productive explorations of innovative research, nor even in the powerfully modeled analytics, as thorough and compelling as the data might be. The paradigm shift more evident is, in fact, in what is missing—in what is "less" present or available in this architectural survey—and here, the instructive finger must be more fully pointed at architectural education itself, ahead of assigning full and immediate responsibility to the culture of practice. Here, the needs can only be sketched with the broadest of pens, but as described above, would certainly include a greater insistence on a direct knowledge and appreciation of materials and construction in design, a more productive set of design research partnerships with practice, and a more thoughtful critique of design methods—leading to advocacy of more diverse design methods.

But these are perhaps critiques in a minor key; the enormity of the urban, landscape, and building design tasks demonstrated within the SOM survey reveals the desperate need for more fully prepared architects—prepared to work across the range of design scales—perhaps particularly at the scale of the city—prepared to work with greater cultural awareness and greater historical sensibility, indeed prepared to work more cross-culturally and collaboratively, and still on the most intimate, focused, and material of terms. SOM, through this juried review of projects, and through this journal of history, theory, and criticism, demonstrates an encouraging commitment to understanding its own trajectory in this landscape of "more," as well as to contributing positively to the intellectual depth of the discipline. Architecture education must respond accordingly—our students must respond accordingly—to this landscape of "more," to these immediate responsibilities, with a new parable: that of the engaged architect, possessed of expanded sensibilities and extraordinary sensitivities. Interesting times, indeed.

The Wintergarden at Manitoba Hydro Place, by Transsolar

Client Blind Spots
Erik Olsen

As I began this essay I turned to SOM Journal 5 for a sense of both how journal submissions have evolved and the thoughts of a previous jury.

I was immediately struck by Juhani Pallasmaa's sentiment that a truly sustainable architecture unavoidably implies "new architectural ethics and aesthetics," which he reinforced with many themes that have become familiar in the drumbeat of sustainable design. This view was restated by most jury members—the jury report laments a lack of "serious commitment to environmental sustainability."

Unfortunately, the submissions and selections for Journal 7, on the whole, do not reflect a sudden evolution toward integration of deeply sustainable thinking. As has become industry standard, most projects include some technology-based measures toward energy efficiency, inevitably include a surplus of hyperbolic language describing sustainable gadgets, and occasionally swing into near-gimmickry. Others take admirable and well-considered first steps toward an "ethic and aesthetic," incorporating sustainability at its roots, but either are not yet sufficiently developed or are simply too simplistic to have been selected by the jury (in this author's view).

Pallasmaa also discussed the role of the client in determining "the final quality of the project." This holds true for sustainability. Although clients increasingly demand sustainable projects as defined by any of the many competing rating systems, they rarely demand the deeply integrated approach which cannot be measured by a rating system. In fact, a truly integrated approach often results in new programming relationships, construction methods, or even comfort expectations which remain "too extreme" for many clients.

For large firms, this problem is compounded by the fact that many—not all—commissions are for large projects and large clients, or smaller but more conservative clients. In our own practice we are familiar with the challenge of reminding such clients that architecture must not only be about delivering a required program, but also creating space which is, at a minimum, humane. Humanity—not technology—as the core of sustainability is often overlooked by these clients. I am especially struck by the fact that the projects I wish to recognize are both located in Asia. Although this may partly be a result of the volume of SOM's work in Asia, I also fear that American clients maintain an exceptional blind spot for the need for humanity in architecture.

Many trends, visible in some of the projects included here and others submitted, demonstrate this blind spot. Although urban responses and interior social spaces are increasingly well-considered, they often remain coupled with deep floor plates which limit access to the façade and daylight, and in some cases provide a questionable masking of the functions within. Where such programmatic opacity is required, the provision of daylight is rejected by the client rather than exploring design possibilities. In both instances, technology is then used as an inadequate substitute for what might have been solved by design. In other cases, heavy reliance on building systems is used in locations which are surrounded by precedents of humane design with limited technological intervention, mostly in the façade.

Based on these examples, this client-driven blind spot appears to avoid recognizing that both basic massing and façade design must work together to create humane space. Two projects in this Journal show potential for meeting this challenge for large-scale projects. Also worth noting is that both projects avoid an excess of sustainability claims relating to systems technology, instead focusing on rational, performance-based design.

Chongqing River Tower demonstrates the emergence of complexity from simplicity with a novel, yet rational, tower form. The shallow floor plans created by the tube design of the residential floors should admit abundant daylight (albeit primarily from the perimeter façade), and the design of penetrations in this tube has been carefully considered to provide natural ventilation—a consideration still rarely seen in tall buildings. The large-scale façade variation and use of terraces introduces a human scale into the traditionally monolithic tower.

Lotte Tower appears even less developed and provides essentially no information on a sustainability approach. However, the overall structural and massing approach is refreshingly rational and performance-based and contrasts sharply with today's trend of purely form-driven towers. As with Chongqing, further development of the façade to provide a humane indoor environment (rather than a sealed crystal palace) appears within reach of the design team.

The opportunity for innovation is most clearly shown in the research projects selected by the jury. SOM's commitment to research is valuable to the entire design community, whether by wholly internal initiatives or cooperative projects such as the Center for Architecture, Science, and Ecology. The capability and enthusiasm for integrated sustainability is present—the challenge remains finding the great client, or better yet, finding a path to transform any client into a great client.

Manitoba Hydro Place: operable vents on the biodynamic double façade, by Transsolar

The Wintergarden, looking south, at Manitoba Hydro Palace, by Transsolar

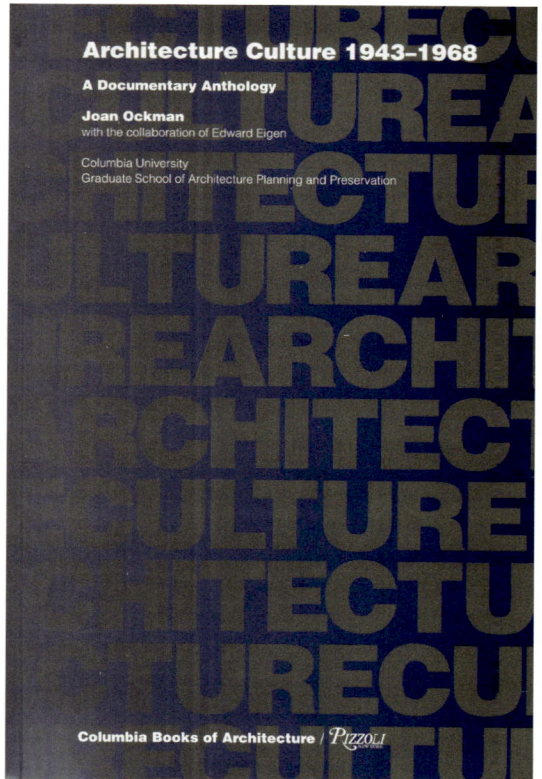 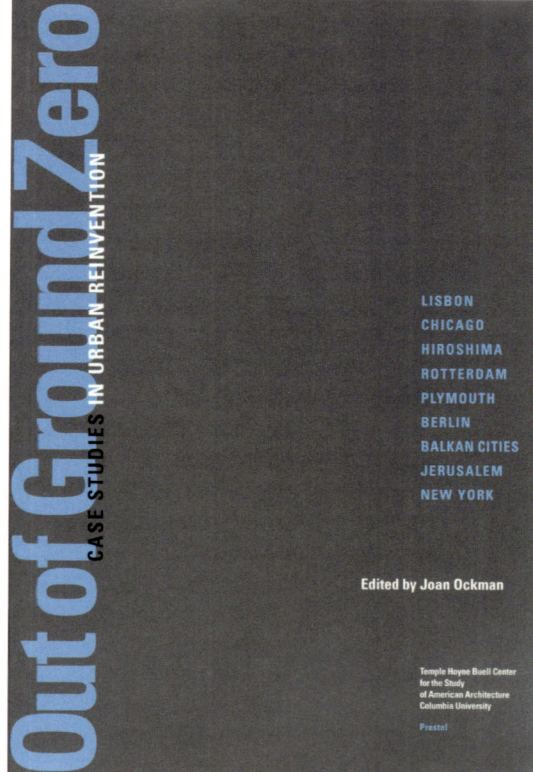

Architecture Culture 1943–1968 (New York, 1993); *Out of Ground Zero, Case Studies in Urban Reinvention* (New York, 2002)

Beyond Image
Joan Ockman

Surprising as it may seem to those who predicted that the apocalyptic events of September 2001 would have a chilling effect on skyscraper construction, those events now seem a blip in the ever-upward history of the tall building, at least to judge from SOM's practice one decade later. Of the twenty-nine projects submitted to last year's interoffice competition, twelve were for buildings above forty-five stories, including three master plans featuring centerpiece highrises. This tally does not count two research projects with direct application to tall buildings nor an observation deck added to an existing skyscraper.

Of the dozen highrises, all but one were for cities in Asia and the Middle East, reflecting not just the impact of economic woes in the United States and Europe, but also the strong imaginative hold that this building type continues to exert in those places. At home, meanwhile, fear of falling seems to have engendered a new kind of *frisson*. The above-mentioned observation deck, dubbed "The Ledge," consists of a set of four mechanically retractable boxes added to the 103rd floor of Willis (formerly Sears) Tower in Chicago. Advertised as an exhilarating and unforgettable experience, and featuring transparent walls and floors of half-inch-thick glass with an almost invisible steel structure, the new addition pushes the envelope of the building—currently the third tallest in the world—out by four feet, producing a sci-fi spectacle. Meanwhile, with its completion date rescheduled for late 2013, and the name Freedom Tower dropped (presumably to erase the memory of its troubled origins), David Childs's fortified One World Trade Center had only one signed commercial lease as of early 2011. This was with the China Center, a real estate company based in Beijing. "The people in China, they recognize the landmark building," stated the company's president.

Yet if the universal sign-language of can-you-top-this still obtains in many contexts, the contradiction between the technical expertise required to design such highly sophisticated structures and the magical thinking that often drives the decision to erect them, both economically and environmentally, remains to be reconciled. While a compact carbon footprint and inhospitality to cars may be easier on the planet than sprawl, as David Owen has argued in *Green Metropolis,* the idea of a "green" supertall building continues to seem counterintuitive. From the latter perspective it is encouraging to know that SOM is devoting considerable talent and resources to new thinking and research about this building type.

What has changed in the way SOM approaches the highrise today? One manifest difference is that preoccupations with image per se have taken a back seat to concerns with individual components, programmatic distribution, and structural and environmental performance. While the latter have always had a determining influence on highrise design and construction, they are now explicitly foregrounded and, indeed, exhibited. In Lotte Super Tower in Seoul, slated to be the second tallest building in the world after Burj Dubai, the architects and engineers have recalibrated the pros and cons of design innovations from the entire recent history of highrise construction. Utilizing an integrated core-diagrid system to withstand lateral loads and efficiently distribute vertical circulation, the building transforms in plan from a square at the base to an octagon at mid-shaft to a circle at the top. This decreases the effects of "vortex shedding," or wind flow around a structure that produces movement in the direction of the downwind side. The tower's taper from bottom to top is also a response to the varying floor-plate requirements of its mixed-use program—retail, office, hotel, observation deck. Each design decision has been based on a logic of optimization and enabled by the computer's extraordinary capacity to model multiple variables. If none of the decisions individually may be said to be radically new, together they add up to a new synthesis of knowledge, generating a unique form. That form, in turn, is projected as a virtuoso image of contemporary construction and engineering, one that goes beyond high-tech fetishism and becomes the subject of celebration in the building's public spaces.

In contrast, in the Chongqing River Tower, aesthetics appears less a by-product of purely structural decisions. An extremely elegant tower located on a riverfront opposite the dense downtown of this city in southwestern China, its "Rubik's cube" massing is high-concept. Alluding to lower-rise precedents like Habitat in Montreal, it also owes something to Herzog and de Meuron's recent condominium at 56 Leonard Street in New York. Yet the seventy-plus-story building presents itself less as a one-off event than as a relatively flexible modular assembly that, at least theoretically, has the potential to be rearranged into a variety of volumetric configurations.

Of the three research projects for non-specific sites that the jury selected for commendation, two, as mentioned, relate directly to tall buildings. In the first case, the research group dealt with topological optimization, developing analyses of structures and shapes like the Michell truss, a concept in variational fluid dynamics originally put forward a century ago by an Australian mechanical engineer. Approached as both a potential new design method and an evaluative tool for performance, research projects of this type represent a major upside for architecture in an economic downturn. In this case, SOM's architects and engineers were able to take advantage of the opportunity to explore experimental ideas in a school-type setting, working together in an interdisciplinary, non-hierarchical spirit. The exciting diagrams and rather futuristic renderings they generated now wait to be tested in actual construction.

The second research project, based on case studies of some of SOM's commissioned buildings, focused on high-performance building enclosures. It addressed a wide range of challenges related to advanced cladding systems, from post-9/11 security issues to climate matters. Among the specific problems that the team studied were blast resistance, dirt resistance, shading under extreme temperatures, transparency and lighting control, and even camouflage (this last in the specific case of the Rolex Tower in Dubai, where "a quiet understated presence" and "shimmering" were among the client's objectives).

The tall or super-tall building makes an instant statement on the skyline; as Roland Barthes famously said of the Eiffel Tower, the only way to get away from it is to be in it looking out. Yet the impact of such structures on cities and their inhabitants goes far beyond iconicity. As SOM's architects are well aware, the role played by these most visible additions to the urban fabric is at least as powerful as their image.

SOM Journal 7
Submissions

ADNEC Arena
Abu Dhabi, United Arab Emirates

Al Hamra Firdous Tower
Kuwait City, Kuwait

Baietan
Guangzhou, China

Castle Quay II
St. Helier, Jersey, United Kingdom

Digital Media City—Seoul Light Tower
Seoul, Korea

Beijing Central Business District Expansion
Beijing, China

Goldsun Hangzhou
Hangzhou, China

Heliotrace Façade System

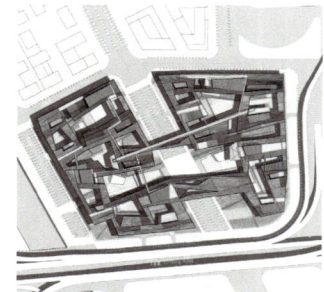

Hongqiao New CBD
Shanghai, China

Lusail Project
Doha, Qatar

Oakland Museum of California
Oakland, California

Olympic Gateway
London, UK

Ssiger International
Cixi, China

St. Louis and Jefferson
National Expansion Memorial
St. Louis, Missouri

Takshing House
Hong Kong, China

Tata Hosur Housing Study
Hosur, Bangalore, India

The Ledge
Chicago, Illinois

The New School University Center
New York, New York

Tianjin Financial City
Tianjin, China

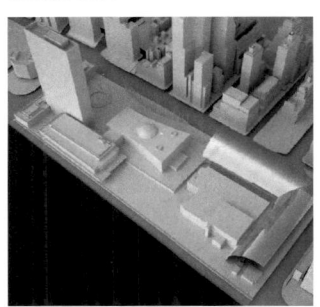
United Nations Headquarters Master Plan
New York, New York

United State Air Force Academy
Colorado Springs, Colorado

The Chongqing River Tower
Chongqing, China
Developed 2004–09

The Chongqing River Tower reconsiders typical mixed-use highrise solutions by creating a unique, porous building volume that maximizes natural ventilation, access to sunlight, and view potential. Situated at the confluence of the Yangtze and Jialing Rivers and positioned opposite the dense downtown peninsula of Chongqing, the River Tower establishes a modular framework to not only negotiate its mixed-use office, hotel, and apartment program, but also to create human-scale experiences within an urban-scale façade. The project represents a delicate balance between simplicity and controlled complexity, in an attempt to meet the developer's directive for efficient, repeatable floor plates, while also addressing the city's desire for an iconic form to establish an identity for a new district.

The basis of design is a six-meter module, which is arrayed to form a forty-eight by forty-eight-square meter floor plate and stacked to three-hundred meters in height. Within the hotel and apartment levels, each floor falls within one of three basic configurations, in which modules are methodically subtracted to allow light and air deeper into the building while maximizing a unit's perimeter to capture views. These three floor plates are rotated around a consistent circulation and plumbing core, creating a varied experience and complex, three-dimensional exterior terraces from a limited number of typical units. Inspired both by the constructed vertical landscapes of Chongqing and the carved and eroded topography of its surroundings, the resulting composition lends a heightened sense of transparency and porosity to the landmark tower silhouette.

At the midpoint of the tower above the office floors, the dramatic sky lobby and restaurant of the hotel draw users high above the surrounding context, offering panoramic views up and down the Yangtze and Jialing rivers and back toward downtown. A skylight in the lobby reveals the heart of the tower: a one-hundred-fifty-meter-tall open-air void, which continues from the hotel through the top of the building. Along the eastern perimeter of the central void, glazed residential elevators glide, creating a constant sense of movement and increasing the experiential connection with the space. The volume brings daylight deep into the tower's footprint and, through the staggered multi-story openings to the building's perimeter, captures and redirects prevailing winds. In the summer, when wind speeds are moderate and temperature and humidity high, increased wind velocity generated by the void contributes significantly to the cooling of the tower's terraces. In the building's initial configuration, a limited number of openings at the base and top of the central void were introduced to contribute to stack-effect ventilation, which proved unable to generate air movement within all occupied spaces of the void. The modified design introduces more and larger openings throughout the full height of the void, leading to a more successful wind-driven ventilation. In the shoulder seasons, as wind temperature and humidity decrease, air movement within the void can contribute to the natural ventilation of the hotel and residences.

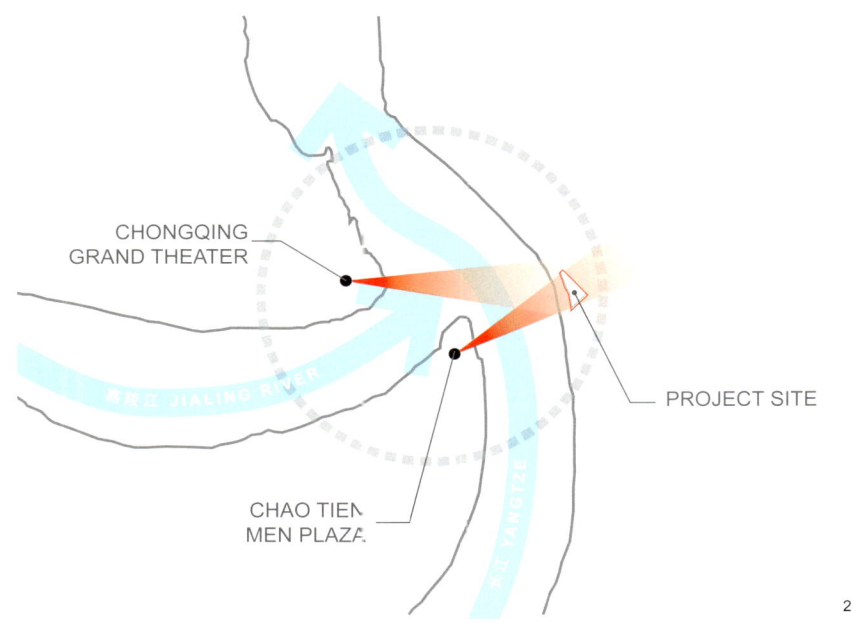

2

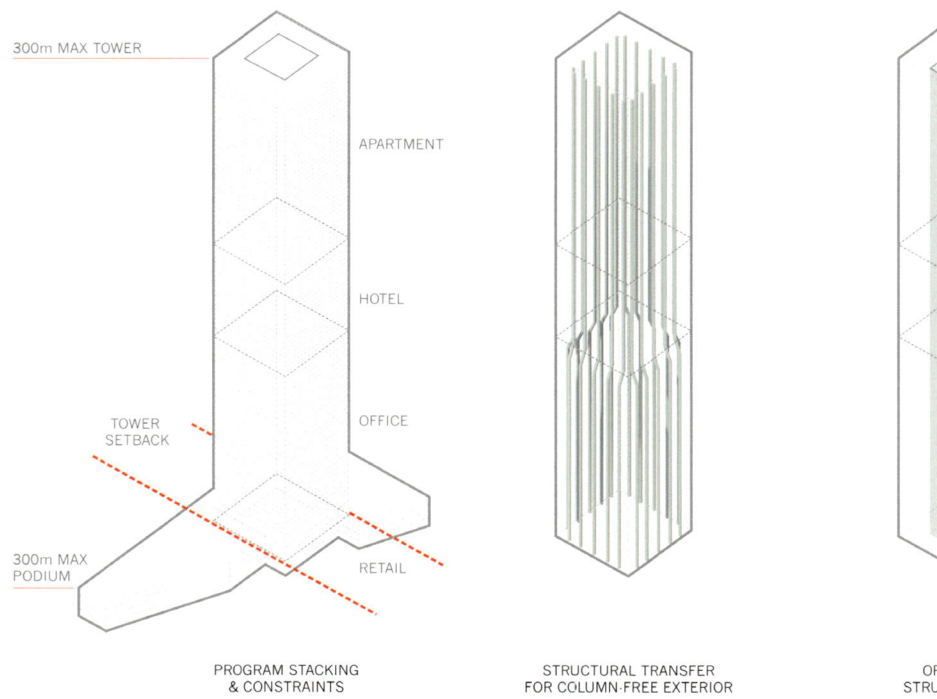

PROGRAM STACKING & CONSTRAINTS

STRUCTURAL TRANSFER FOR COLUMN-FREE EXTERIOR

OPEN VOID IN STRUCTURAL CORE

4

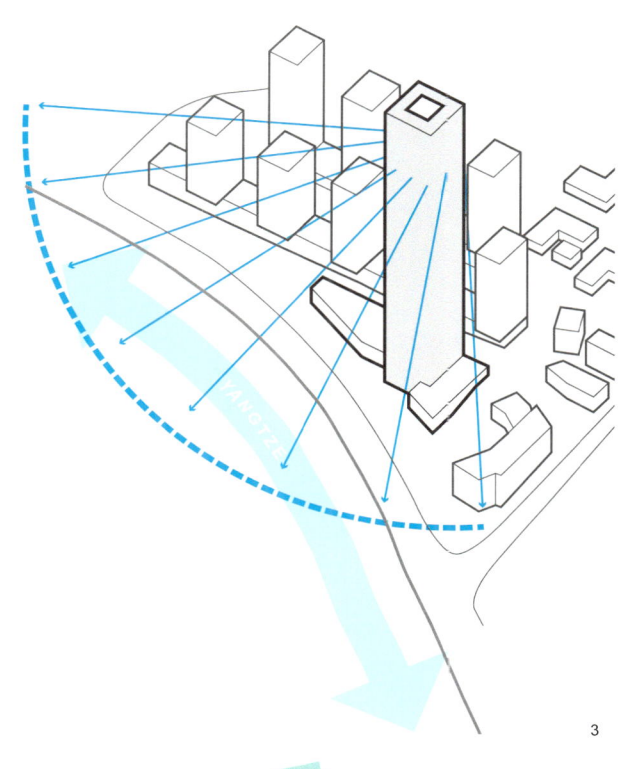

1 Downtown Chongqing
2 Project location and its relationship to two of Chongqing's landmarks
3 With its position along a bend in the Yangtze, the tower offers views that wrap nearly 270 degrees around the site
4 Tower build-up diagram

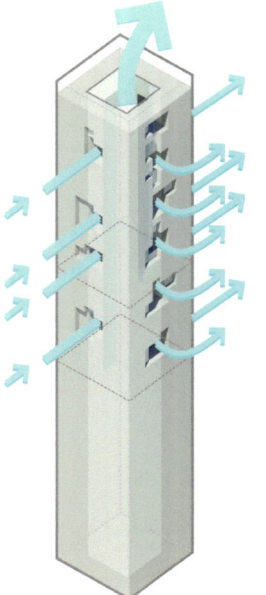

VOLUME VENTILATED TO EXTERIOR

PERIMETER TERRACES

BUILDING COMPOSITE

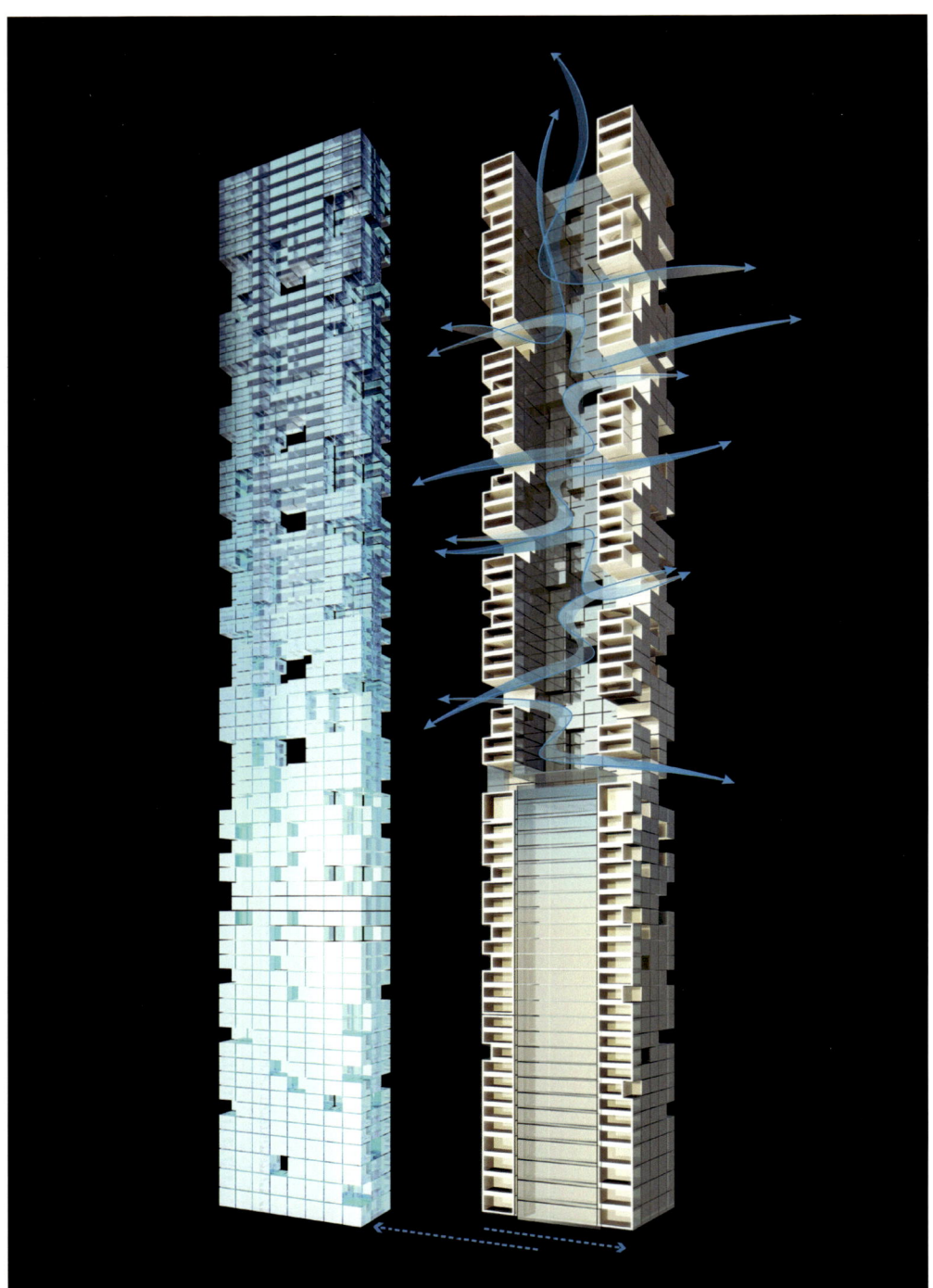

6

7

8

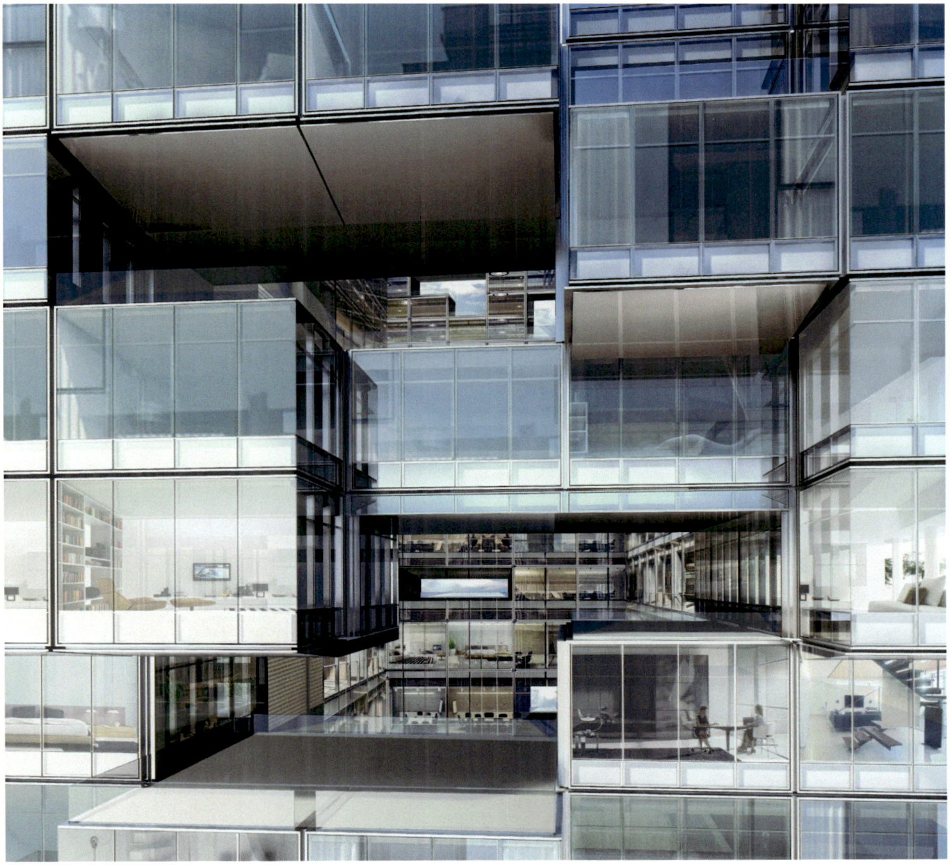

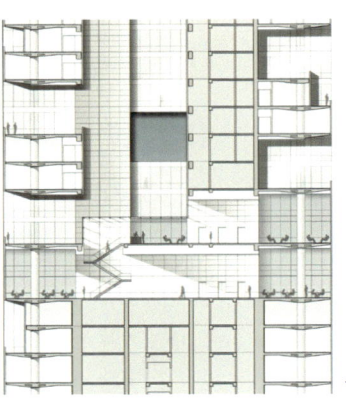

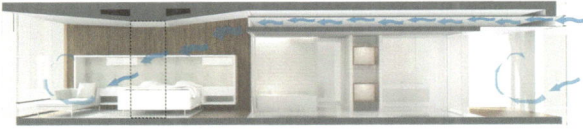

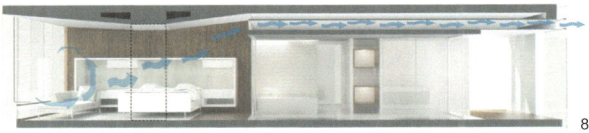

5 Section perspective through open-air void
6 View of multi-story opening
7 Section through hotel sky lobby
8 Room conditioning sections

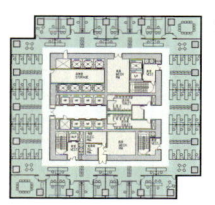
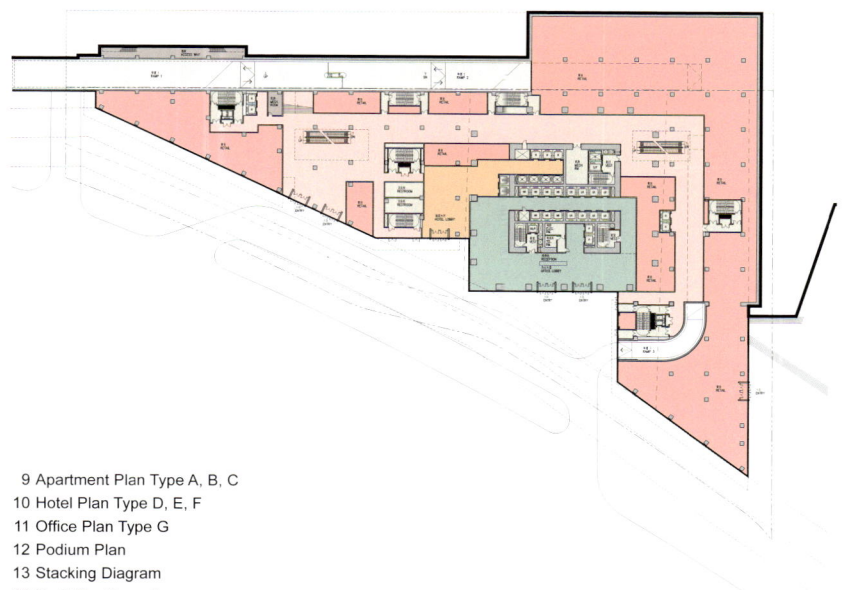

9 Apartment Plan Type A, B, C
10 Hotel Plan Type D, E, F
11 Office Plan Type G
12 Podium Plan
13 Stacking Diagram
14 North/South section

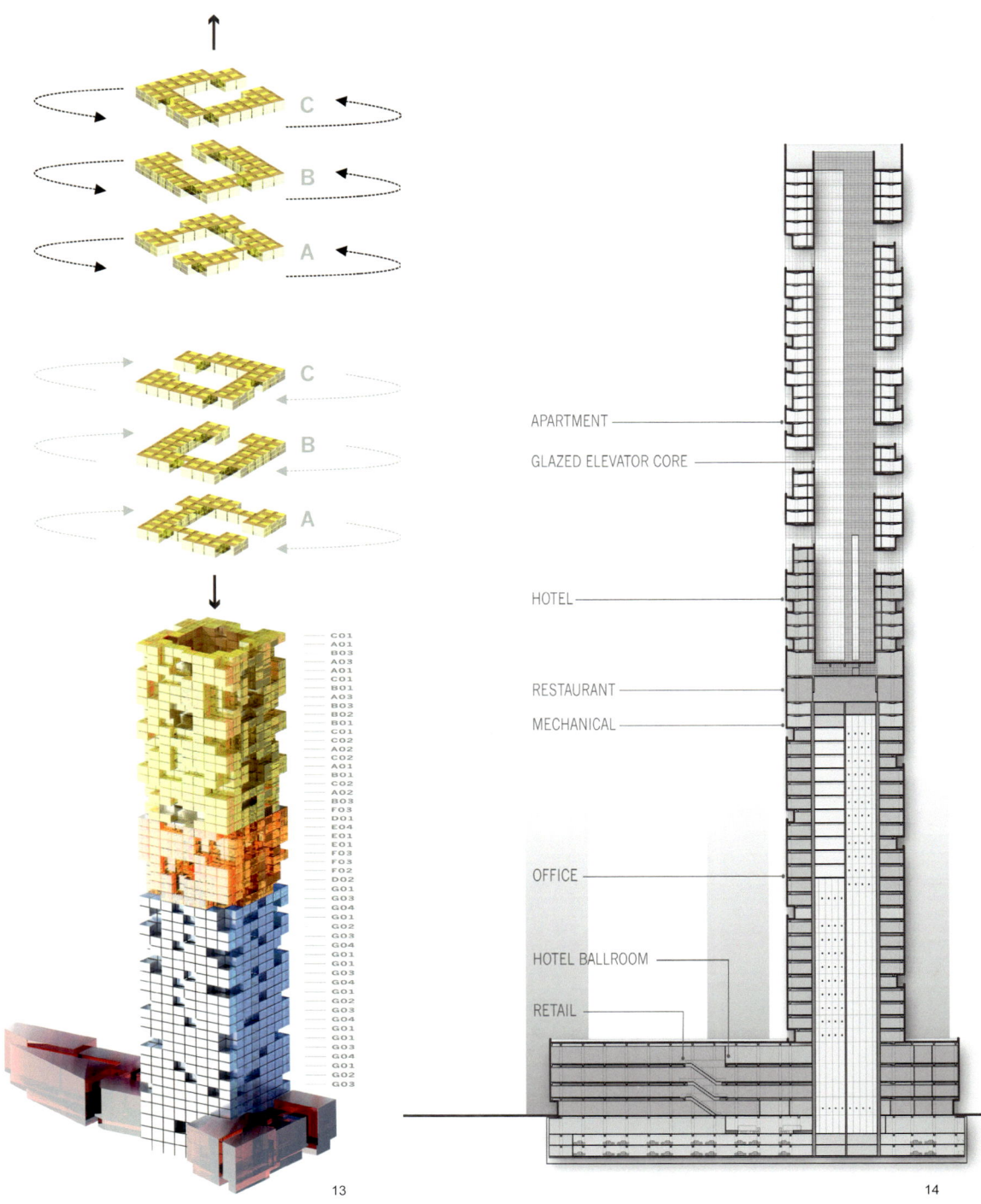

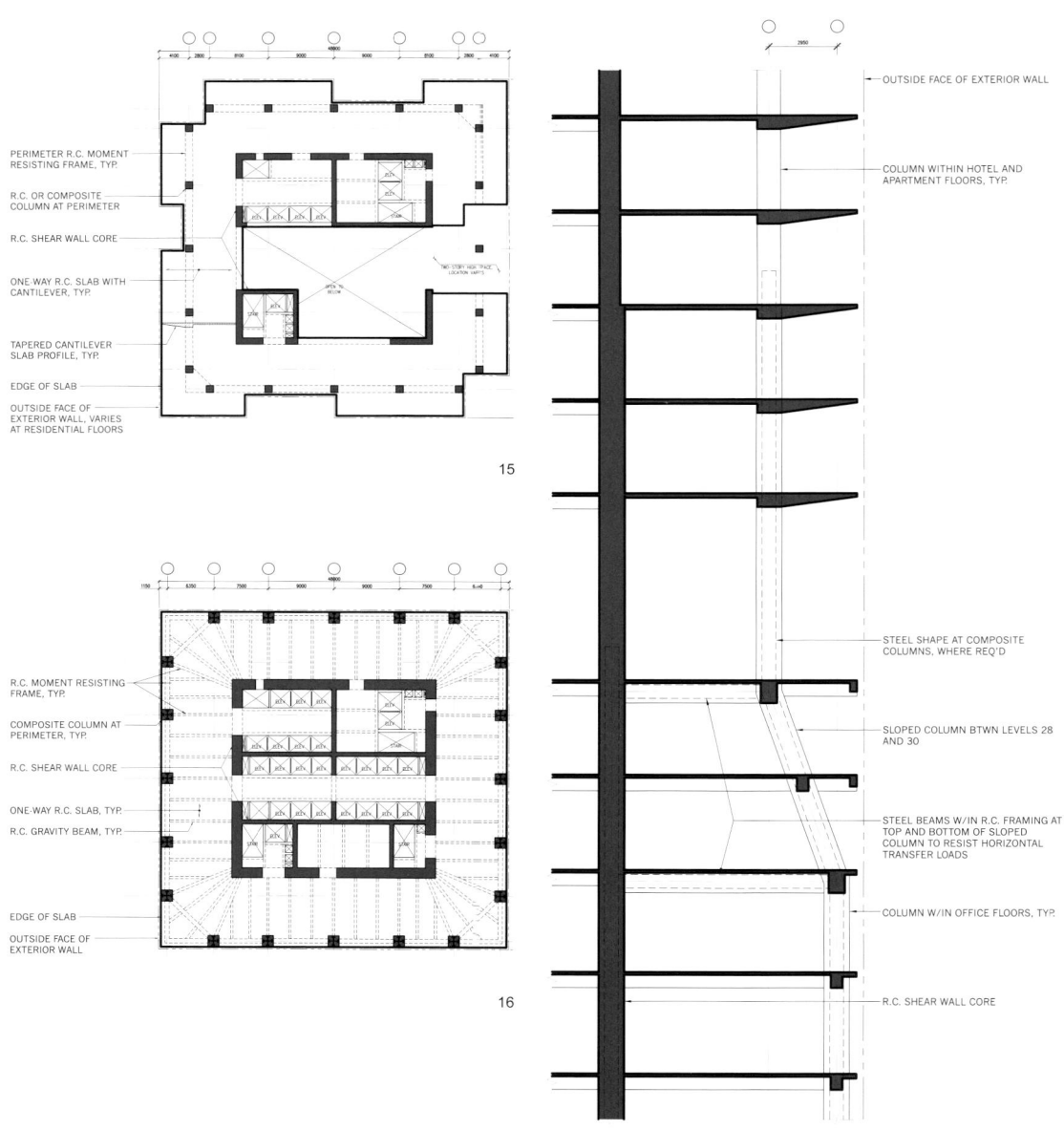

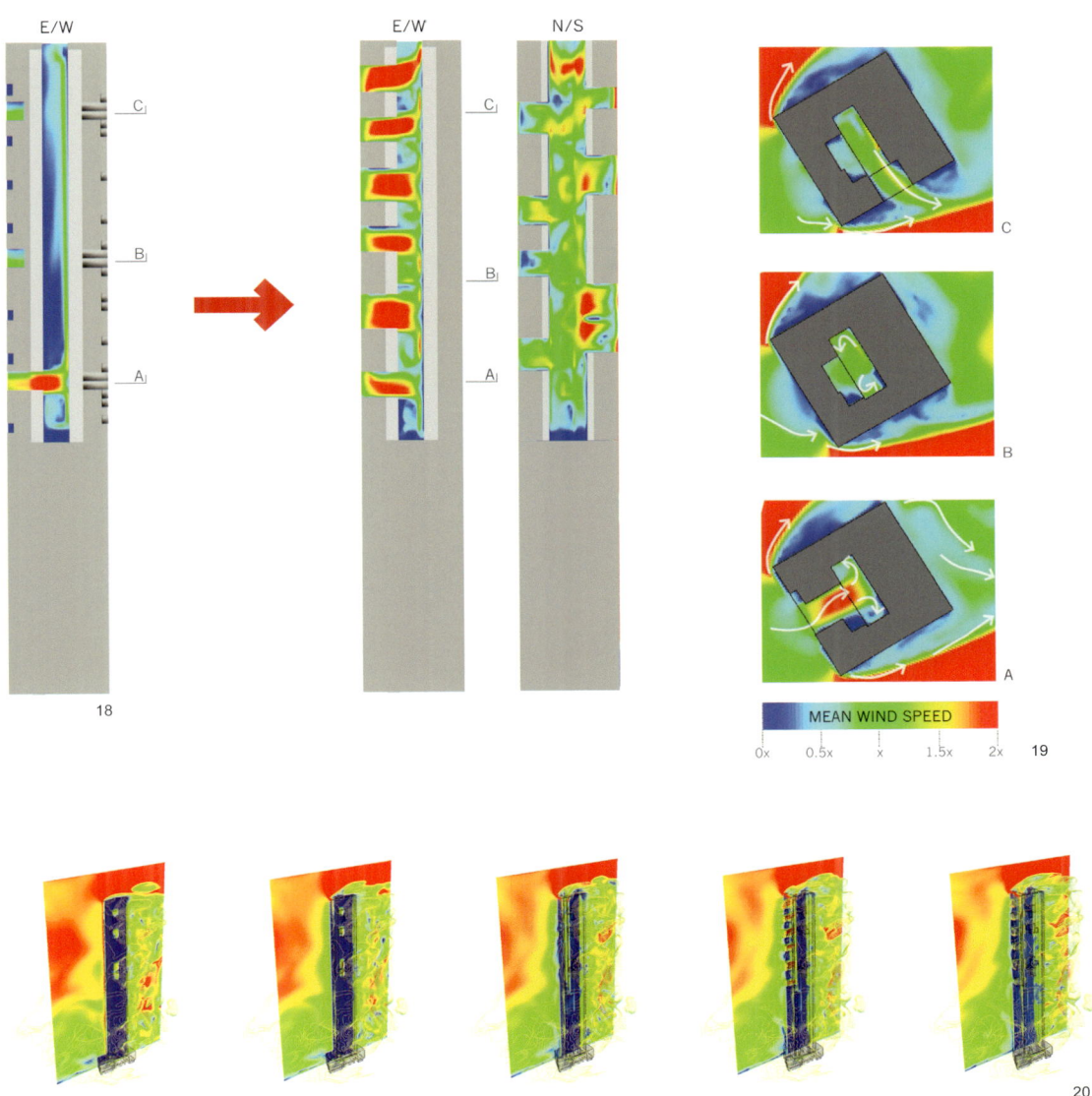

15 Typical residential level
16 Typical office level
17 Section through column transfer at hotel to office transition
18 Initial tower ventilation study: stack ventilation creates air movement in sixty-three percent of void
19 Final tower ventilation study: wind-driven ventilation creates air movement in ninety-four percent of void
20 Sectional wind study

41

21

22

21 Duplex unit
22 Corner unit
23 View from Nanbin Road
24 Residential terraces >
25 Aerial view over downtown Chongqing >

John Jay College of Criminal Justice
New York, New York
Designed 2003–05

SOM's design for the John Jay College of Criminal Justice adds nearly 625,000 gross-square-feet of new classrooms, laboratories, auditoriums, and student lounges to the existing school, doubling its size. Addressing the need for social spaces for students and creating a cohesive identity for the school was also a key component of rethinking this urban campus.

After the September 11 attacks on New York, enrollment at John Jay increased dramatically. Outgrowing its facilities, which had undergone a previous expansion in 1988, the school decided it needed to grow even further. The existing college comprises the eastern half of the block between Tenth and Eleventh avenues and Fifty-Eighth and Fifty-Ninth streets, and is spread over a few buildings in the vicinity. The primary focus was on connecting these discrete spaces into a unified campus. This premise guided the project's transformation of a bleak multi-story parking lot on the western half of the block into a completely new urban campus that refocuses existing facilities and ties the campus together as a whole.

Following previous expansion strategies, the college proposed a linear extension of the building westward. Originally the school occupied Haaren Hall, an early twentieth-century building fronting Tenth Avenue. In 1988 a new building was constructed immediately adjacent to Haaren and left the western half of the site a parking lot. SOM's design proposed a new building that would occupy the entirety of the vacant block. A vertical mass containing faculty offices, conference center, and moot court is located along Eleventh Avenue, matching the scale of adjacent buildings and giving a visual presence to the college from the West Side Highway and Eleventh Avenue. A low rising plinth of dense social and academic programs occupies the mid-block portion of the site where a roof terrace acts as new outdoor green space and traditional campus quad.

Internally, a cascading avenue connects the original Haaren Hall and North Hall buildings to the new building allowing indoor access between Tenth and Eleventh avenues. This social spine is programmed with open plan lounge spaces, study areas, and gathering spaces that maximize interaction and student activity. Classrooms flank this internal avenue and allow for efficient circulation between classes. Additionally, this active social and circulation zone negotiates the steep grade change between the avenues allowing for dynamic sectional relationships between the original building and Eleventh Avenue to the west.

At over 65,000 square feet, a significant outdoor space serves as a new campus green for the college. This green roof will become the central gathering space for students and faculty. The Commons is landscaped with large grassy areas for recreation, decked areas for outdoor dining and lounging, paved paths for circulation between buildings, and planted with trees for shade. At either end, the Commons connects to both the existing Haaren Hall building and the tower through large expanses of glass that provide entries and light into the building.

Inspired by the artist's use of subtle variations in color to achieve elaborate patterns, the building enclosure is organized to create a dynamic experience as one circulates around the building. Vertical fins are arranged in horizontal bands. The spatial compression of these fins in perspective creates more or less density in the patterns they create. These metal fins are colored on one side and reflective on the other, so that completely different effects are visible, depending on the direction in which one approaches the building. Approaching from the east the building appears red and is visually connected to the brick exterior of the existing Haaren Hall building. From the west, the building presents a new identity expressed in glass and reflective slivers that alludes to the glass towers along the avenue. Significant programs and public spaces are framed in glass to highlight entries, auditorium, dining areas, and the large moot court. These spaces—and especially the moot court—express the activities within and enlighten the mission of John Jay College to the city.

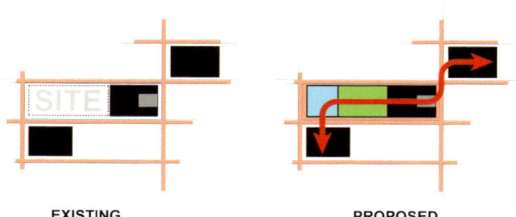

EXISTING　　　PROPOSED

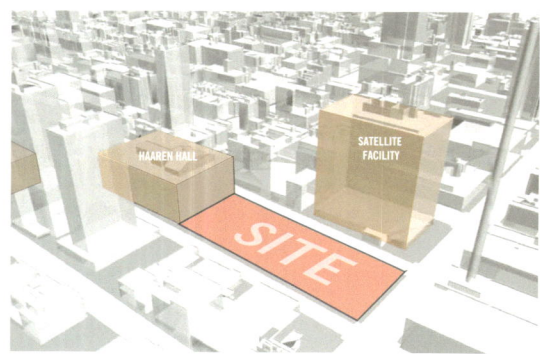
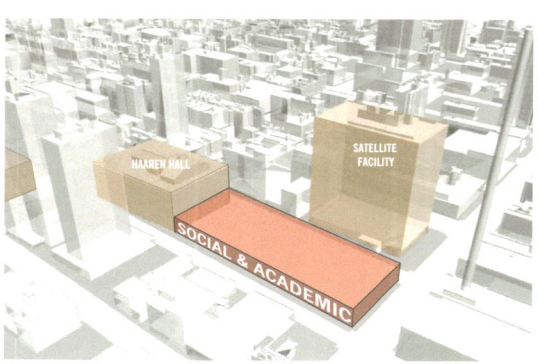

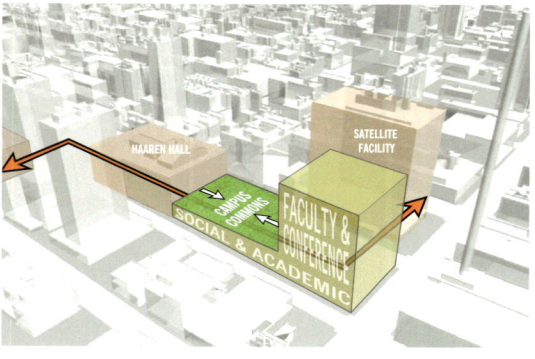

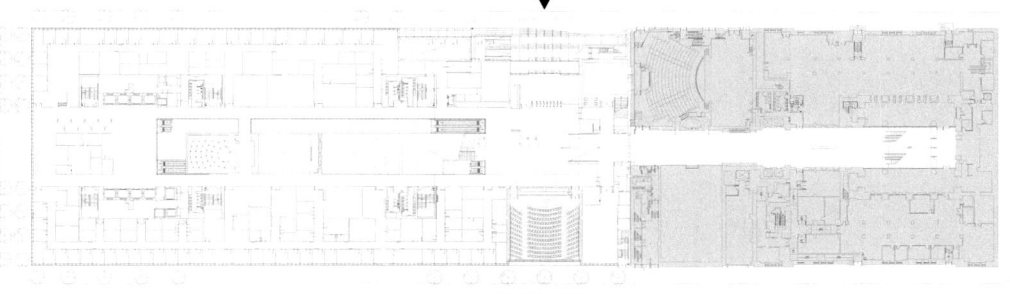

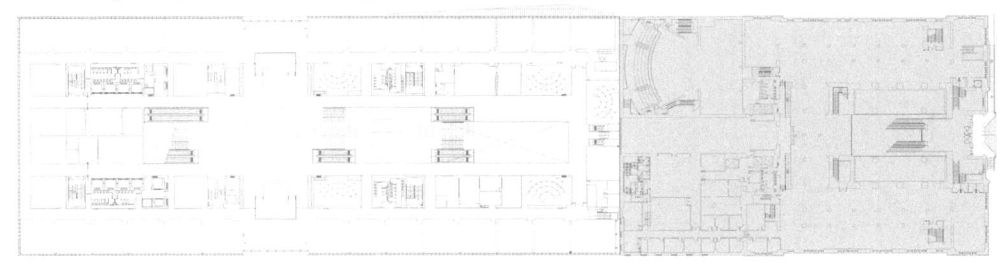

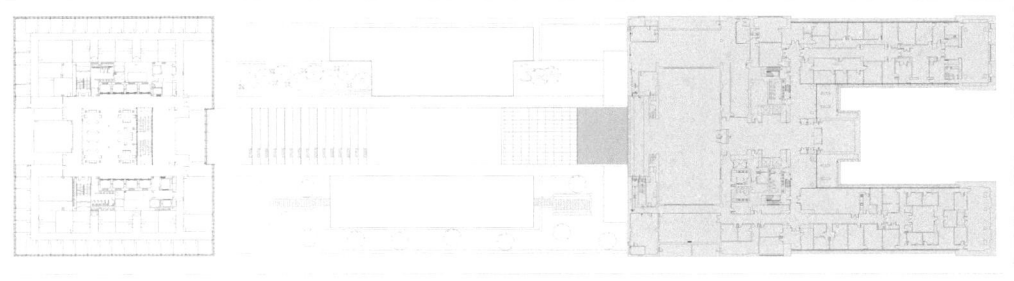

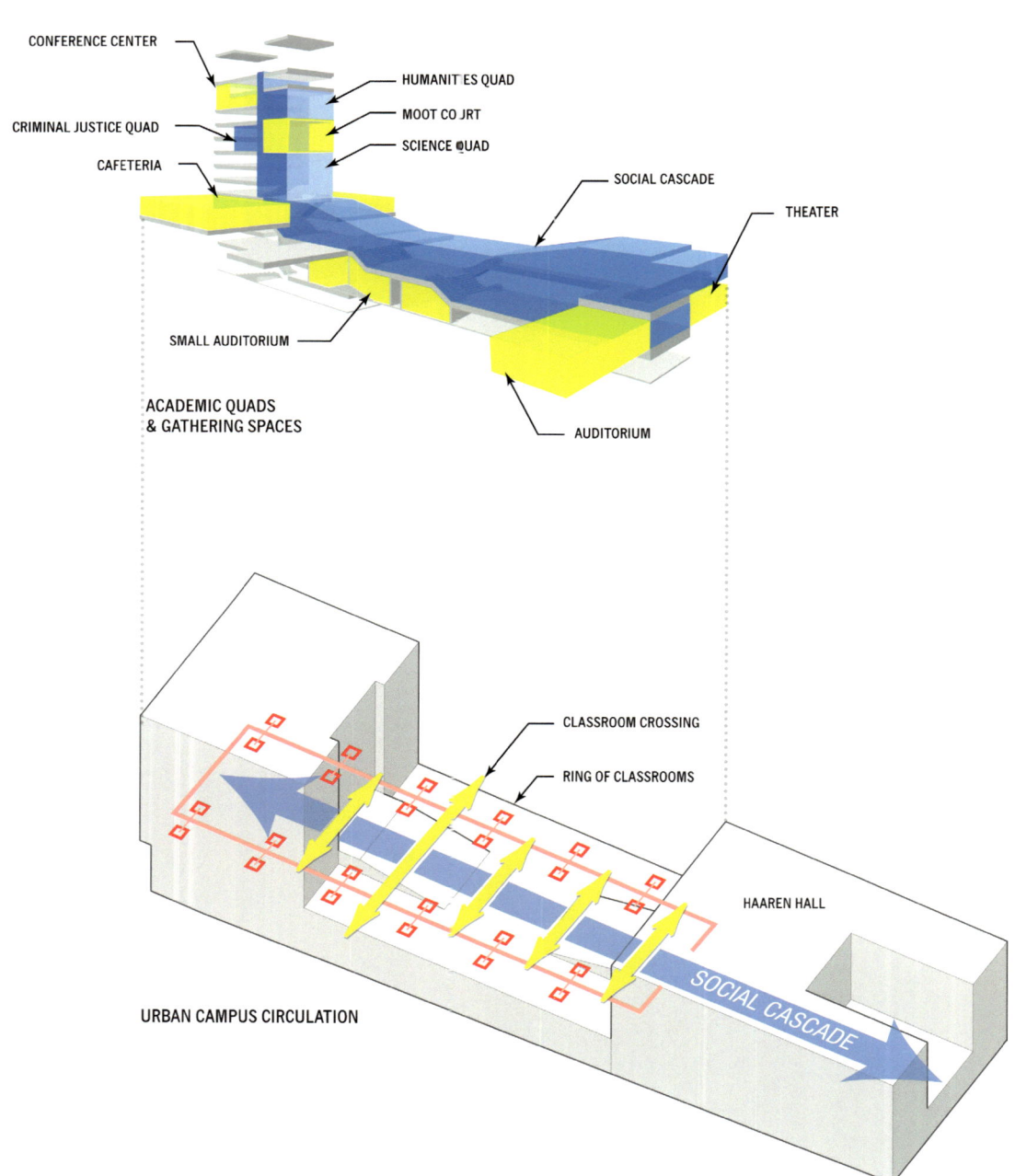

<<1 Aerial view of campus site
<<2 Creating an urban campus
  3 Floor plans level 3, 4, and 9
  4 Campus circulation diagram
  5 Sectional model through Social Cascade

The expansion of John Jay College of Criminal Justice allowed the creation of a proper "campus" for the college. The Social Cascade that runs the length of the building from east to west, and connects multiple floors sectionally, is a dynamic space for student nteraction. Lounges, auditoria, study spaces, and social spaces line the cascade and activate this internal avenue. Above it is a large campus that gives the school much needed access to outdoor green space.

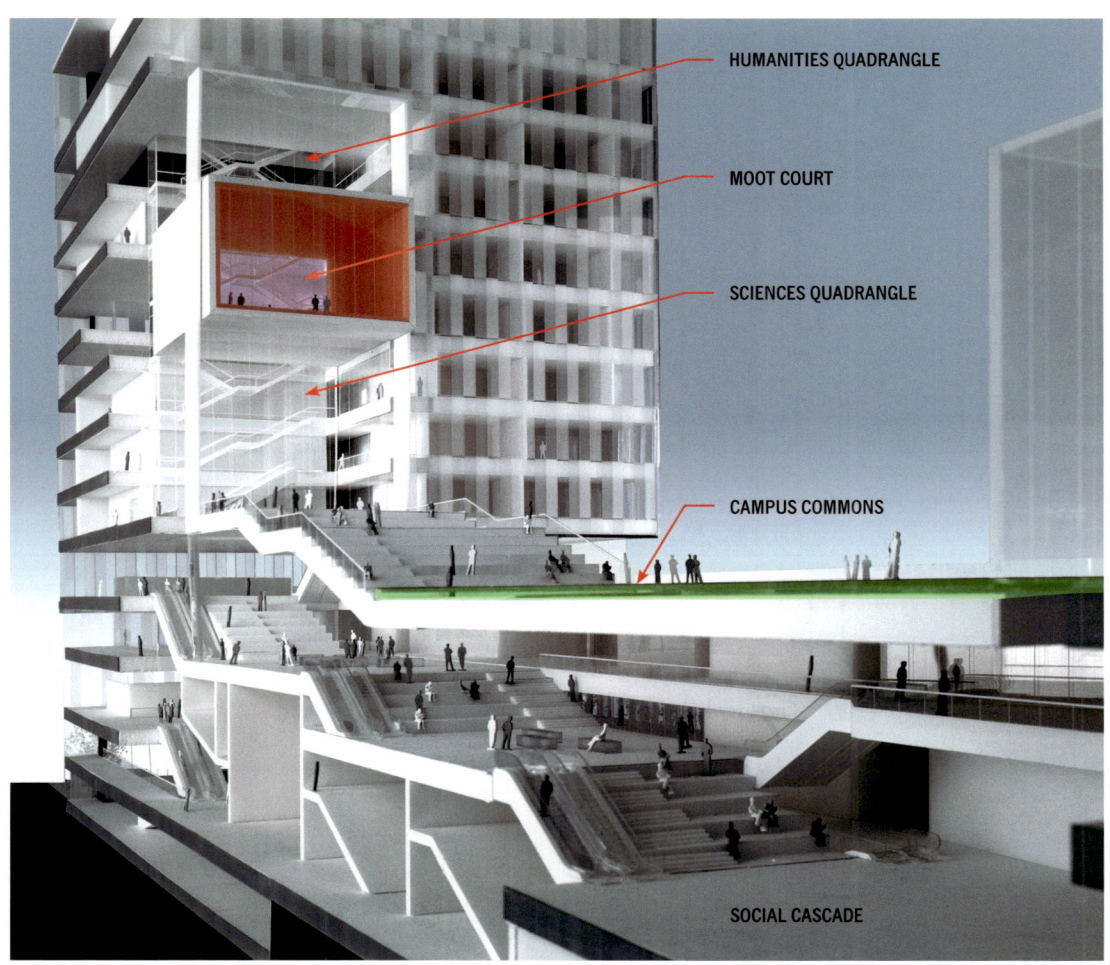

PROGRAMMING

ACADEMIC DEPARTMENTS — 67,938 SF
Psychology
LPS Crim. Justice Admin
English
Mathematics
Sciences
Public Management
SEEK
Government
Foreign Lang and Lit
African - American Studies
Puerto Rican/Latin Am Studies
Communication Skills

GENERAL ADMINISTRATION — 5,124 SF
VP for Student Development
Admin Conference Space
Sponsored Programs
Institutional Research
Faculty Senate

ASSEMBLY & EXHIBITION — 3,300 SF
Black Box / Moot Court
Alternate

STUDENT ACTIVITY SPACE — 62,730 SF
Faculty/Student Lounge
Food Service
Bookstore
Student Clubs & Organizations
Student Government

STUDENT SERVICES — 32,559 SF
Freshman Programs
Registrar
Career Development
Counseling
Admissions
Student Financial Services
Doc Program Forensic Psych
Svcs Students with Disabilities
Bursar's Office
Student Activities Campus Life
Consolidated Counter
Testing
Graduate Admissions
Health Services

GERALD W. LYNCH THEATER

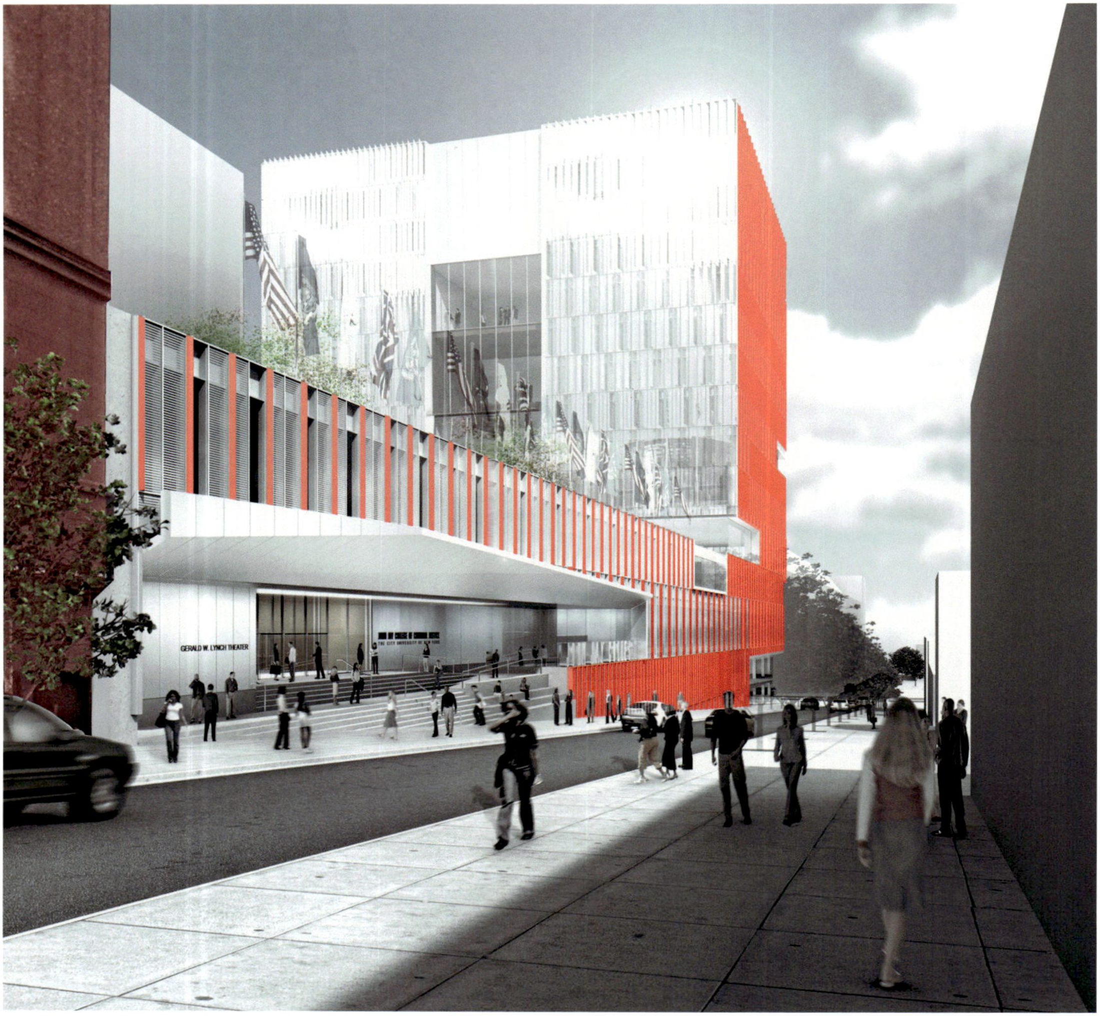

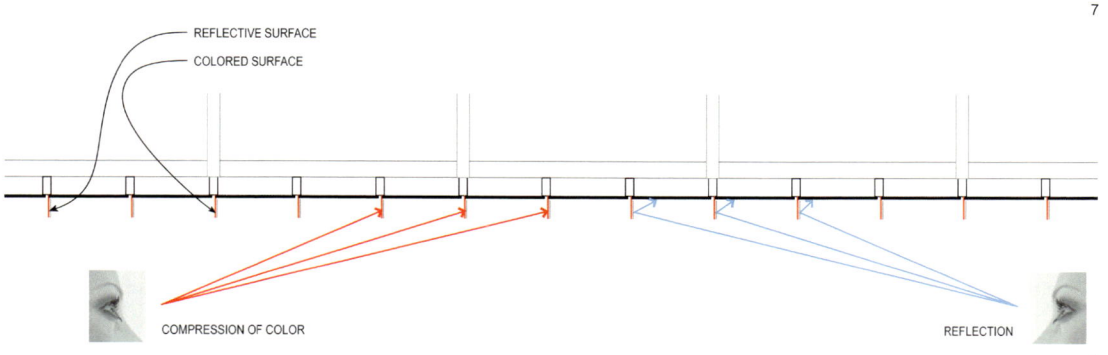

7

REFLECTIVE SURFACE
COLORED SURFACE
COMPRESSION OF COLOR
REFLECTION

8

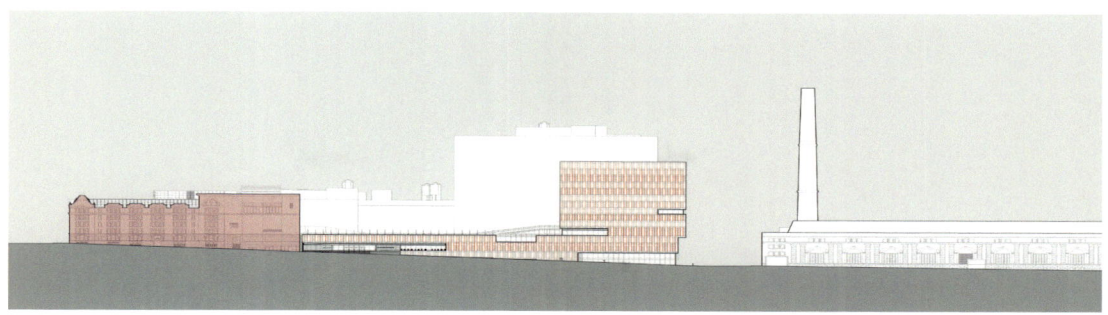

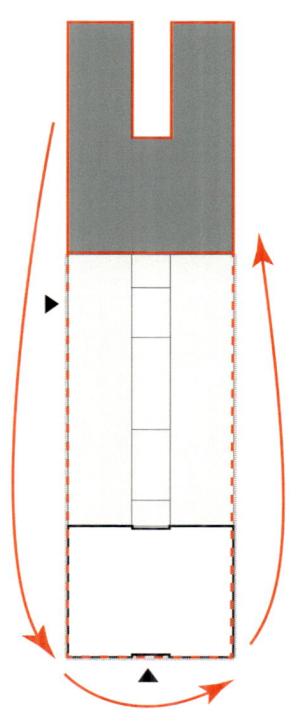

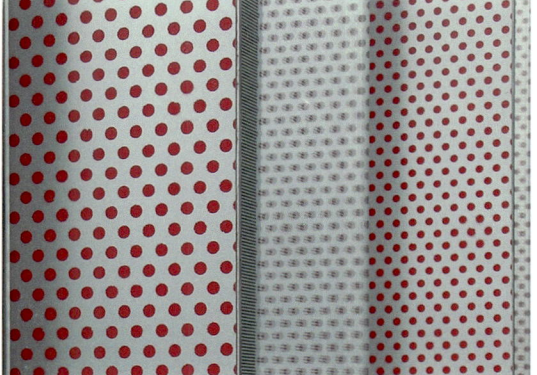

< 6 Campus programming
7 View from Fifty-Ninth Street and Tenth Avenue
8 Dynamic façade
9 Elevation
10 Façade detail
11 Color orientation
12 Façade under construction

14

<13 View from Social Cascade looking west
<14 View from Social Cascade looking east
 15 Aerial view
 16 View from Fifty-Ninth Street

Lotte World 2
Seoul, South Korea
Designed 2005–07

The Lotte World 2 tower is a design rooted in performance. The massing of the tower is driven by its mixed-use programmatic organization and wind engineering that closely align the architectural characteristics of the project with the engineering required in the construction of very tall highrise towers. The super tower is designed as a precision instrument: its faceted enclosure is a machined object; its efficient structural diagrid is tuned to optimize resistance to gravity loads and lateral loads; and an "inside-out" core minimizes core penetrations. Buildings at this scale require innovations in design and building systems, since building performance on all levels becomes more critical.

The tower is located in the Lotte World 2 retail and entertainment complex along the Han River, south east of the city center. The development is also adjacent to the Lotte amusement park, which is the world's largest indoor recreation complex. The surrounding area is a mixture of thematic variations, from high-end retail and its branding precision to the immense amusement park rooted in whimsy and fantasy. In contrast to the themed approach of the context, the design for the landmark tower is an expression of architectural simplicity and engineering performance that establishes its own identity within the complex.

Rising 555 meters above Seoul, the tower's geometry gently tapers and changes shape as it rises. The tower transforms from a 70-by-70-meter square at the base to a 40-meter-diameter circle at the crown of the building. The building's unconventional profile responds to both programmatic logic as well as a structural response to wind forces. Containing retail, offices, hotel, and observation deck, the building's tapering form adapts the changing lease span requirements of each program. Larger retail and office functions occupy the lower portion of the tower, where floor plates are large and deep; while hotel and observation functions occupy the upper portion, which have shallow floor plates and allow for the best views. Furthermore, the transition from square to circle allows simple rectilinear floors for efficient planning of retail and office spaces; and rounded out floors at the top offer 360-degree-views of the city. Structurally, the tapering and changing geometry minimizes building oscillations by varying vortex shedding pressures upward, which reduces the likelihood that the tower will oscillate at its natural frequency. In buildings with very consistent shapes and smooth surfaces there is a tendency for swaying perpendicular to the direction of the wind. If these wind forces become "organized," very large forces need to be counteracted by the building's structural system. Through wind engineering and by optimizing the tower shape, the forces exerted on the tower become weaker and subsequently the structural system could be made more efficient.

The structural system of the tower's main perimeter is diagrid. Columns are made diagonally to better balance the gravity load resisting system with the lateral load resisting system. Columns at the base of the building are more vertical and steeper to best respond to gravity loads, while more horizontal or shallower columns best respond to lateral wind forces at the top, where they are strongest. The diagrid also allowed a more natural relationship between the building's geometry and its structural resolution. The tapering and transforming geometry of the building combined with the optimized diagrid structure allows the tower to be constructed with thirty percent less steel than a conventional steel framed highrise. The result is a tower that is structurally stiffer and safer than a conventional tower while reducing the amount of resources needed to construct the tower. Through engineering and design the tower can be constructed more efficiently and with less material which greatly reduce the environmental impact of the project.

The mixed-use function of the tower required a complex vertical organization of circulation and services and demanded a creative organization of the core to maximize efficiency and structural performance. The core contains all services, express elevators, and circulation, and is the main artery of the tower. Each program com-

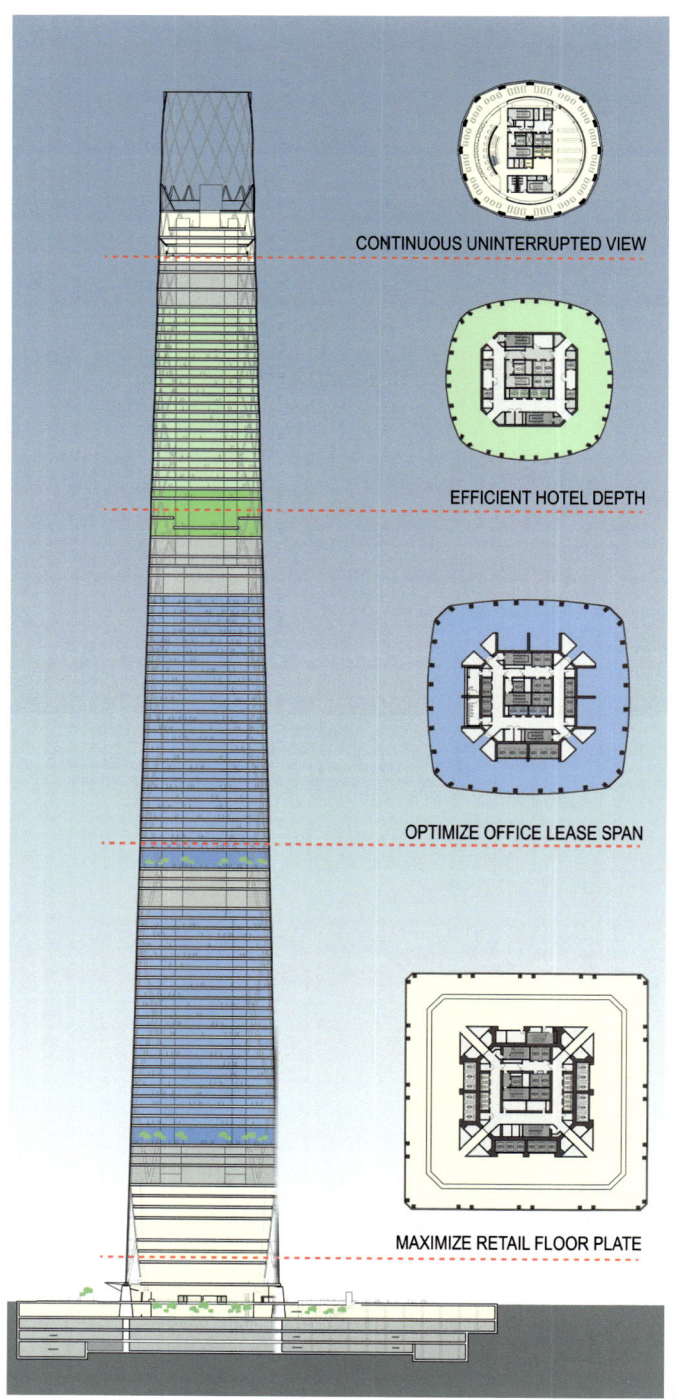

ponent operates almost independently of others, with dedicated elevators, mechanical and safety spaces creating a complex puzzle. The tower core proposed an inversion from typical core configurations that puncture core walls in order to serve each floor mechanically. An "inside-out" concept was developed: mechanical systems were placed outside main structural shear walls to greatly reduce the number of shear wall penetrations. For the lower two-thirds of the tower a series of buttresses effectively increased the structural footprint of the core and allowed for mechanical systems to have flexible access to each floor without impact to structural shear walls.

The tower combines a bold iconic form with intense performance-based design. Through deep investigation of building systems and alignment of architectural ideas with engineered solutions, the tower raises the standard of super-tall highrise design. Rather than the energy intensive proposals of the nineteen-seventies, the iconic towers of tomorrow will stress performance and environmental sensitivity.

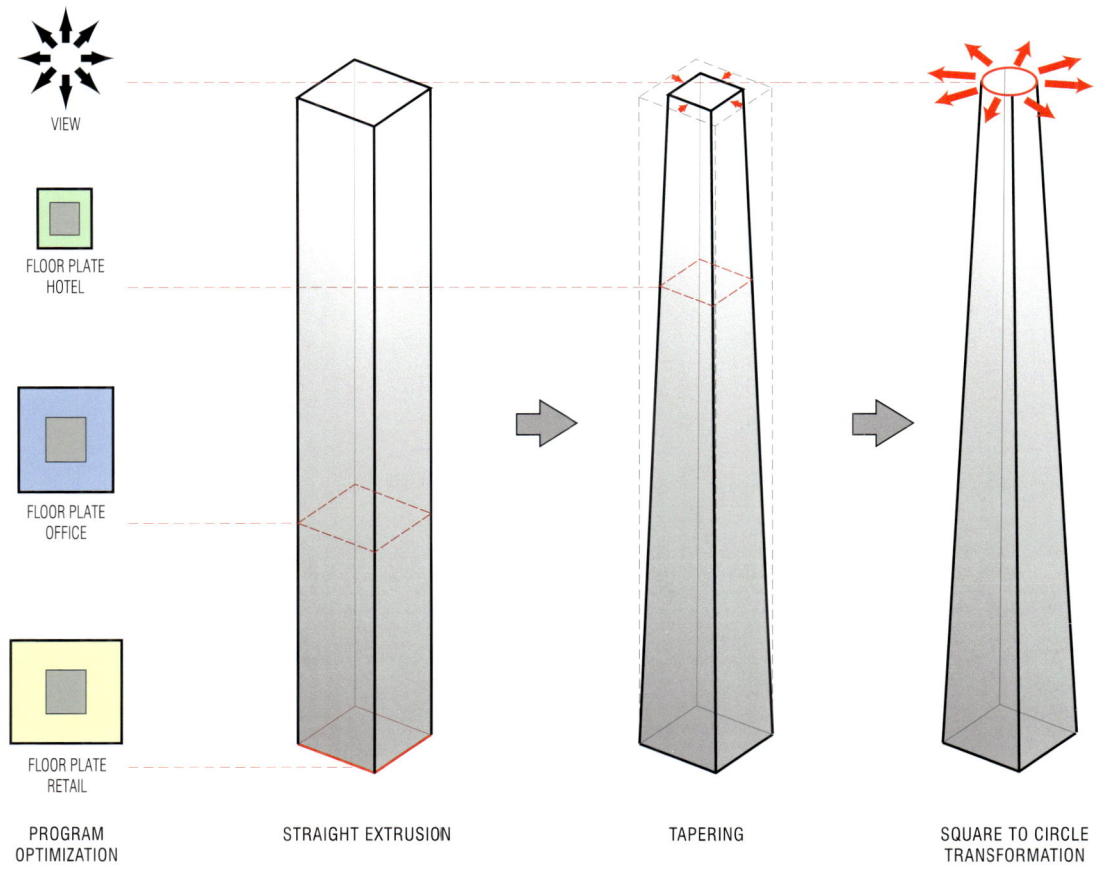

555 M
500 M
Moment Frame
Conventional
Structure
DIAGRID
30% REDUCTION IN
STEEL

4

1 DIAGRID WORKPOINT GEOMETRY
NOT TO SCALE
A SIDE DIAGRID SLOPE CHANGE AT B1
NOT TO SCALE
B CORNER DIAGRID SLOPE CHANGE AT LEVEL 3
NOT TO SCALE

5

1820'
REDUCED
WIND LOAD
CONVENTIONAL
STRAIGHT EXTRUSION
TAPERING REDUCES
EFFECTIVE WIND LOAD
CHANGING GEOMETRY
DECREASES VORTEX SHEDDING
SURFACE ARTICULATION
FACETTING BREAKS UP WINDS

6

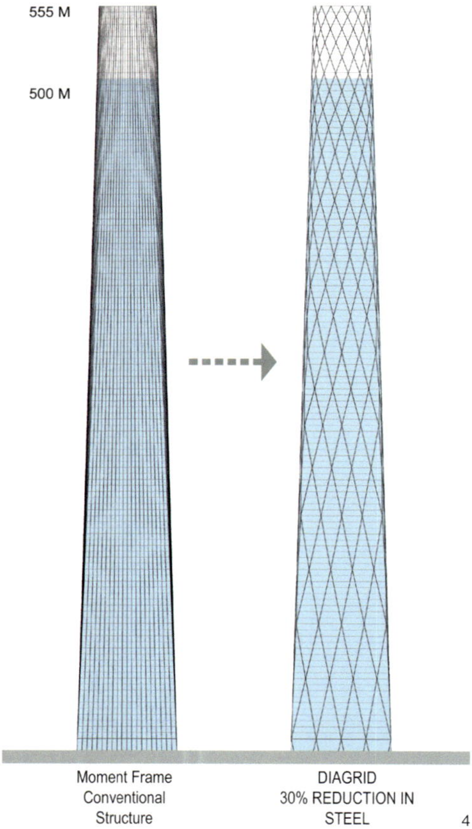

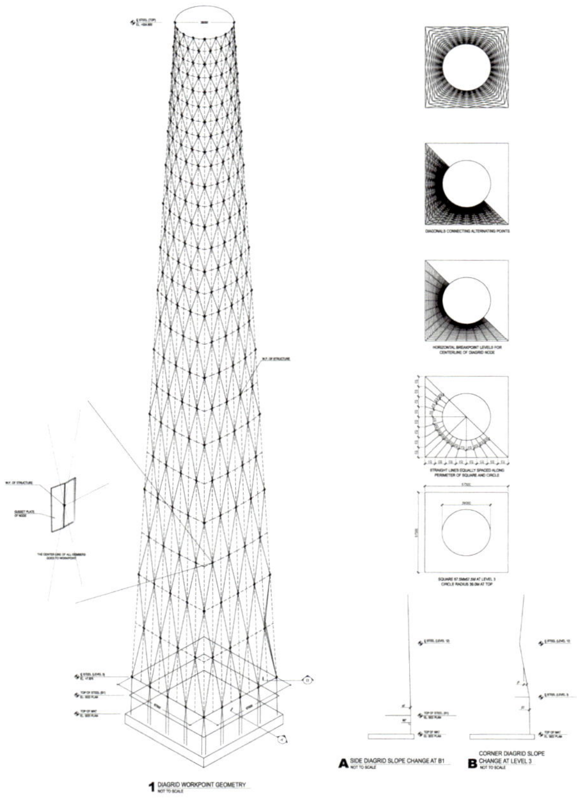

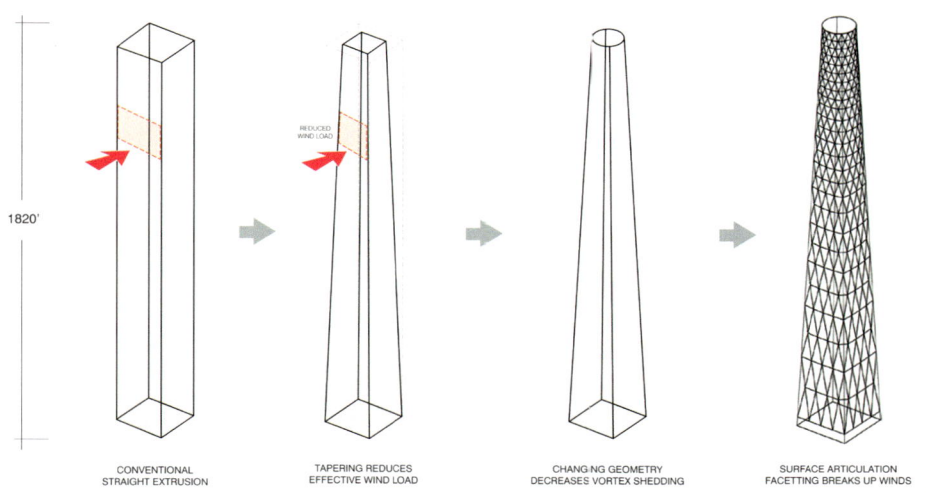

<<1 Aerial view of downtown Seoul
 <2 Program section and typical floor plans
 <3 Optimized building geometry
  4 Diagram showing thirty-percent reduction in steel using the diagrid structure versus the moment frame
  5 Diagrid workpoint geometry
  6 Structural optimization
  7 Axonometric of node and façade expression
  8 Stress analysis under service and ultimate loads
  9 Weld sequence details of diagrid nodes

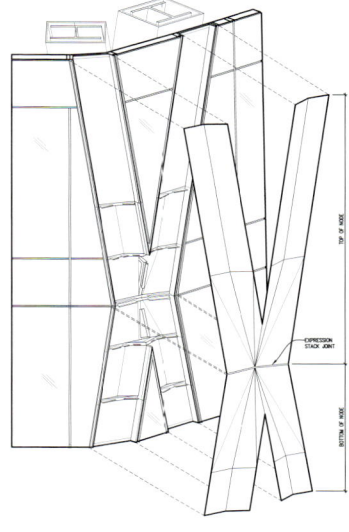

AXONOMETRIC OF NODE AND FACADE EXPRESSION

7

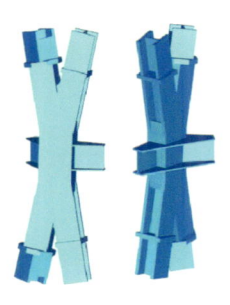

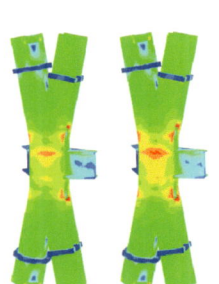

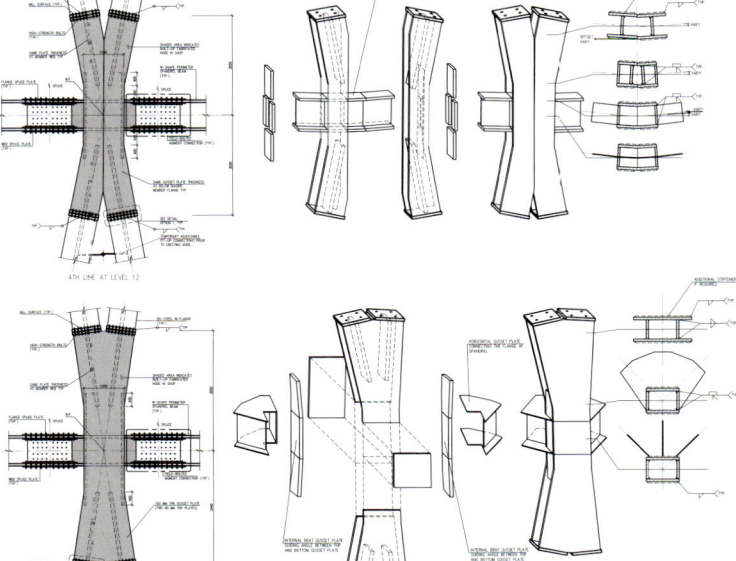

STRESS ANALYSIS UNDER SERVICE AND ULTIMATE LOADS

WELD SEQUENCE DETAILS OF DIAGRID NODES

8

9

65

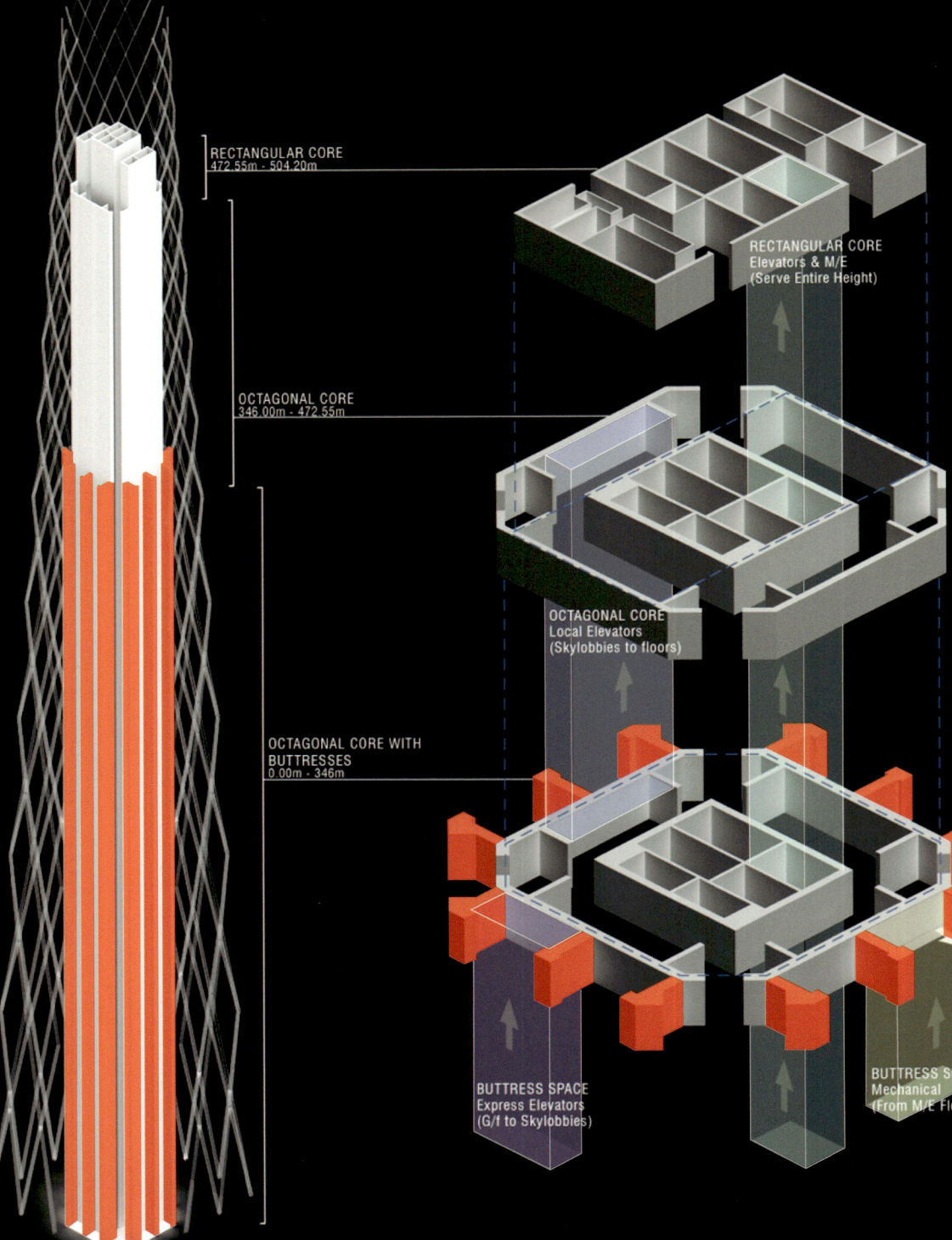

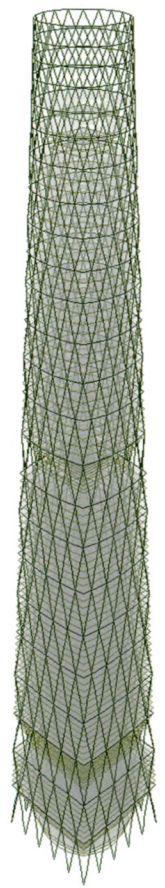
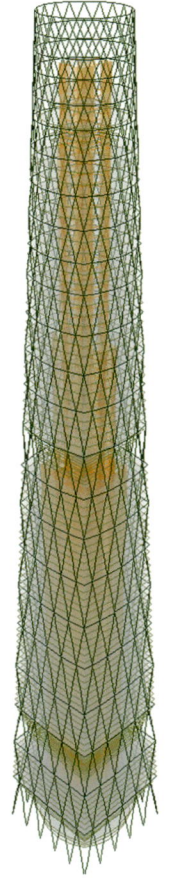

SHEAR WALL CORE
AS LATERAL LOAD
RESISTING SYSTEM

EXTERNAL DIAGRID
AS LATERAL LOAD
RESISTING SYSTEM

CORE-DIAGRID AS
LATERAL LOAD
RESISTING SYSTEM

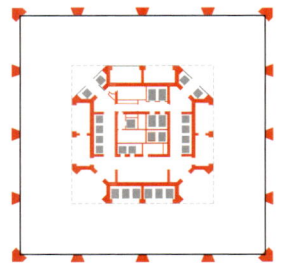

10 Inside-out core and structural concept
11 Axonometric and floor plan diagrams
   showing lateral load resisting systems

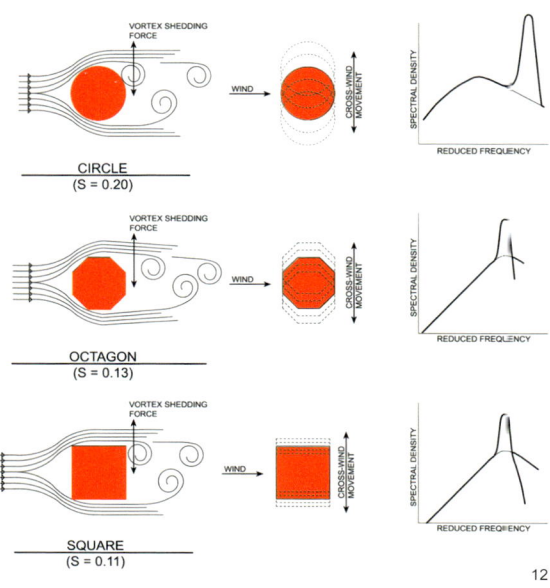

12 Building geometry optimized for vortex shedding and reducing wind loads where they are the greatest
13 The transforming geometry, taper, and faceted surface, break up wind forces and reduce lateral loads on building
14 Diagrid structure optimized for gravity loads at base and steeper columns and lateral loads at top with shallower column angles
15 Graph showing Lotte tower diagrid angle's structural efficiency

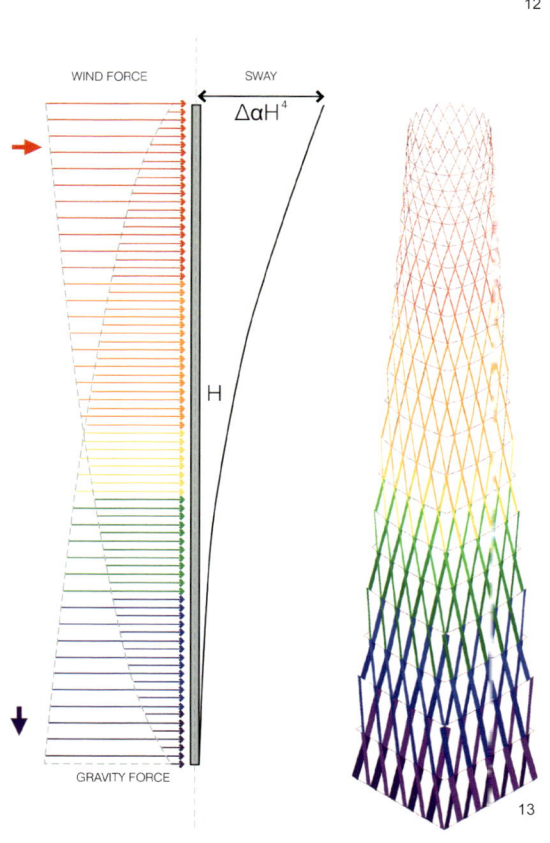

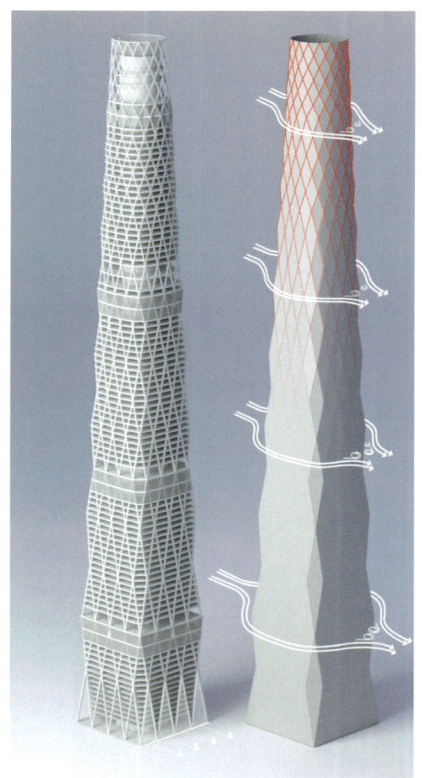

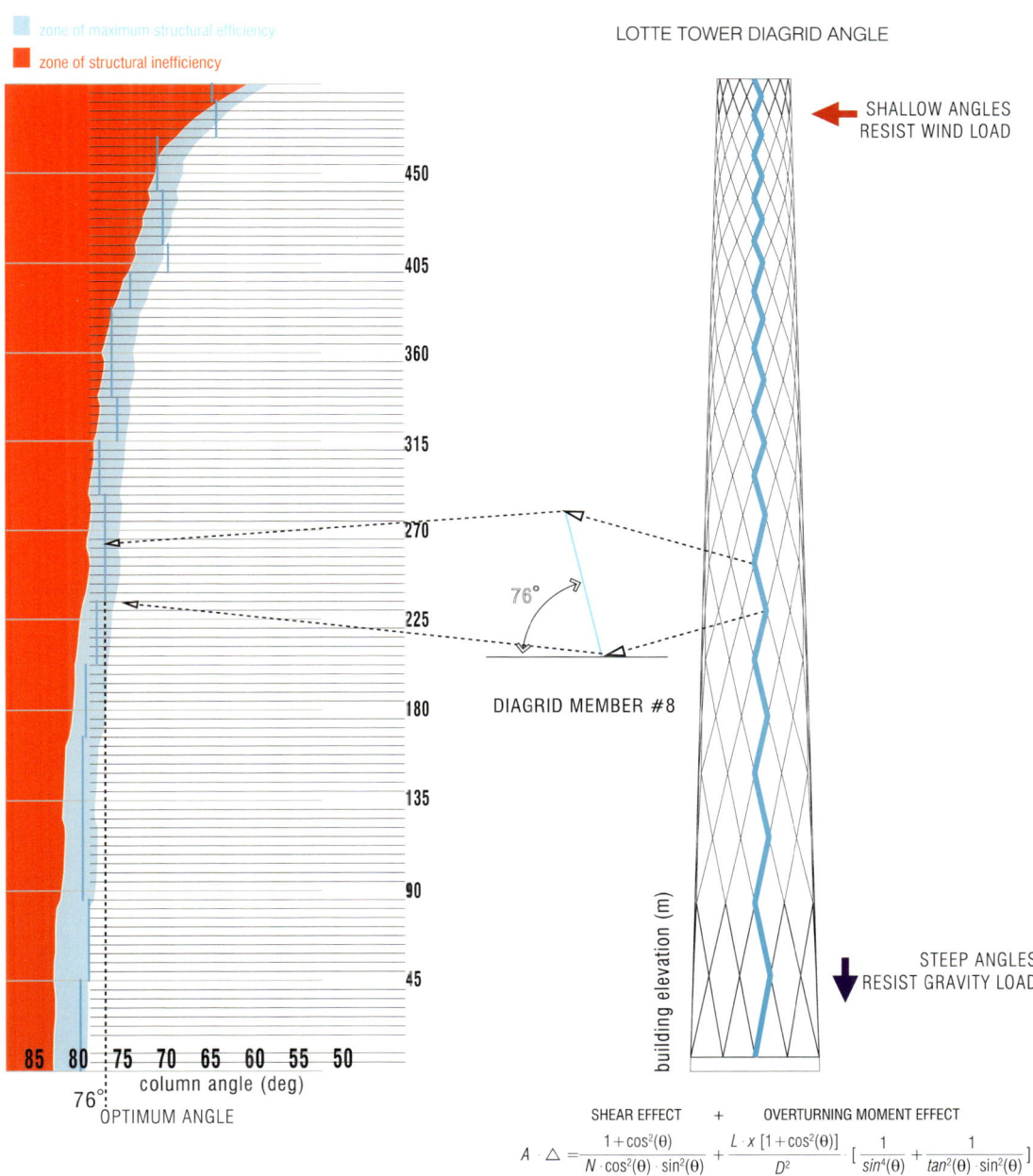

16

16 Curtain wall detail
17 Curtain wall system
18 View of tower from the south

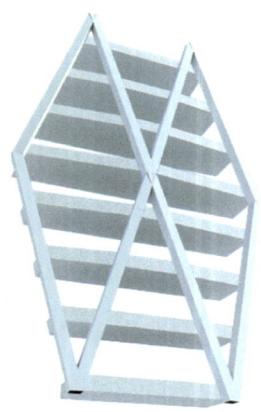

SLAB AND STRUCTURAL DI-
AGRID

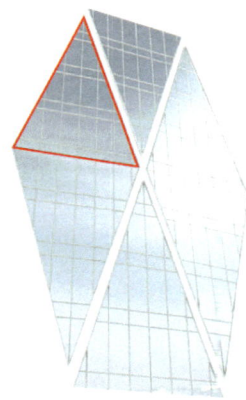

TRIANGULAR GLASS
PLATES

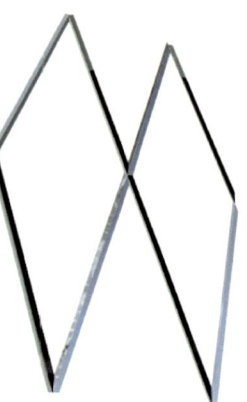

POLISHED ANGULAR
REVEAL

COMPLETE SYSTEM

17

20

21

19 View from plaza showing the art wall of pixilated and programmable LED fixture grounding the tower at the pedestrian level
20 Interior rendering showing art wall
21 LED fixture mock-up. The diamond pattern references the diagrid skin of the tower
22 Observation Deck view >
23 Sky Restaurant view >
24 Building crown view >

22

23

Project Floyd
Geneva, Switzerland
Designed 2009

Project Floyd is located in an area of Geneva characterized by a unique combination of prestigious international organizations and extensive parklands. The design establishes a strong identity for the building among its illustrious neighbors, while responding sensitively to the surrounding parkland.

The design meets the client's aspiration of consolidating its four existing premises within a single, landmark headquarters building and explores an architectural expression that celebrates and heightens the relationship between the building and its context. The design draws references and connections not only from its immediate context, but also distant landmarks and views across the Lake Geneva and the Alps.

The building's form grows from a single geometry, unique to the site, which is manipulated with a blend of architectural and sustainable strategies to effectively reduce the real and perceived impact on the site. A central courtyard is carved out to create a garden on the ground plane, maximizing views and daylight to the floors above. By elevating the northeastern and southern corners of the building, the simple courtyard form is manipulated to increase permeability across the site, opening it up to the local neighborhood, facilitating direct pedestrian connections with local transport hubs, and providing perceived continuity with local parks through a merging of the boundaries between building and landscape The garden created at the heart of the site eloquently integrates the building with its surroundings, while providing an inspirational setting to promote the well-being of the employees. The headquarters meets the ground in only two spots, allowing easy access to the garden from the northeast and southwest corners of the site. The building has a double cantilever (sixty and forty-eight meters) in order to increase permeability and establish strong visual links with the lush environment.

The natural landscape introduced on the building's grounds provides an inspiring entrance to the headquarters and references the neighboring Parc Barton and Botanical Gardens. The headquarters meets the ground at the most prominent southern corner of the site which has been reserved for the entrance lobby. The lobby is carved from the massing and creates a six-story atrium that provides a striking first impression and reinforces the building's identity. The entrance lobby is filled with natural daylight and is animated by informal meeting spaces that overlook the lobby at the upper office floors. At the reception area, employees and visitors are introduced to the continuous landscape stair that weaves throughout the building, interconnecting the entire workplace.

In parallel with the architectural design, the peripheral structural system directly corresponds to the building form and achieves a column-free office space, providing maximum internal flexibility and future adaptability. Each of the three main tubes are formed of six-story deep trusses on each face, which are tied with cross bracing at the top chord roof line and the sloped bottom chord level, which complete the formation of the multi-story tubular box frames.

All office floors benefit from spacious, column-free floor plates spanning eighteen meters. A variety of interior configurations can easily be implemented within this fluid workspace, providing long-term flexibility to accommodate the client's evolving needs. Taking into account research on international best practices in office spaces, the design incorporates natural ventilation and open workspaces, using low partitions to allow ample exposure to natural daylight and ease of communication. Every floor has a collaborative work area oriented to the landmark Jet d'Eau, containing pantries, lounges, smoking rooms, and general gathering spaces. The headquarters has been carefully planned to provide a functional and efficient workplace for all employees. The double-aspect open plan design allows for natural ventilation during moderate seasons via the quilted skin. During hot and cold seasons, the comfort levels are enhanced through geothermal technology, by chilled beams and a radiant ceiling. Fundamental to the new headquarters is a desire to change the existing client's business culture of closed-off working environments to a much more flexible workplace that promotes collaboration. The new workplace incorporates a continuous element throughout the building, an approach which simultaneously breaks down silos between departments, and allows the workplace to have both horizontal and vertical connections. This unique organizational feature—embedded through all floors—engages the employee/visitor at the entrance lobby and subsequently weaves throughout the building toward all key building programs, ultimately terminating with the panoramic views at the restaurant and roof terrace.

The quilted façade design enhances panoramic views and maximizes natural daylight, while sheltering the office spaces from direct sunlight and heat gain by decreasing direct solar incident angles. The high performance glass façade creates a dappled pattern of shadows, supplies warm light to the offices, and provides a breathing façade to minimize energy demand in moderate seasons. The intelligent geometry maximizes the amount of daylight that infiltrates the building, as well as enhancing the views from within. The site's highly visible location allows the curtain wall system to offer unique visual experiences to passers-by, whether traveling by train, car, or on foot.

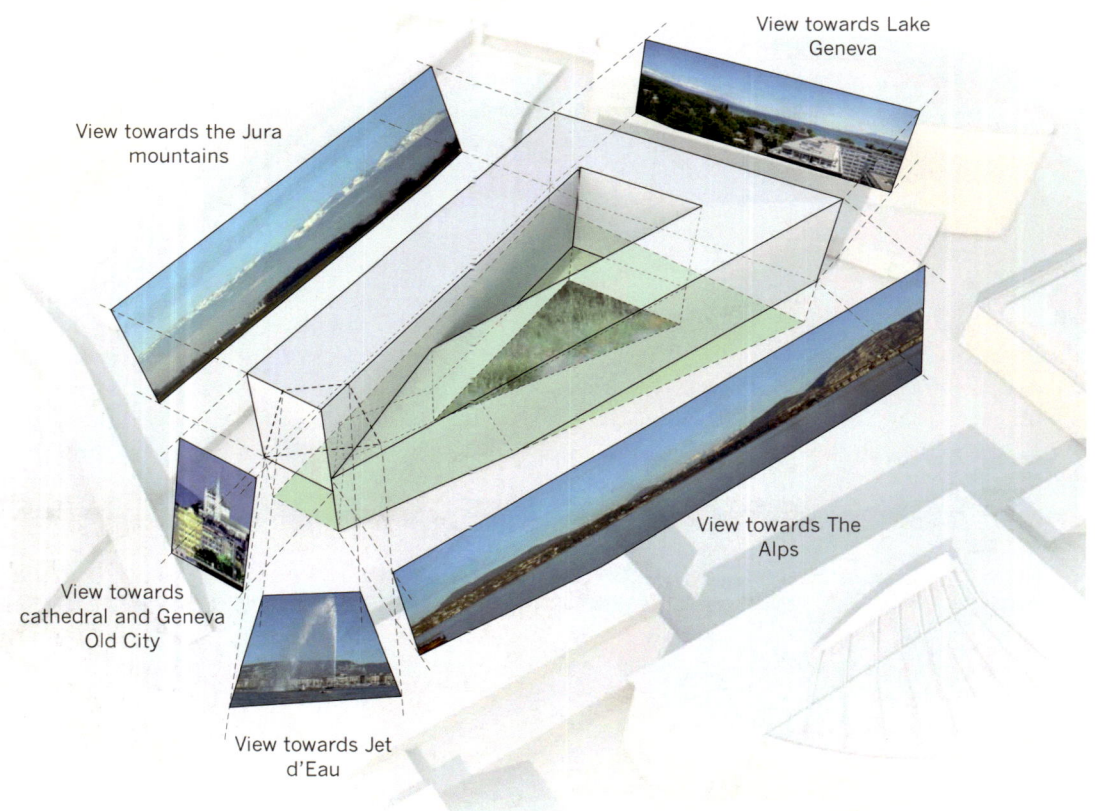

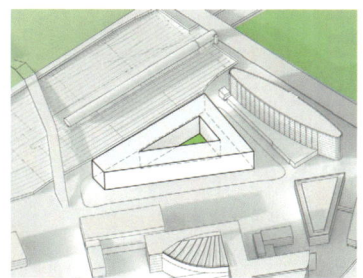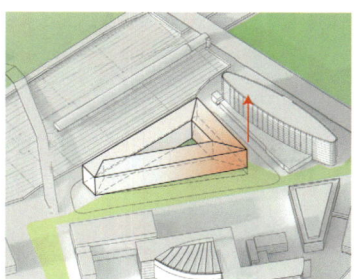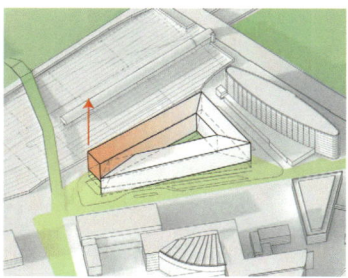

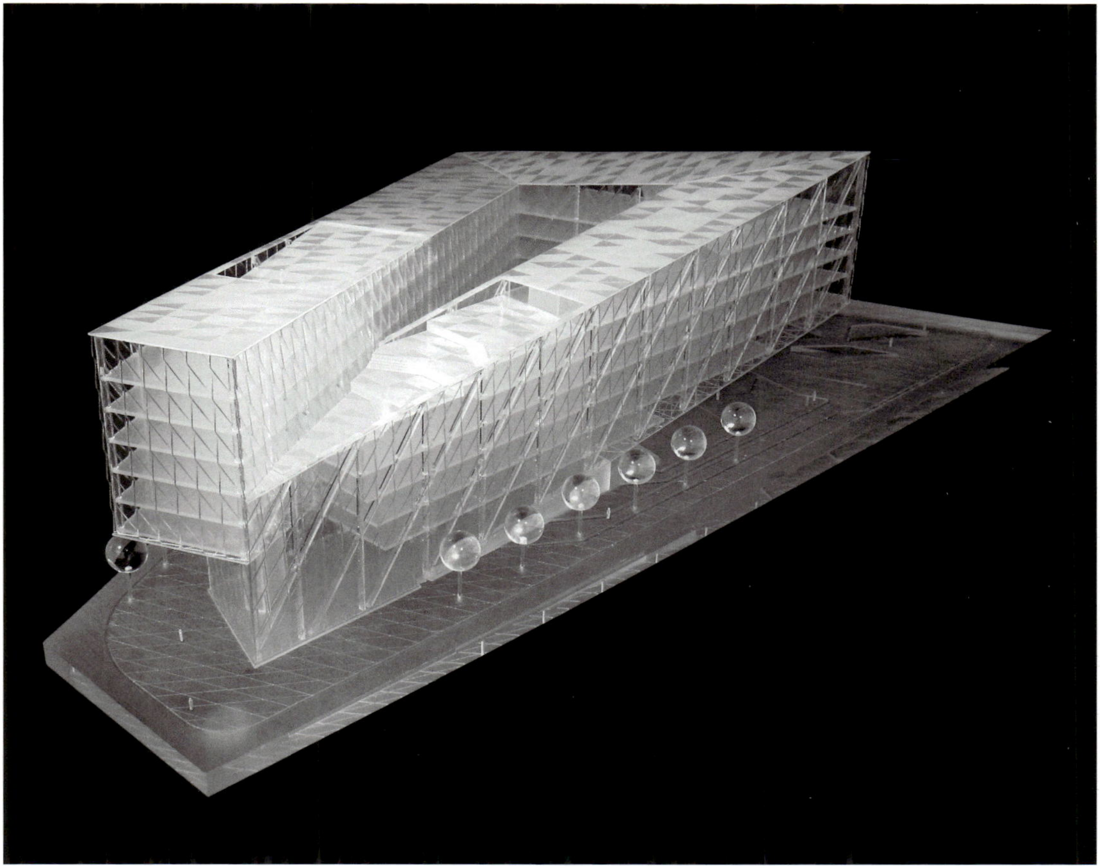

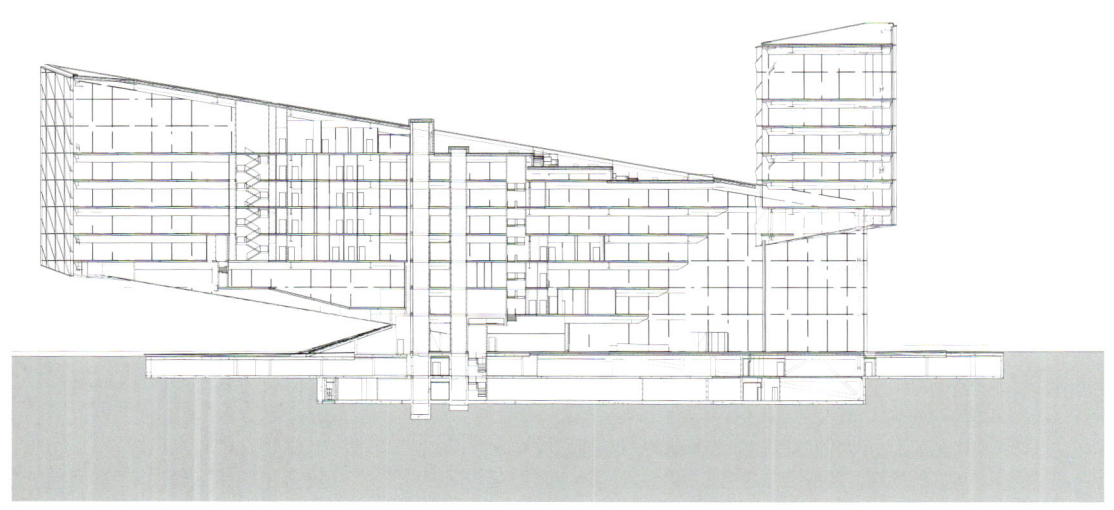

5

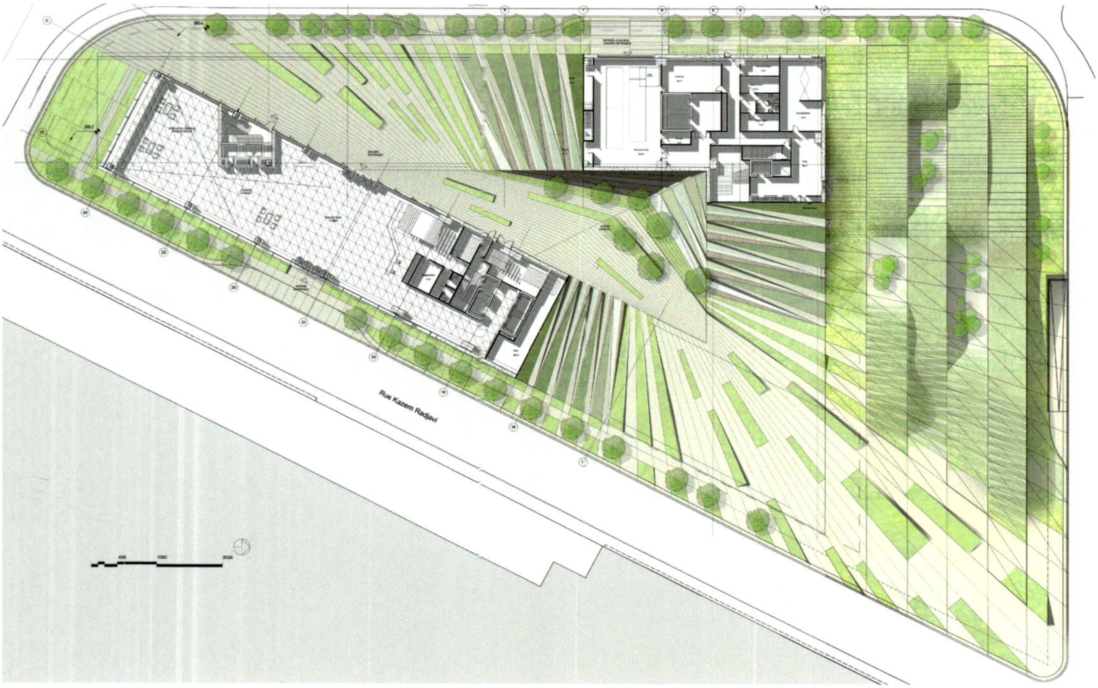

6

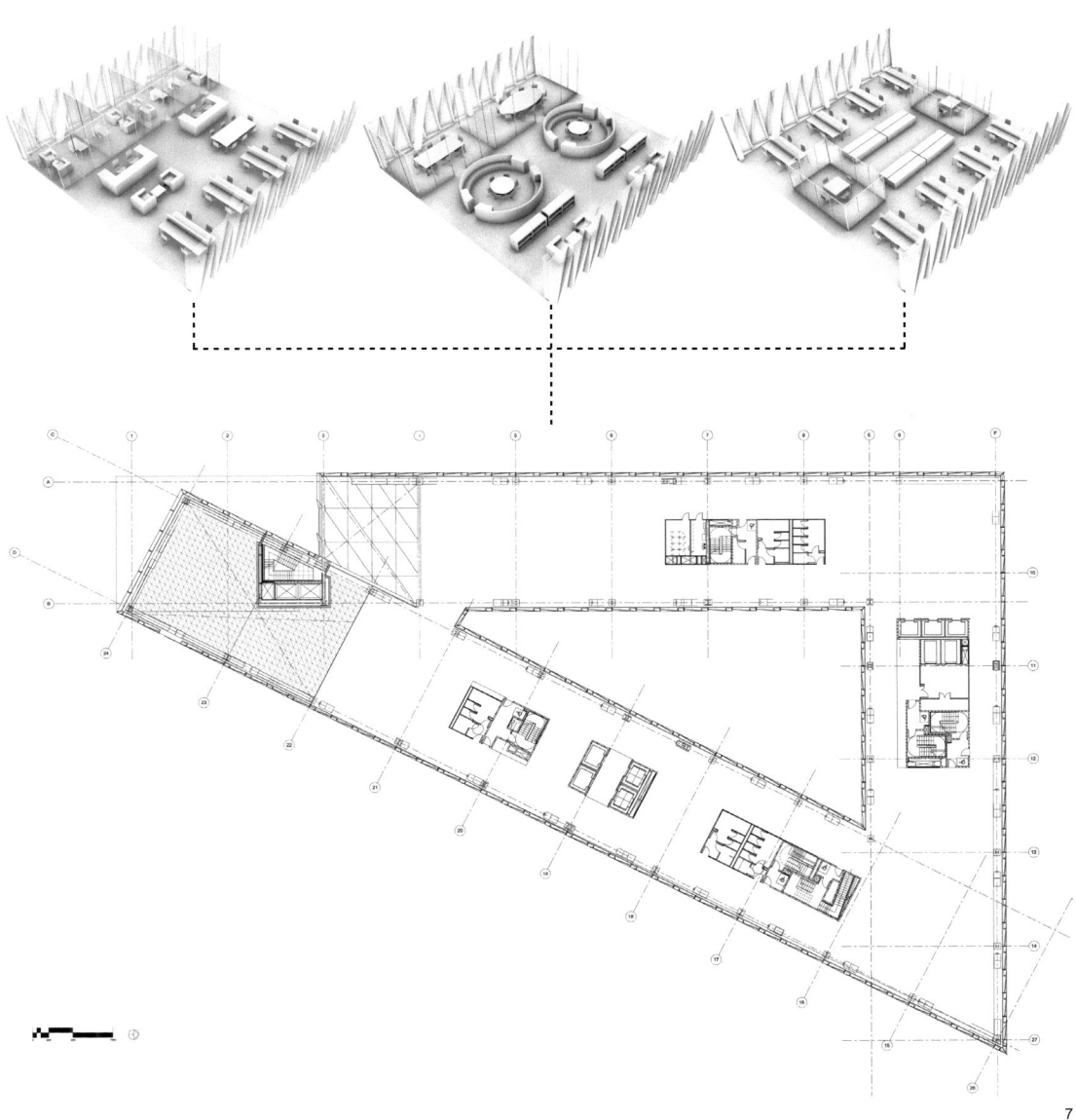

<< 1 Aerial context plan
 < 2 Building formation diagram
 < 3 Conceptual view diagram
 < 4 Concept model photograph
    5 Section through lobby, auditorium, and restaurant
    6 Illustrative landscape plan
    7 Adoptable eighteen-meter office configuration and typical office plan

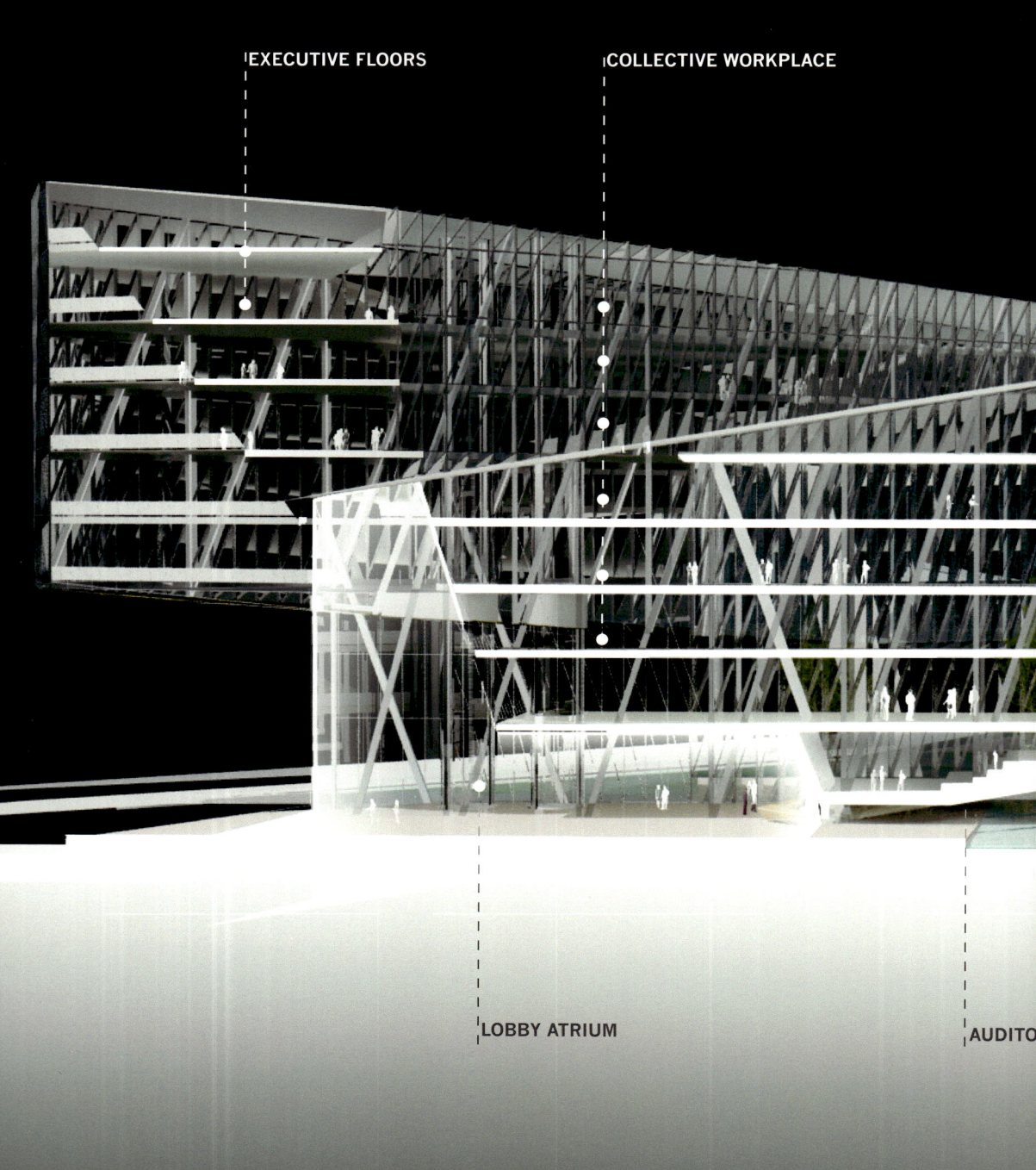

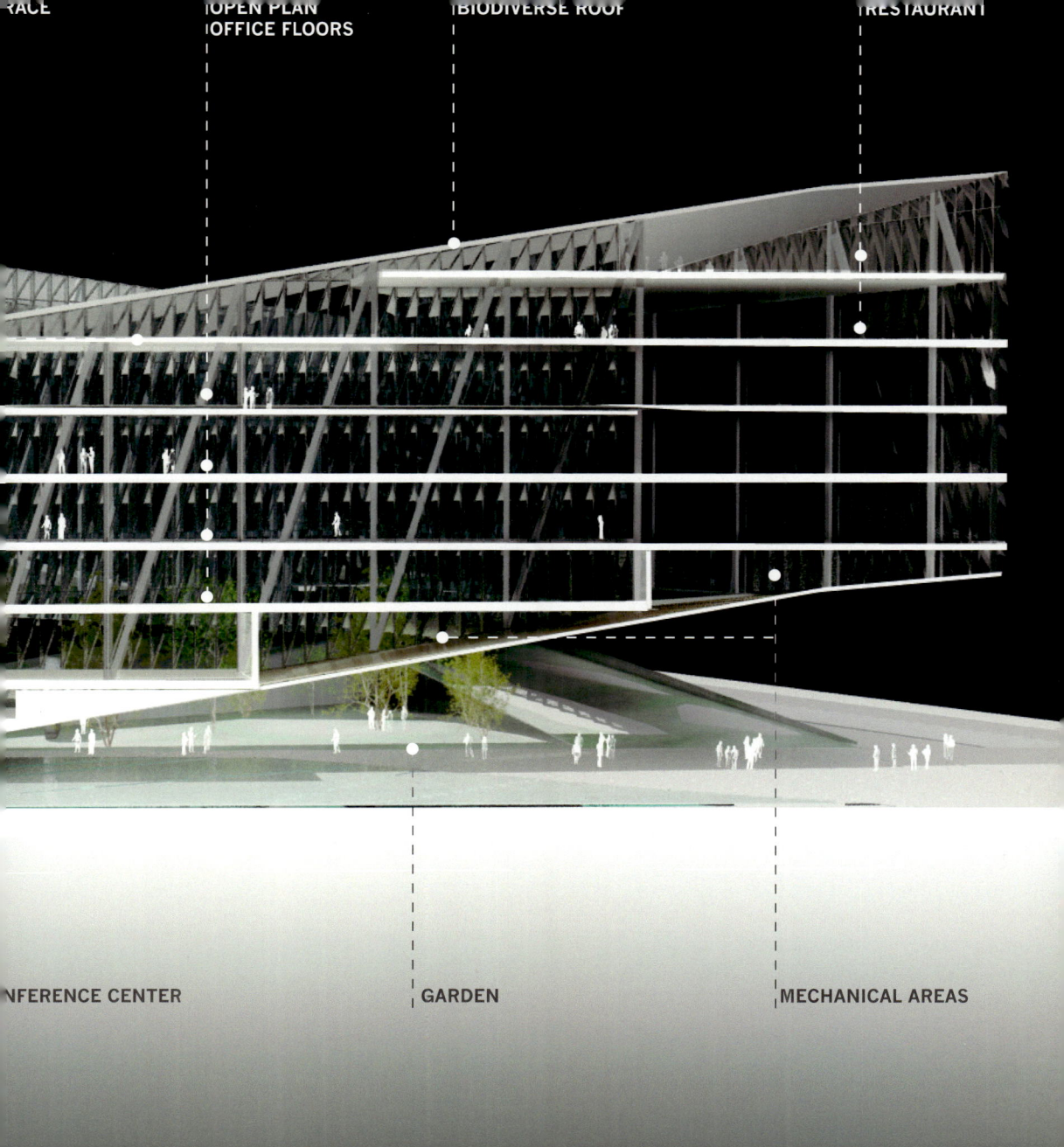

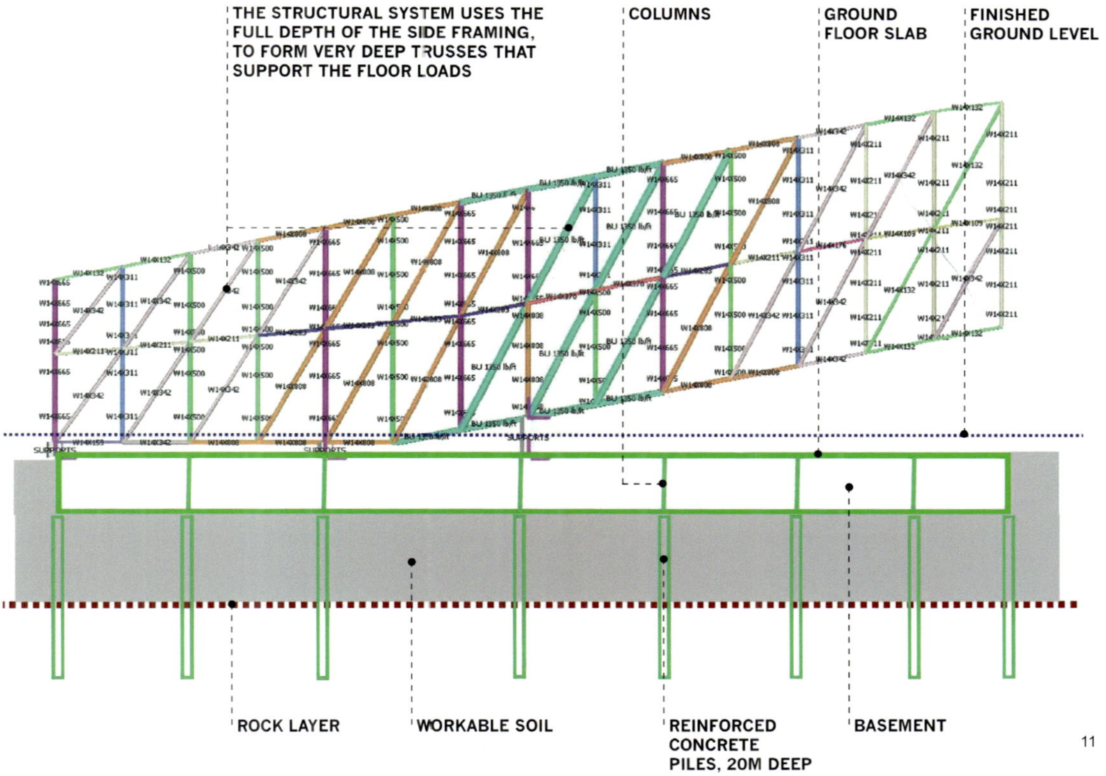

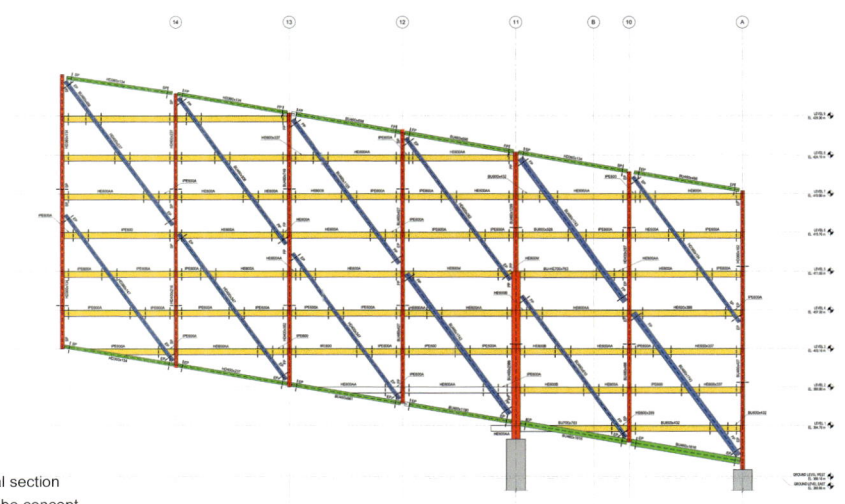

< 8 Longitudinal section
9 Torsional tube concept
10 Perspective showing cantilevered structure
11 Structural diagram illustrating sixty-meter cantilever
12 Structural diagram illustrating forty-eight-meter cantilever

85

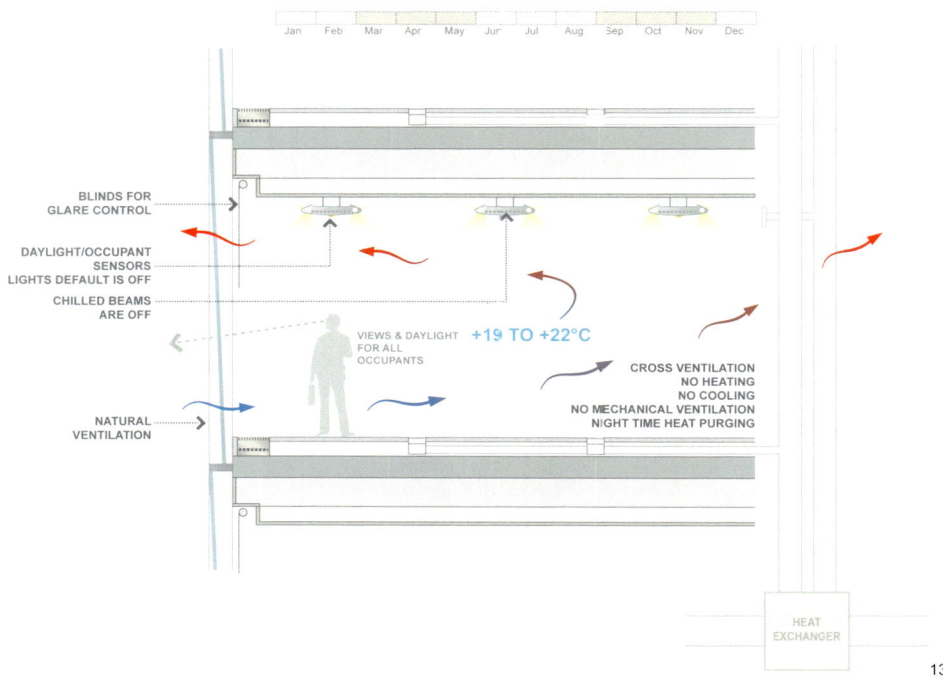

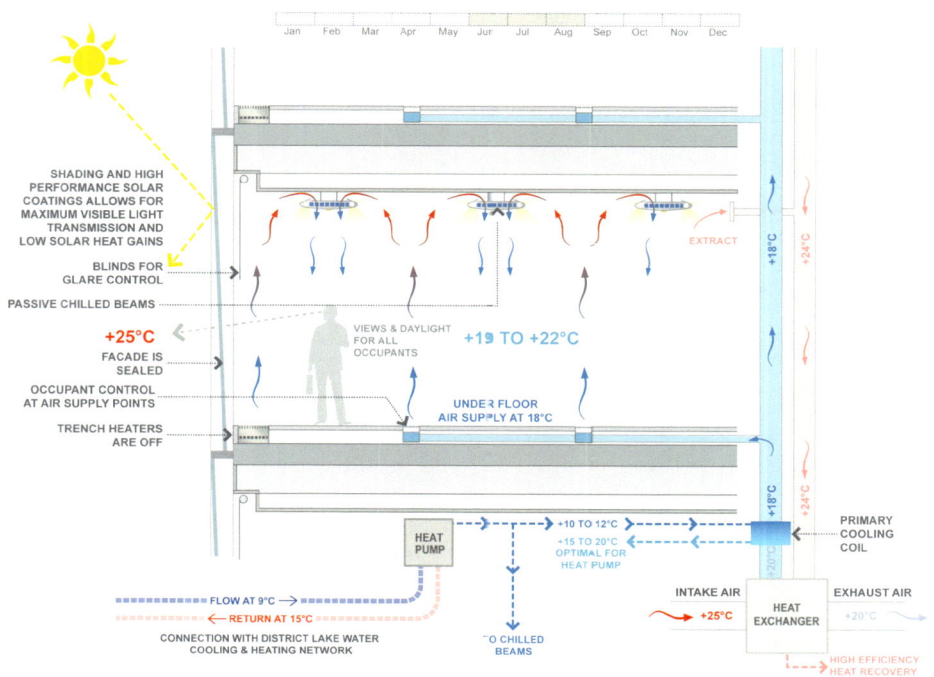

13 Moderate season ventilation strategy
14 Warm season ventilation strategy
15 Project Floyd garden
16 Sustainable design concept
17 Lobby atrium diagram >
18 Courtyard view from Rue de Desert >
19 Main lobby view >

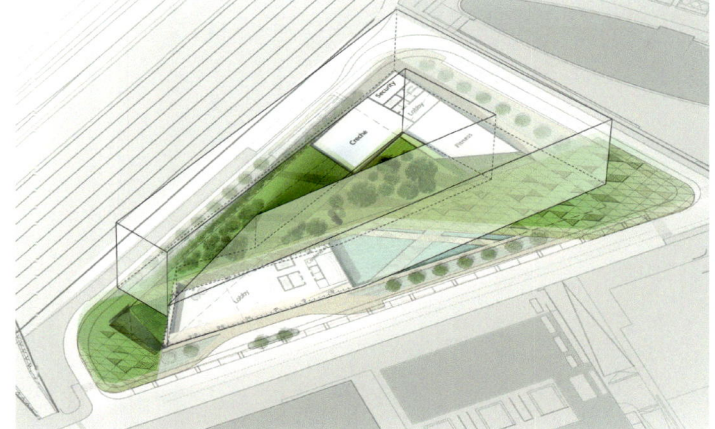

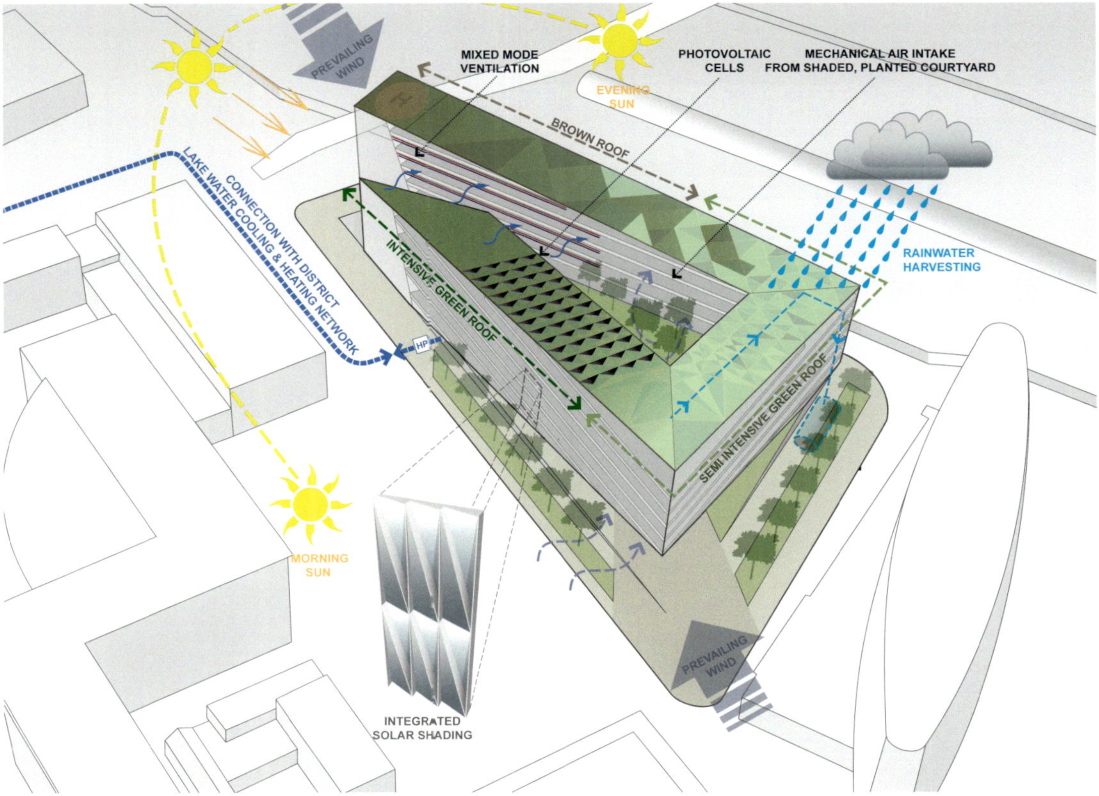

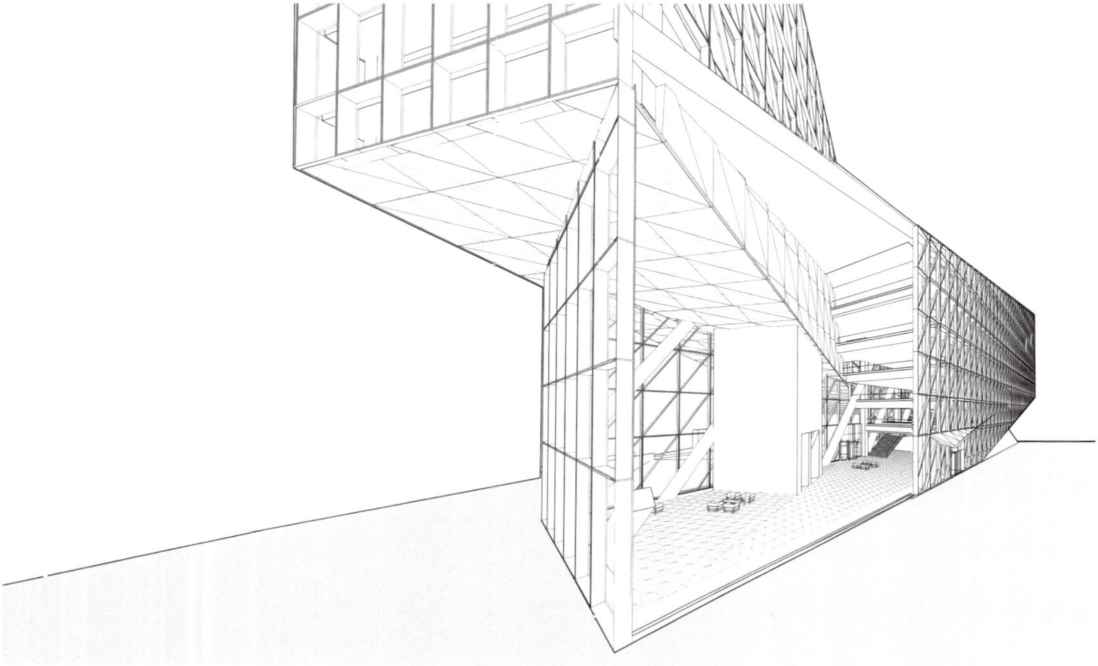

17

18

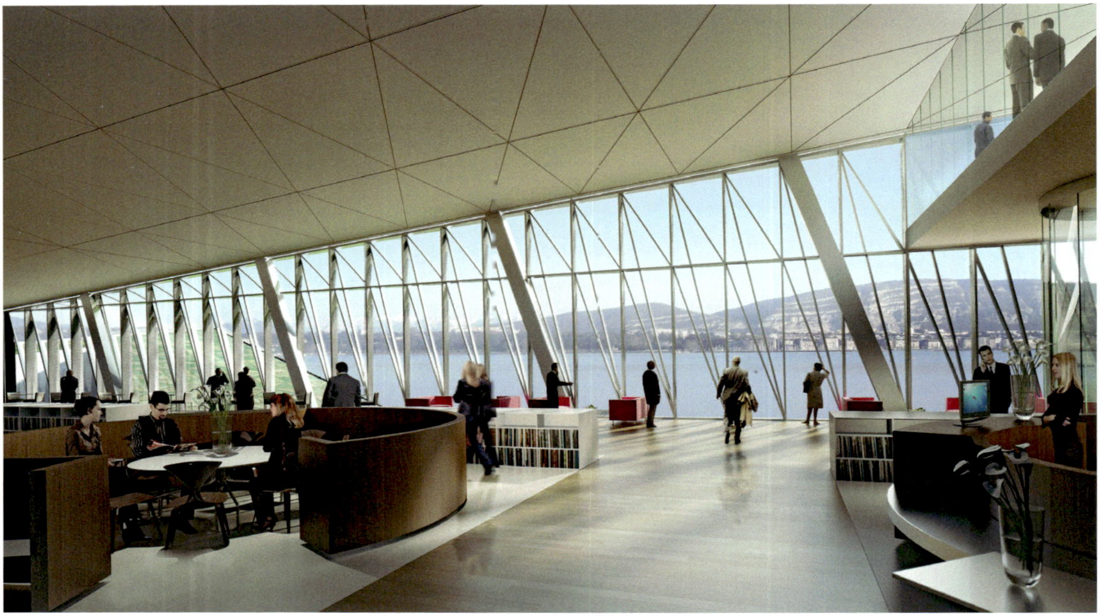

20

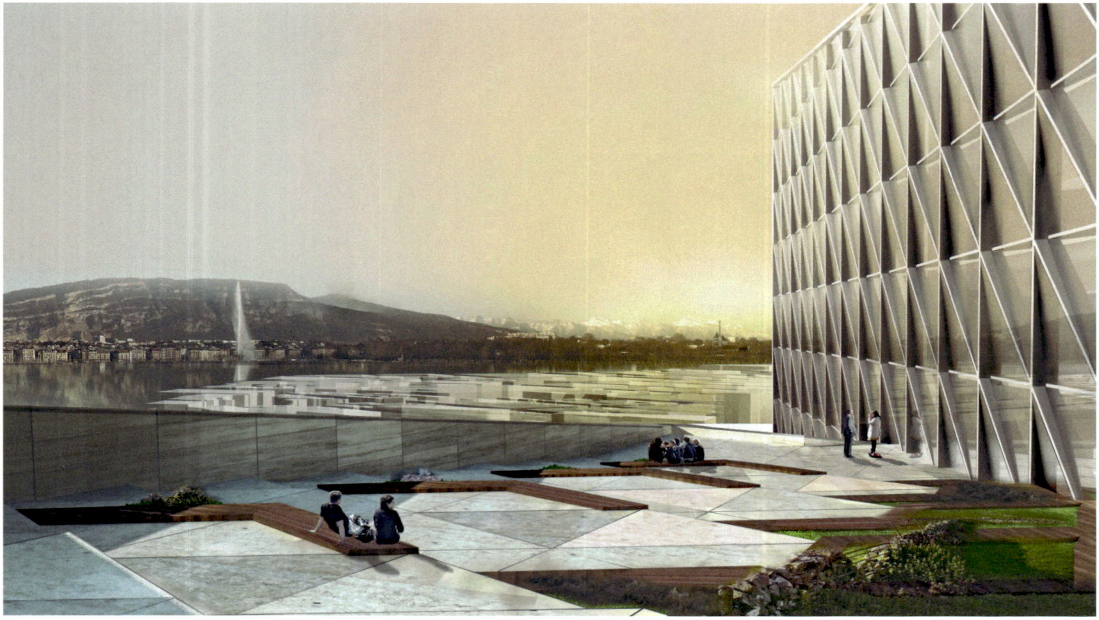

21

20 View from office level
21 View from rooftop terrace
22 View from Rue Kazem Radjavi

PSAC II
The Bronx, New York
Designed 2008–11

Strategically located on the outskirts of Manhattan, PSAC II (New York City's Public Service Answering Center, better known as the home of 911) is located on a prominent nine acres of land at the intersection of the Hutchinson River and Pelham parkways in The Bronx. The site is significant, nestled between Robert Moses Greenways and the Richard Meier-designed Bronx Development Center.

In order to diminish blast exposure, the 240-foot-cubic building references classic Renaissance fortress design through its setbacks, rotation on the site, and its use of sculpted landscape. With its edges facing the Hutchinson River and Pelham Parkway, the cube appears as diamond-shaped, deflecting forces at its perimeter while minimizing the visual mass of the large structure. A large berm of native grasses encircles the building, disguising blast setbacks, while enhancing both the visual and security requirements.

The siting of the building, bermed landscaping, and serrated façade, reinforce the idea of "approaching edges." In all cases, the architecture is approached obliquely, with a continually changing appearance. The serrated aluminum and charcoal grey-toned metal of the façade give the building dynamism and visual anonymity, creating a defensive camouflage. Depending on the viewer's direction of travel on the Hutchinson River Parkway, it gives a darker charcoal or lighter silver appearance. Windows and mechanical louvers inserted within the façade, intentionally disguising the program behind.

At the intersection of site, landscape, and building, the transparent security pavilion stands in contrast to the serrated façade of the main solid structure. A courtyard garden beyond provides outdoor relief space for the employees of the emergency answering center. Reinforcing the idea of "approaching edges," the exterior berm, sloped entry, and planted roof converge at this point to form the main gateway of the secure building. The glass entry pavilion stands at the intersection between defendable building and open landscape beyond.

The pure cube form offers flexibility and efficient planning for the functional demands of the workplace within. Internal free section and multi-story spaces reflect the cube design work of Le Corbusier and Walter Gropius.

At the heart of the building is the 50,000-square-foot, thirty-foot-high call center floor. The high demands for communication, IT, and MEP (mechanical, electrical, plumbing) are serviced by adjacent floors directly above and below. As an emergency answering center, the facility is designed to be self-sufficient to offer twenty-four-hour-a-day, seven-day-a-week service, even if utilities are interrupted. Communication, IT, and mechanical systems are duplicated within the building for full back-up operations, providing reliable continuous service.

As a secure, 24/7, blast defensive facility, the building offers few opportunities for a sustainable and progressive workplace. Windows are restricted, even for the ground floor lobby and cafeteria areas. In addition, employees may be reluctant to use the outdoor courtyard at night or during the winter. However, the project does manage to introduce sustainability and nature to this highly stressful environment.

For this reason, the team is integrating the AMP (Active Modular Phyto-remediation) Wall, which was published in *SOM Journal* 6. This is a phytoremediation wall that uses the roots of plants to clean the air and provide a natural element to interior spaces. It is organized into a row of eleven eight-foot-wide, twenty-foot-high totems, forming an interior "green zone."

The call center floor gets indirect, diffuse light that emanates from serrated ceiling panels hung above, providing a calm space for emergency dispatchers to operate. The serrated ceiling reflects the building's rotated siting and two-tone façade "edge" theme on the interior of the building. This 911 emergency answering center will be staffed by both the police and fire departments, creating a new unified response center for the City of New York's five boroughs.

< 1 Aerial view of New York City
  2 Aerial site rendering
  3 Section and plan showing employee courtyard

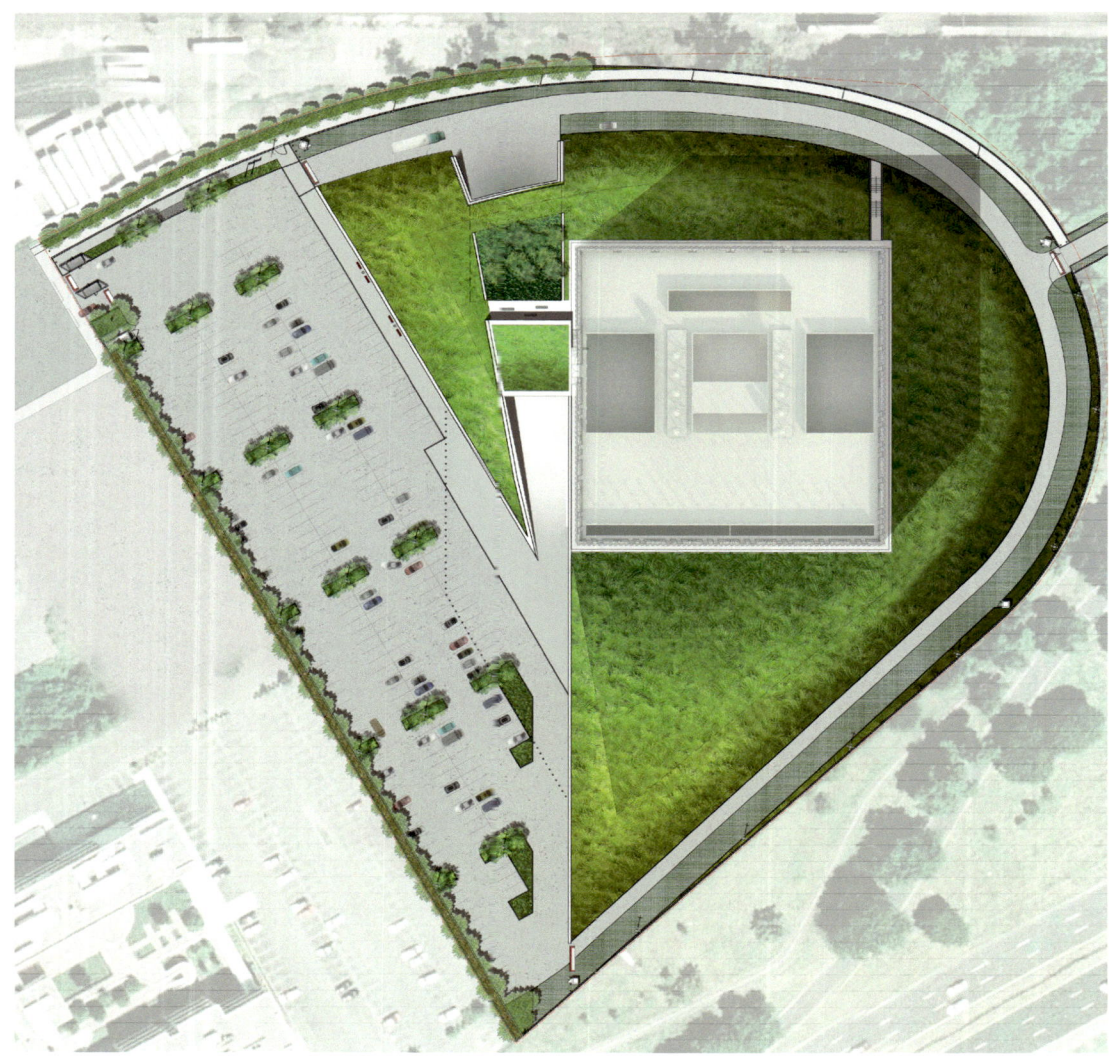

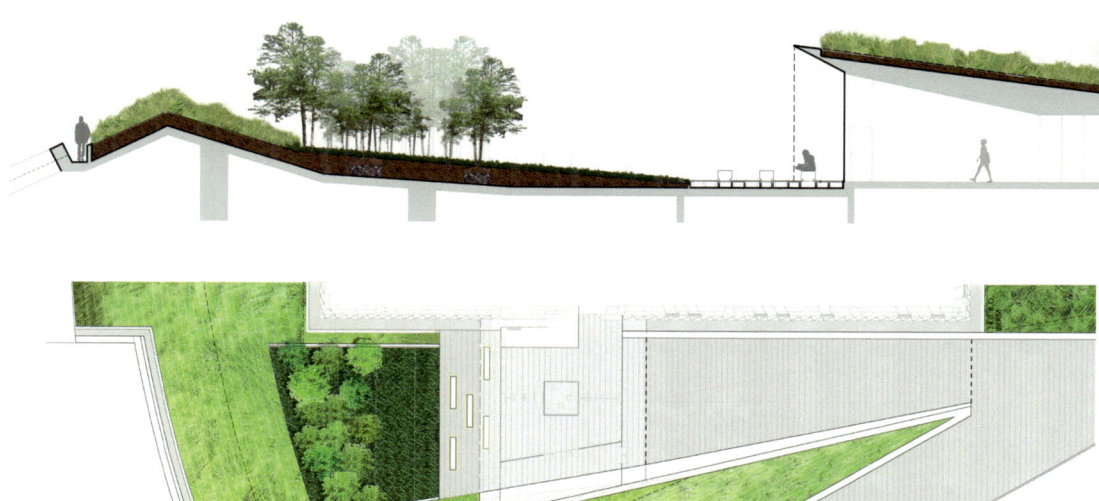

4 View of call taker floor
5 Detail view of call taker floor
6 Section of call taker floor
7 Axonometric view of call taker floor and administrative
  floor showing 50,000-square-foot floor plate
8 Ground floor plan

4

5

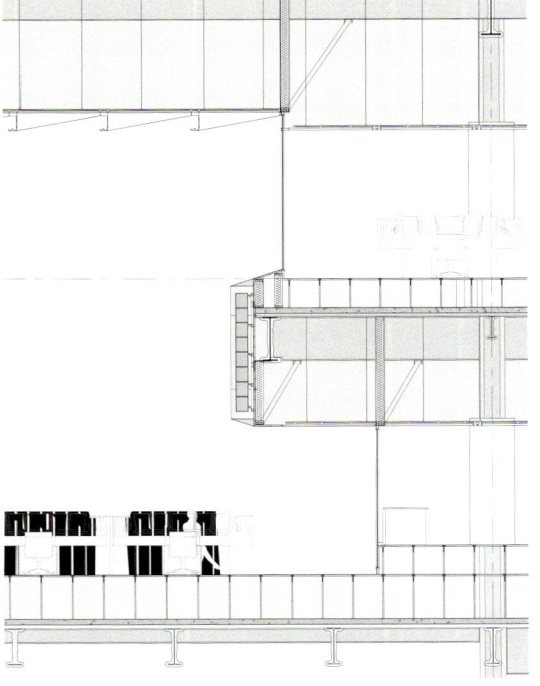

6

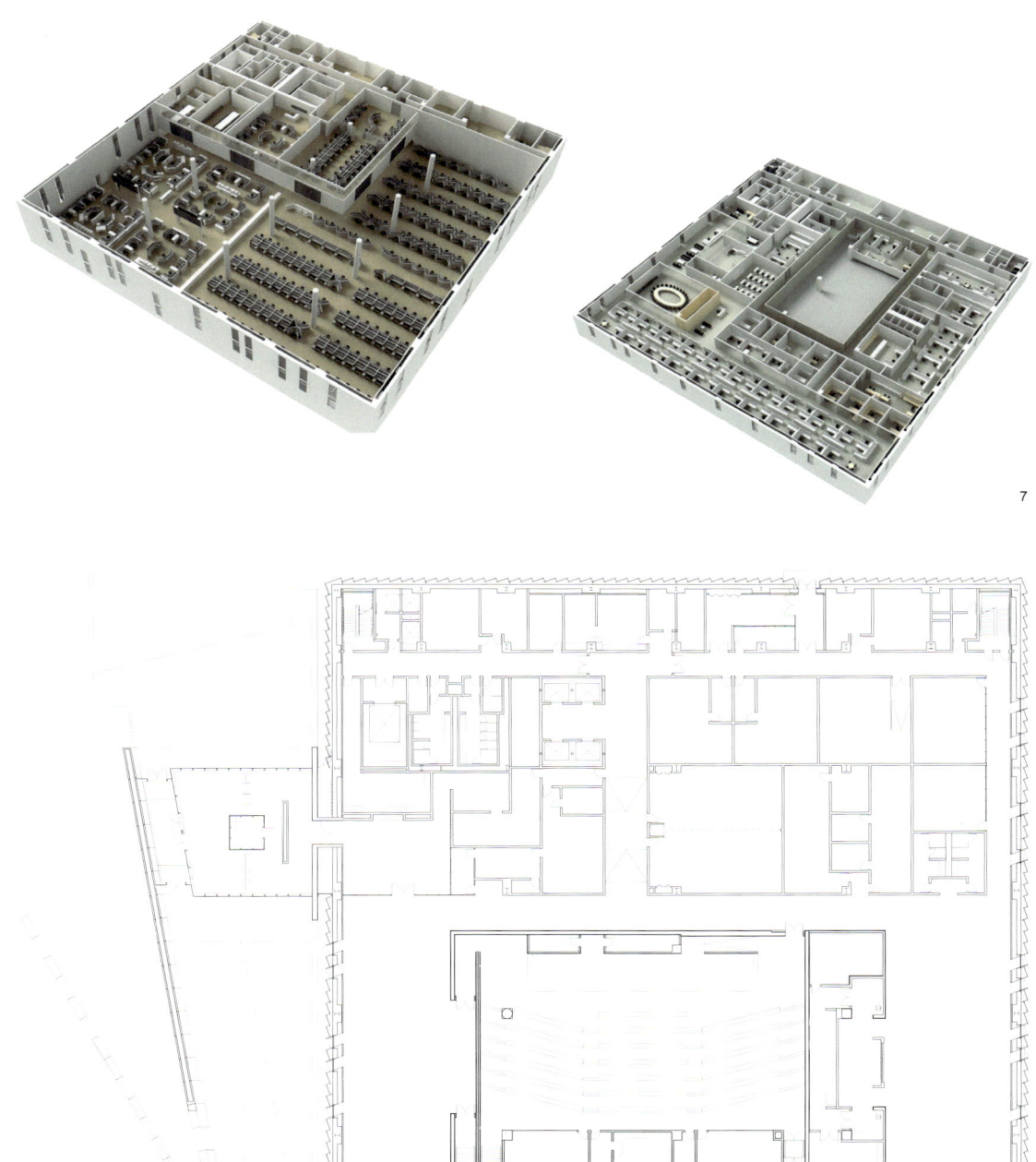

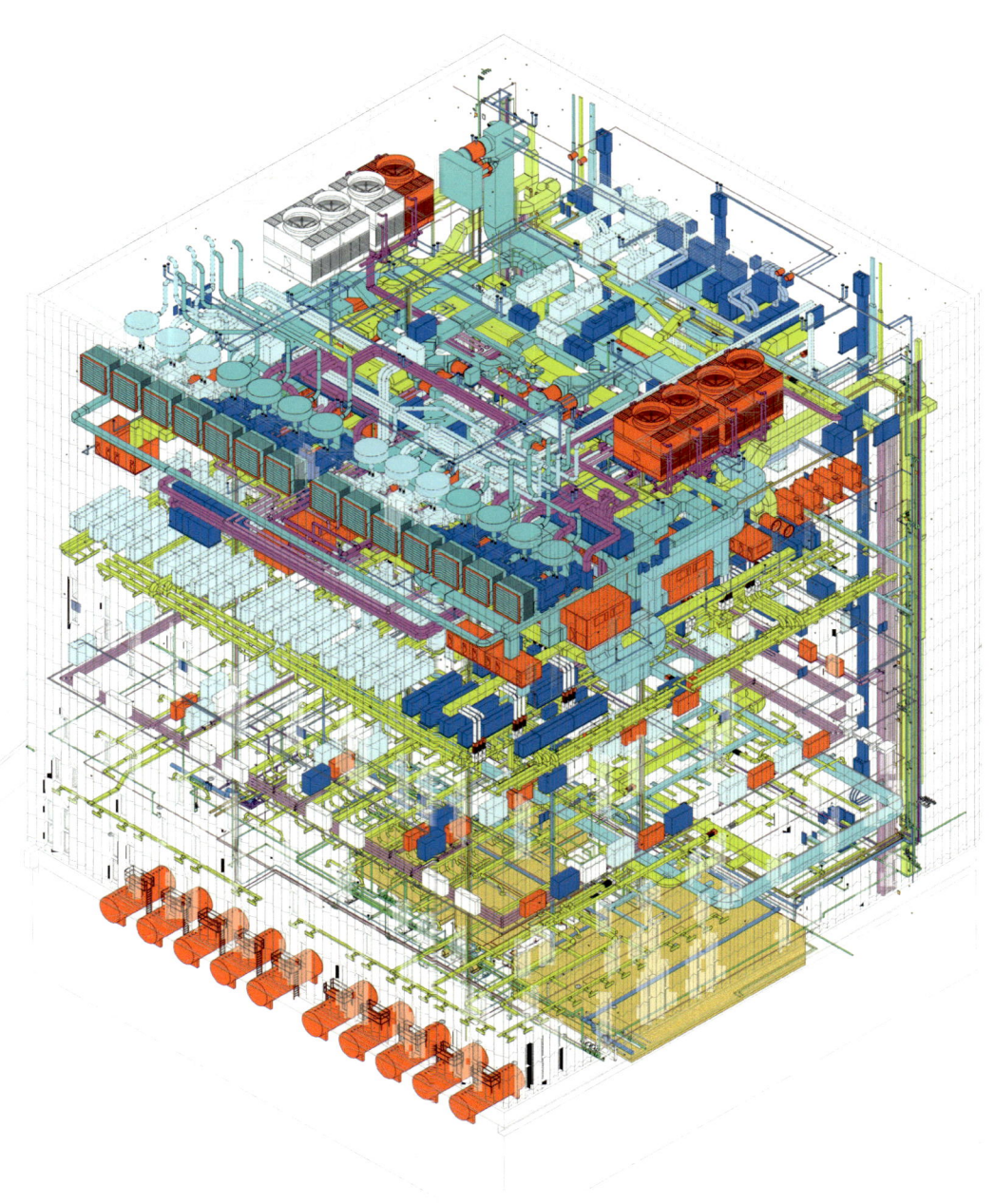

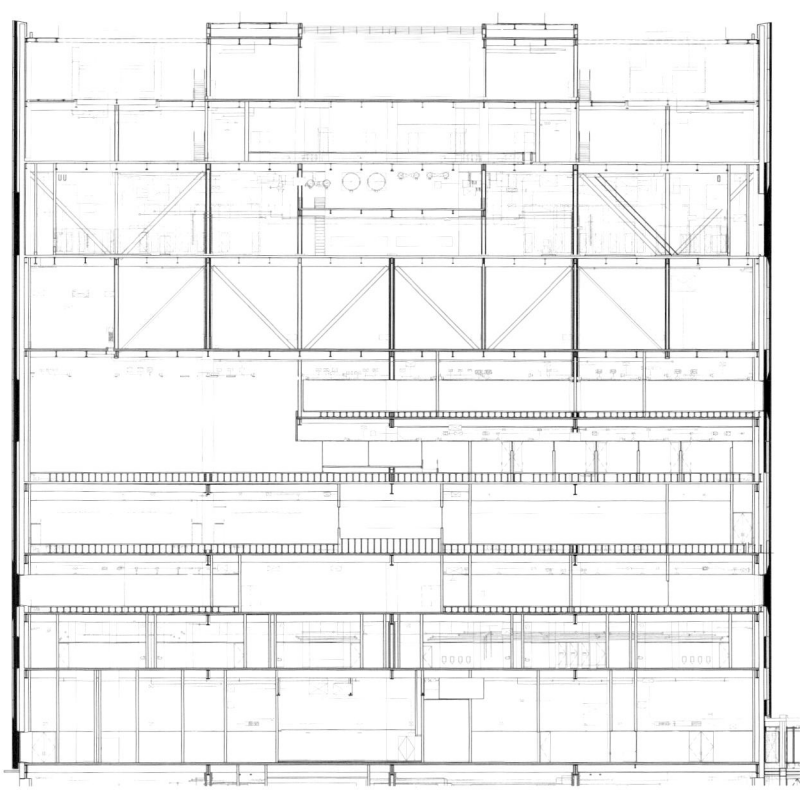

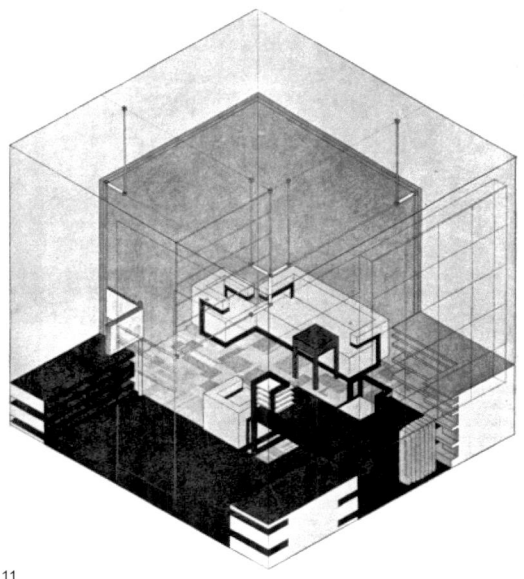

9 BIM (REVIT) model showing all mechanical equipment and structure
10 BIM stacking section showing complex floor heights
11 Gropius's plastic experiment of an office design from the nineteen-twenties

12 Section and plan of unitized panel system 1
13 Section and plan of unitized panel system 2
14 Model elevation of building exterior
15 Detail of brushed aluminum façade
16 Axonometric model of auditorium
17 Interior rendering of auditorium with recycled barn oak cladding

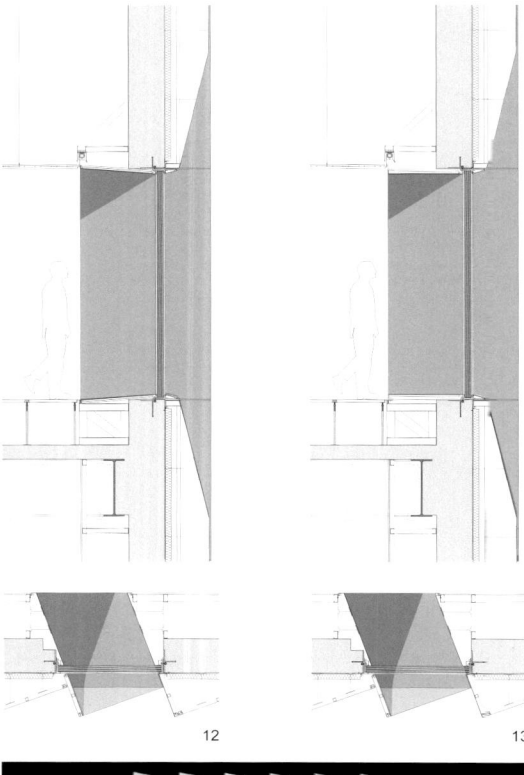

12 13

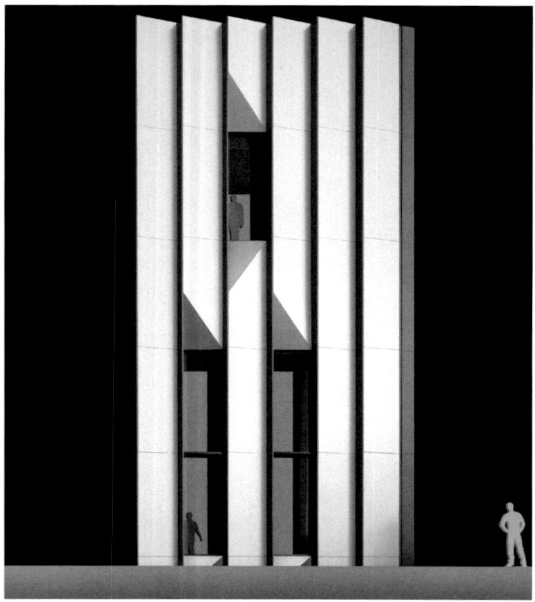

14

15

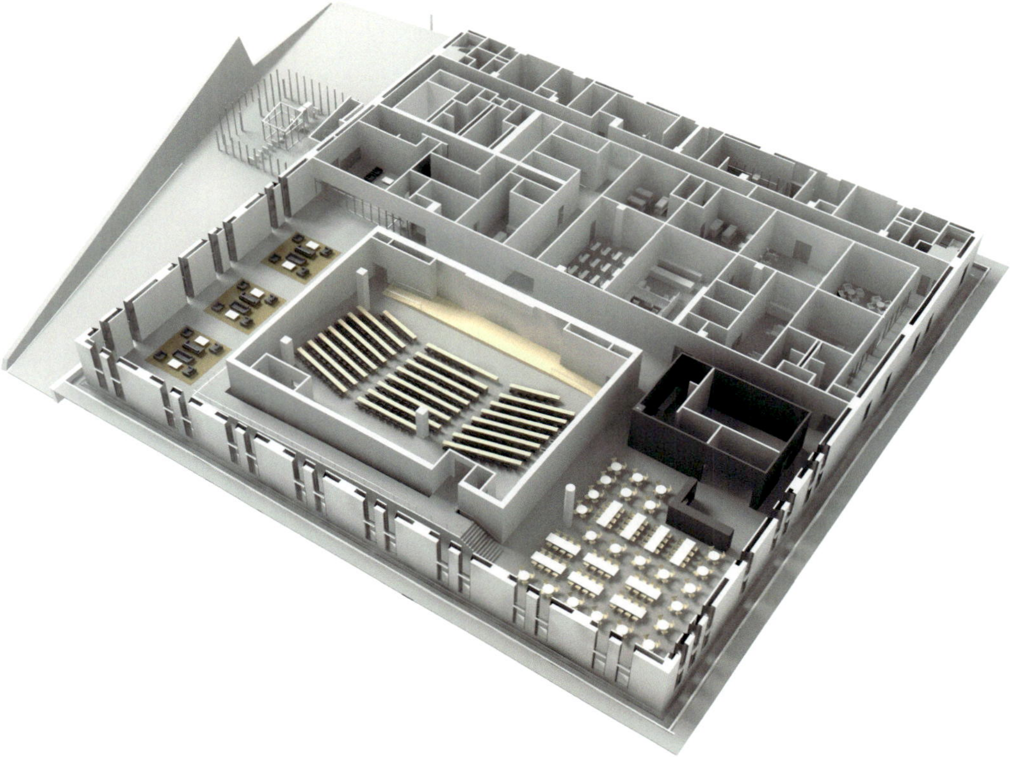

18 Interior rendering of cafeteria
19 Interior rendering of lobby showing AMP (Active Modular Phyto-remediation) Wall System
20 Exterior rendering
21 Glass pavilion entrance rendering

20

21

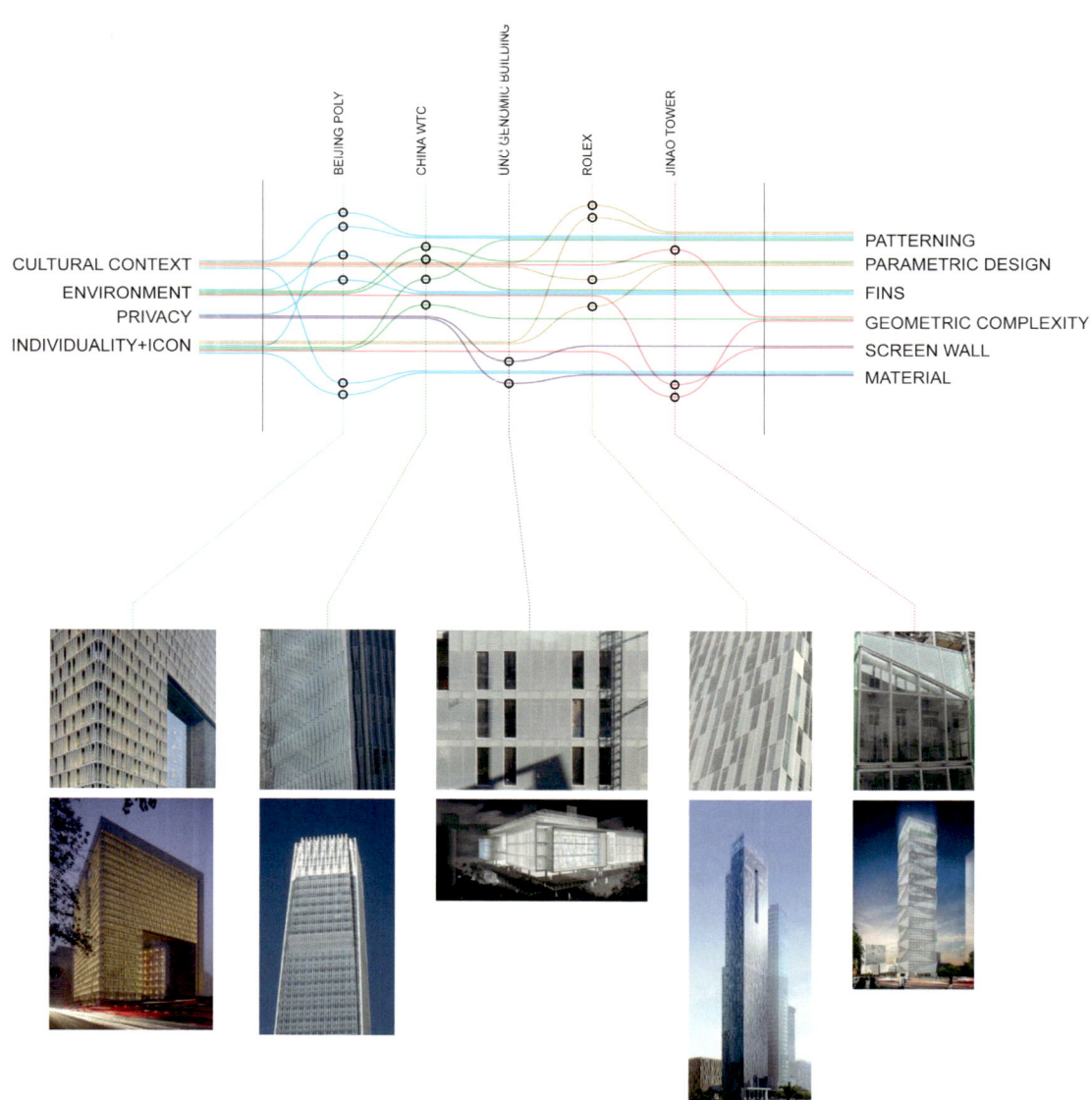

High Performance Building Enclosures
A Cross Section of Curtain Walls

Since the early decades of the twentieth century, modern architecture's ongoing project has over time become reliant on a series of tectonic innovations which underpin (almost literally) the entirety of the global built environment. These include the glass curtain wall, the electric elevator, the steel frame, and the plenum ceiling, each of which represent paradigm-changing technologies that reshaped our understanding of the built urban environment. For the purposes of this exercise, we have limited our focus to the most visibly prominent of these ingredients—the exterior wall. Through a process of (seemingly) unending refinement not unlike the microchip in scale and ubiquity, flexibility, and capacity, the exterior envelope is often called upon to be all things to all users. Bearing this in mind, we thought it valuable to consider how five different walls, all of which are either built, or being built, perform relative to contemporary demands placed on them. These demands, or imperatives, address four major issues (cultural context/environment; security; privacy/individuality; and iconography), using seven techniques or tropes.

While the exterior envelope is rarely, if ever, considered in isolation from the overall design of the building which it encloses—conceptually revisiting the performative aspects of only the exterior envelope allow projects to be considered at a medium to micro scale, linked referentially to the macro scale ambitions of the buildings which they enclose. Considered across this selection—the walls use visual tropes of patterning and camouflage, parametric design, exterior fins or screens, biology, materiality, and complex geometry to respond to their respective issues.

Typologically it is interesting to note that four of the five are highrise buildings, and that all of these are mixed-use towers—a fact that is not necessarily revealed by virtue of their enclosure strategy. All of these buildings were designed in the first years of this century and have since informed the design of at least a generation of progenitors.

The exterior wall as a building component is called upon to address new issues particular to our time: issues of cultural context, environmental performance, security, and identity.

POLY BEIJING

CONCEPT: A combined headquarters and rental office building is located on a trapezoidal site with major south and west exposures. Because these elevations receive the most intense solar gain in Beijing, they have been designed using a deep, staggered sunscreen of stone fins anchored by an exterior maintenance balcony which both shades, and allows maintenance of, the interior glazing. These fins provide deep shadow over the glass and are carefully oriented to minimize disruption of views from the interior.

DOCUMENTATION: Originally conceived as cubic elements spanning vertically, the solution evolved to one in which smaller pieces were aggregated around a mechanically fastened vertical tube for stability and consistency. A repetitive pattern is embedded in what appears to be a highly random, screen-like expression.

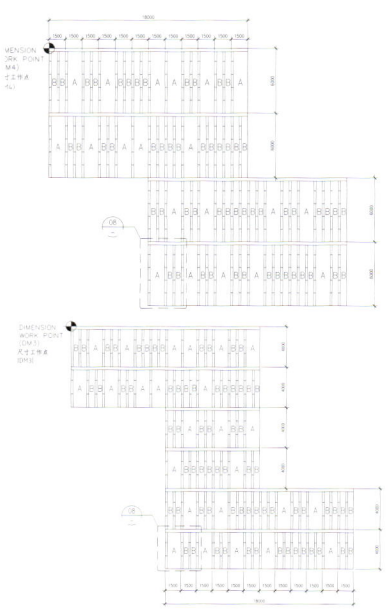

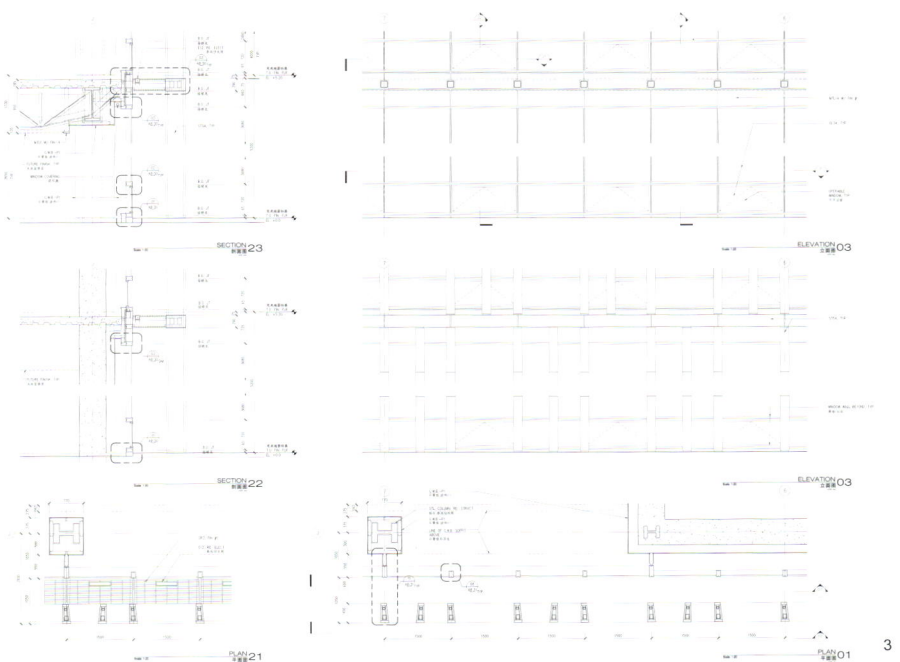

3

IMPLEMENTATION: The stone screen wall has been successful in representing values of permanence, strength, and longevity. In addition to solving problems of heat load, the building does a good job of providing panoramic views which open out to the city with a combination of floor-to-ceiling glass in the office interiors and dark mullions which visually recede.

1 Repeating module of the exterior stone sunscreen
2 Southwest corner condition showing monumental openings in the outer stone screen to admit daylight deep into the inner atrium
3 Curtain wall drawings showing exterior stone screen: plan, section, elevation
4 Night view of completed building

CHINA WORLD TRADE CENTER

CONCEPT: The tallest building in Beijing is designed to meet the strict standards required for LEED Gold certification. Achieving this while also maintaining the maximum amount of perimeter glazing for the office and hotel functions required the introduction of a series of frosted glass fins to both shade the glass and visually unify the vertical expression of the tower elevations, which themselves gently undulate as the tower rises from the ground, creating a rippled, textured surface of contrasting light and shadow.

DOCUMENTATION: The challenge of the exterior wall's development lies in the legibility of the glass fin, which while relatively deep when seen at the scale of an individual glass panel, is miniscule in contrast to the scale of the tower. As a result, a polished stainless steel cap that is elliptical in profile was introduced; its curved surface creates a continuous highlight in the sun. The face is then intermittently routed out to contain LED point fixtures which illuminate the tower at night.

IMPLEMENTATION: The wall has performed in excess of the design expectations by providing a scrim of visual texture which mediates the admission of light to the building interior. Following installation, the fins have proven to intensify the admission of indirect lighting deep into the floor plate interior, especially in the hotel rooms at the top of the tower. All of this has been achieved with a solution which minimizes horizontal surfaces that catch the famously prodigious dirt in Beijing's atmosphere.

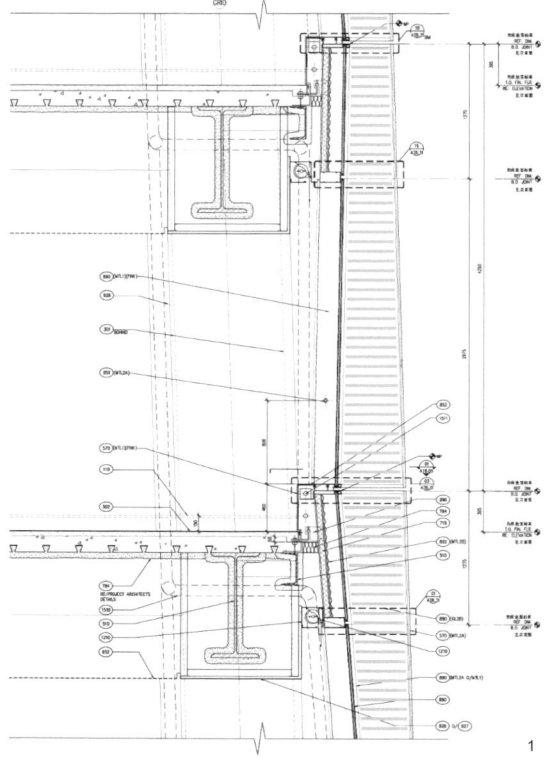

1

2

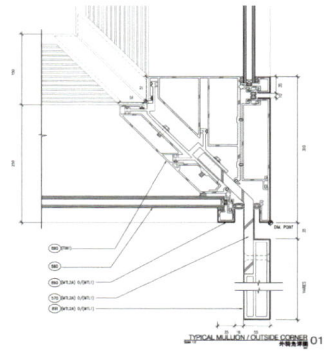
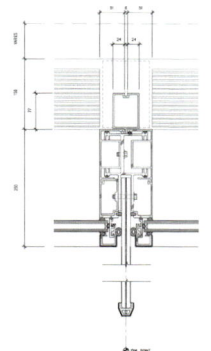
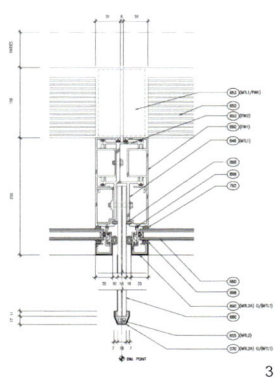

1 Detailed wall section illustrating floor assembly and exterior glass fin
2 Final full-scale visual mock up of exterior wall
3 Detailed drawings of window mullions and exterior glass fins at corner, widest, and shallowest conditions
4 Detailed view of the upper register of the tower
5 Oblique view of final visual mock up

UNC CHAPEL HILL

CONCEPT: The demands of a large research program were met with a plan that articulated the program into three distinct concrete volumes. To emphasize the connection between the programmatic volumes the design team employed a glass jacket that contains the program volumes and creates the building's unified appearance while addressing the environmental, contextual, and privacy issues of the client and site.

DOCUMENTATION: The challenge of the exterior wall's development lies in the design of the glass surface. This enclosure employs a fifty-five percent ceramic frit reverse dot pattern allowing controlled natural light to enter the spaces, presents a semi-opaque surface to address the contextual relationship to adjacent masonry campus buildings, and creates a level of privacy for the occupants. Critical to the concept of a unifying jacket is the use of full height glass and minimal expression of mullions and joints. This enables the glass to be seen as a monolithic surface.

IMPLEMENTATION: Presently under construction. The fabrication and assembly of the exterior wall is a unitized panel system.

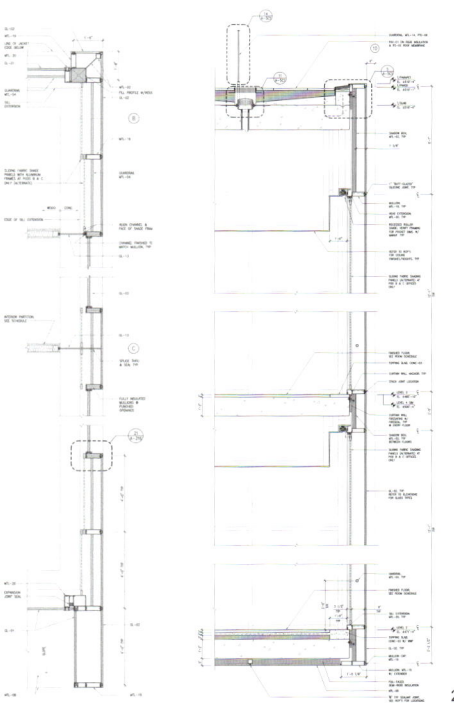

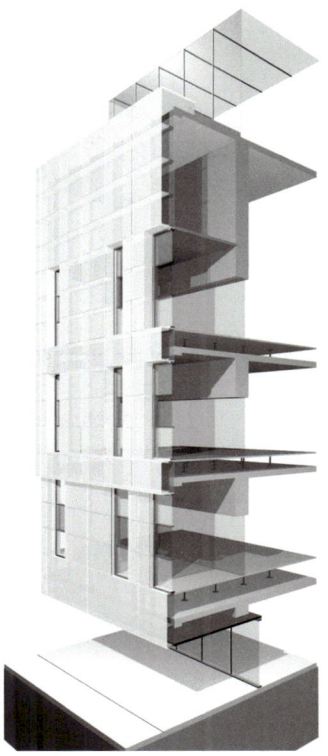

1 Detailed view of the final exterior wall assembly
2 Section through the jacketed glass wall enclosure
3 Sectional study model
4 Construction photograph showing installation of fritted and clear glass panels

ROLEX TOWER

CONCEPT: Located among the hyper-designed urban setting that is Sheik Zayed Road in Dubai, the Rolex Tower establishes a quiet understated presence among competing tall buildings. Recalling shimmering desert mirages, the tower utilizes a patterned exterior wall to balance transparency and translucency, creating an animated manipulation of reflections and light.

DOCUMENTATION: The design team utilized parametric modeling to help inform the optimum pattern to achieve the desired appearance of a shimmering object.

IMPLEMENTATION: Working in collaboration with the owner and exterior wall fabricator the design team studied many options of frit pattern density and transparency. On-site mocks were used for final selections of frit color and glass.

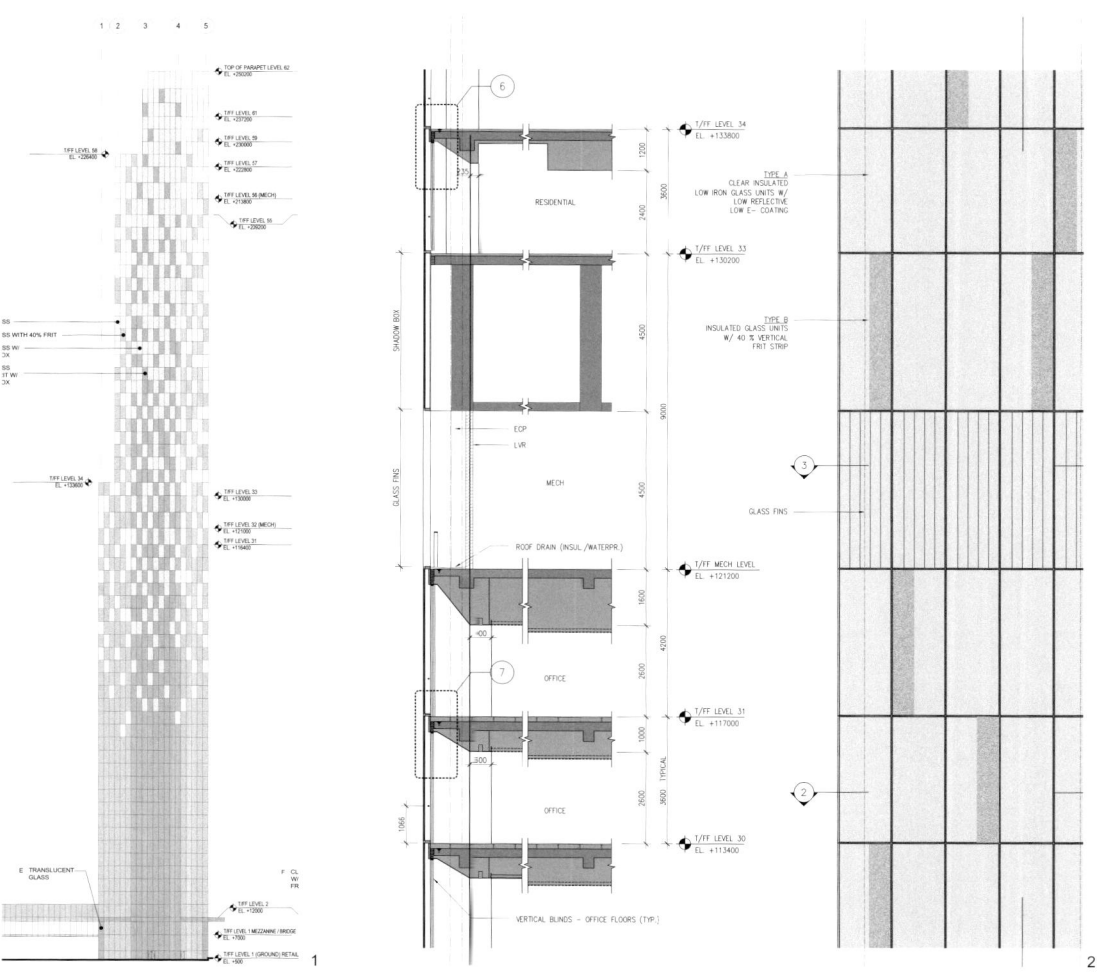

1 Pixellization of east elevation
2 Section and elevation detail of exterior wall assembly
3 Night view of completed building
4 Building crown with vertical slot and diminishing fritted panels visible at top
5 Interior view of fritted seam between screen pattern and clear glass on a typical floor

JINAO TOWER

CONCEPT: A gently folded exterior glass envelope shields a second, fully glazed interior enclosure within a unique, sculptural envelope defined by its undulating profile. Prevailing winds at the site were anticipated to generate a negative pressure on the leeward side of the tower causing air within the cavity to move, cooling the inner glass wall by up to twenty degrees Fahrenheit. The naturally ventilated wall cavity is subdivided in four-floor-high divisions which align with each of the primary diagonal folds. Interior steel catwalks allow the inner wall to be maintained.

DOCUMENTATION: The challenge of the documentation and fabrication of the wall resides in its inherent ability to effectively move air within the cavity and around the tower. This was carefully studied in digital form during the design process using an extensive CFD (computational fluid dynamics) analysis which were refined and informed by the plan and sectional geometries. Subsequently a series of full scale mock ups were constructed on the tower superstructure and evaluated.

IMPLEMENTATION: The final exterior enclosure is now being applied to the tower superstructure. While its thermodynamic performance cannot yet be evaluated, the design team looks forward to measuring the long term performance of this double wall condition executed at a very large scale. Anticipated energy savings have had a significant impact on the sizing and performance requirements of the building mechanical system.

1

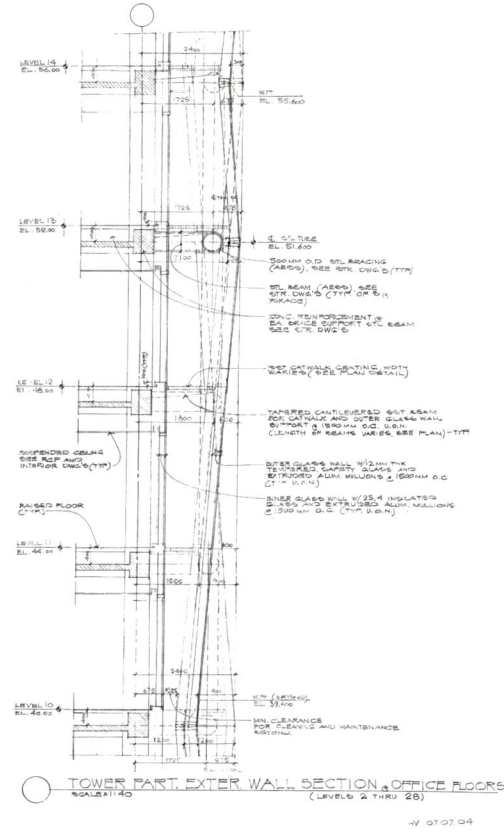

2

1 Sectional study of double-wall condition and interior floor assembly
2 Large-scale wall section showing four-story-high atmospherically connected thermal chamber within which air is allowed to move around the main building enclosure
3 Construction photograph showing installation of outer glass panels over structural braces
4 Final full-scale performance mock up
5 Construction photograph showing diagonalized exterior steel bracing

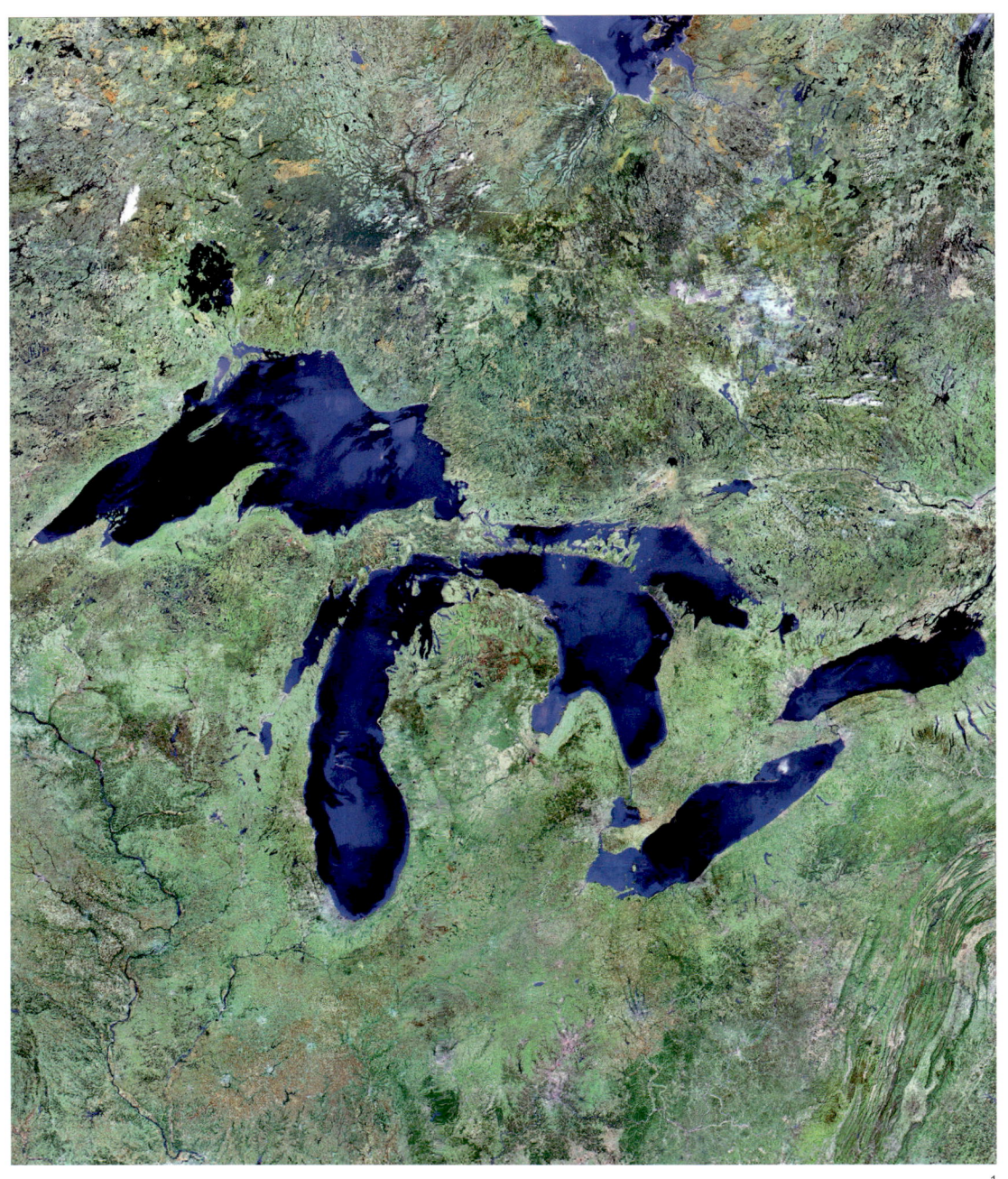

Hundred-Year Vision for the Great Lakes and St. Lawrence River Region
Developed 2009–ongoing

The paramount challenges of our time are to reverse the environmental consequences of global pollution and to manage the voracious consumption of natural resources by urban, agricultural, and industrial megalopolises like the bi-national Great Lakes and St. Lawrence River region of North America. The order of magnitude of these worldwide challenges places a leadership obligation on the urban design field.

The City Design practice of SOM has been effectively using the firm's fresh-thinking approach to problem solving and its graphic communication techniques in a pro bono initiative to stimulate an environmental and economic renewal of the vast ecosystem and network of cities that surround the world's largest fresh-water resource. The Hundred-Year Vision for the Great Lakes and St. Lawrence River Region is intended to engage a broad public and their leaders in adopting a new strategic perspective. It is calling for a new vision for this remarkable region and the source of one-fifth of the world's fresh water, which today has no comprehensive revitalization plan in place.

A Global View of Water

An accelerating global population shift from rural to urban areas has, for the first time, made cities the home for the majority of humanity. While urban scale and density offer the best promise for high-efficiency sustainable living, the limits of urban development are directly proportional to the amount of water available to support human life and productive activity.

Fresh water is not equally distributed around the world, and the need for it will only become more critical as climate change and population growth continue. Today, hundreds of millions of people across the globe lack a sustained source of fresh water—a number projected to grow exponentially, so that by 2050 over forty percent of the world will face the prospect of water shortages.

Indeed, SOM has already seen this in its City Design practice, which has declined planning projects—for some of the hundreds of new cities needed to meet explosive population growth—because of inadequate sources of local water.

Regional Challenges

This issue is particularly acute in the Great Lakes region, whose watershed includes more than ten percent of the US population and thirty percent of the Canadian population—a mega-region of over 50 million people. This "cradle of the carbon economy" produces a combined annual GDP of more than $2 trillion—greater than all but six nations—and is the primary economic crossroads of the world's largest bi-lateral trade relationship. Concomitantly, the Great Lakes contain over twenty percent of the world's fresh water and eighty-four percent of North America's water. Their shorelines create the foreground to hundreds of cities and span over 11,000 miles—larger than America's Atlantic, Pacific, and Gulf Coasts combined. But, to date, there is no plan in place that takes a comprehensive view of how to protect the Great Lakes and St. Lawrence River watersheds. As Cameron Davis, senior advisor to the administrator of Great Lakes issues notes, "People see how vast the Great Lakes are and mistake that vastness for invincibility."

Today, the lakes and their region face challenges both numerous and diverse. Air pollution from coal-fired power plants adds mercury to the waters. Agriculture creates high-nutrient and pesticide runoffs that end up in the lakes. The combined sewer outflow and pharmaceutical waste from cities causes damage, and urban populations, both American and Canadian, deplete local water tables. Furthermore, nearly everything in the region still depends on fossil fuels to work. Something has to change if we hope to conserve and protect these rare fresh waters, build cleaner cities, farm more responsibly, and live and work more in balance with nature.

The Need for a Hundred-Year Plan

This work began in 2009 as SOM's contribution to the centennial commemoration of Daniel Burnham's Plan of

2

LONDON
WARSAW
VIENNA
MARSEILLE

3

St. Mary's River
St. Clair River
Detroit River
Lake Superior
Lake Huron
Lake St. Clair
Lake Erie
Niagara Falls
Niagara River
Lake Onta
+601'
+578'
+572'
+569'
+243'
210'
750'
923'
Lake Michigan
1,330'
802'
vertical exaggeration 1,000x
379
60
223
89
236
35
150
2,212 mi

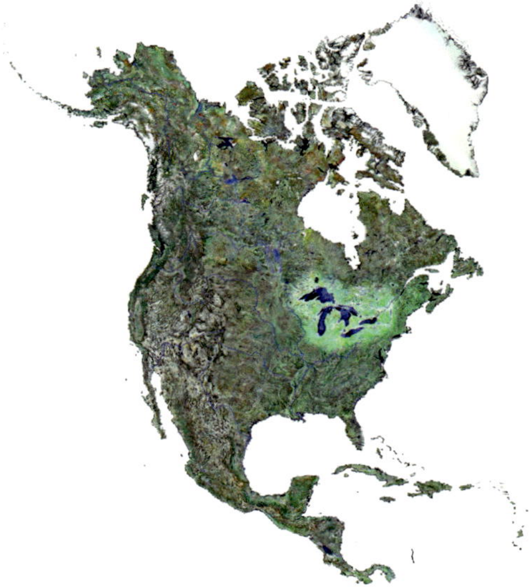

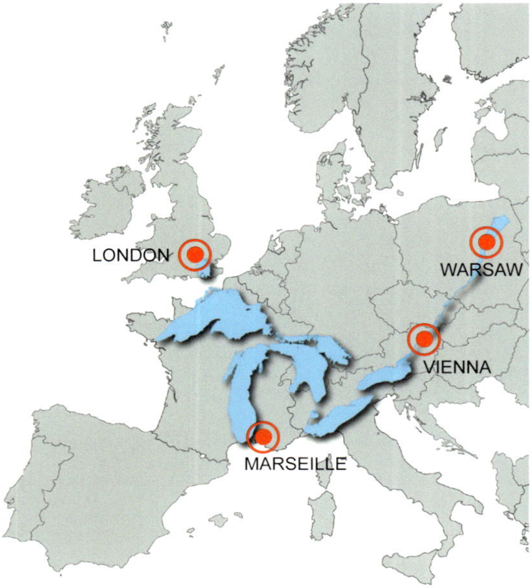

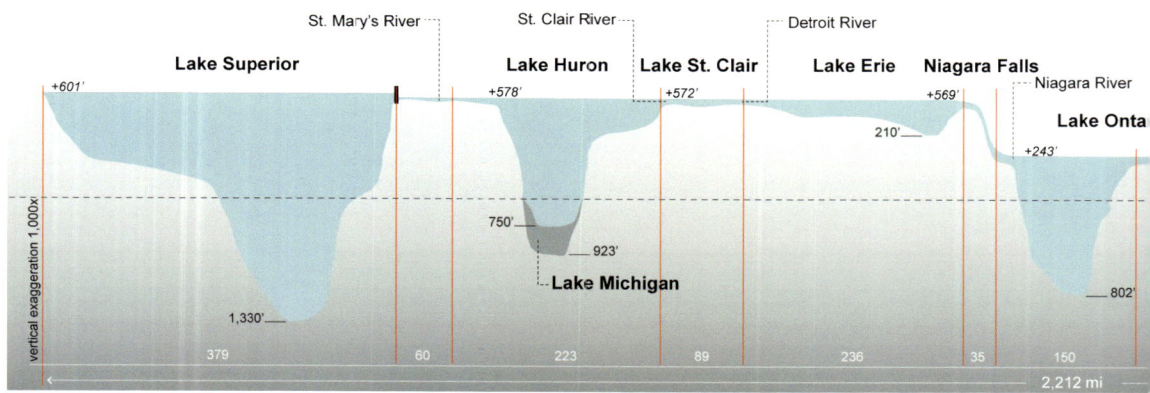

< 1 The Great Lakes and St. Lawrence River Region
2 The Great Lakes and St. Lawrence River Region Watershed
3 The scale of the Great Lakes and St. Lawrence River Region is vast; it would reach from London to Marseille to Vienna to Warsaw
4 The Great Lakes were formed at the end of the last ice age (about 10,000 years ago), when the Laurentide ice sheet receded. The retreat of the ice sheet left behind a large amount of meltwater, which filled up glacial depressions and created the Great Lakes Basin. The Great Lakes are a connected, navigable system. They flow into one another before reaching the St. Lawrence River and finally the Atlantic Ocean. Consisting of Lakes Superior, Michigan, Huron, Erie, and Ontario, they form the largest body of fresh water on Earth by surface area and volume. Less than one percent of the Great Lakes and St. Lawrence River Region water is renewable.

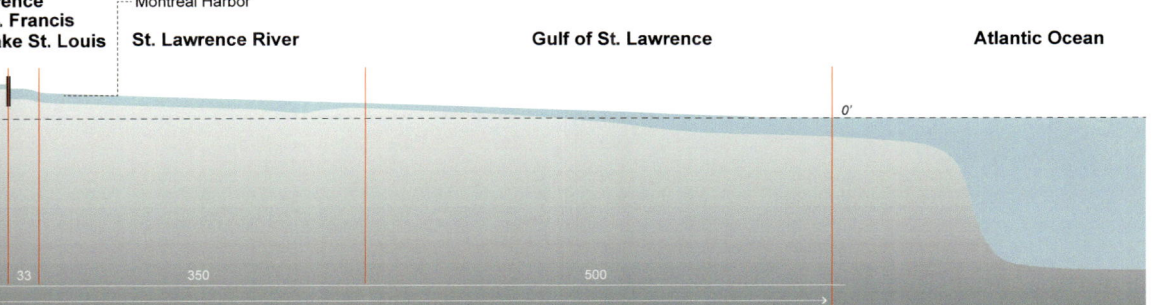

Chicago, which in 1909 defined the city's environment as a massive, three-state region and which set forth a transformative vision that has taken a century to realize. The celebration inspired SOM to ask, "What should the next hundred-year plan address?" With the support of the Chicago partners and the studio's resources, the City Design team conceived and crafted this research and advocacy initiative on its own time, seeing the project as a Burnham-scale, hundred-year vision for the modern era. It extends his regional approach to planning to the vast expanse of cities and rural areas centered on the Great Lakes, setting forth broad strategies for water, energy, the environment, cities, agriculture, industry, education, transportation, tourism, recreation, and even local governance. In doing so, it fills a much-needed void in regional conservation and planning efforts.

Forgetting Political Boundaries

Building a coalition for positive change will be a challenge among two different systems of national governance, tribal nations, major metropolitan areas, and more than 15,000 local governments. Uniting this diversity, however, is a unique pride of place and a love of the great inland seas that drain into the Atlantic Ocean and connect to the Mississippi River.

The key to SOM's early success in this endeavor was the introduction of the problem-solving approach and graphic vernacular of architecture to a complex policy issue, providing a fresh and compelling perspective. The resulting publication, *Recognizing a Global Resource: The Need for a Hundred-Year Vision for the Great Lakes and St. Lawrence River Region,* produced an immediate and memorable understanding of the problems and possibilities that require sustained engagement. In the process, it bridged political and jurisdictional divides that have long hampered efforts at regional cooperation. It has become a rallying point around which dozens of cities, foundations, and non-profit organizations have gathered in support of a comprehensive vision for the future of the Great Lakes. "SOM has helped us see things that were not readily apparent, that will be helpful to us as we plan and take action in the future," notes David Ullrich, Executive Director of The Great Lakes and St. Lawrence Cities Initiative.

Scientists, politicians, environmentalists, business and public policy audiences have been energized by SOM's first draft. The high-impact communication of the work has effectively focused attention on the opportunities and challenges associated with the future of the Great Lakes. This idea is quickly captured by Lynn McClure of the National Parks Conservation Association: "The holistic approach that the hundred-year vision takes has really challenged the Great Lakes community to extend beyond our own goals and examine how we connect to others in the region. SOM has started the dialogue. It's up to all of us to advance this truly remarkable vision."

As a regional advocacy initiative, the project continues to gain momentum. SOM has already engaged dozens of organizations with a stake in the future of the Great Lakes, including the Great Lakes Commission, major colleges and universities, and local institutions such as the Shedd Aquarium in Chicago. The studio has presented its "Call for a Comprehensive Plan Initiative" lecture to audiences across North America, from the 2010 TED (Technology Entertainment and Design) Conference in Minneapolis, to the Design Futures Council in Atlanta. International leadership has even taken notice, inviting SOM to speak to both the International Joint Commission in Windsor, Ontario, and a Congressional Breakfast in Washington, DC. The Great Lakes and St. Lawrence Cities Initiative—an organization representing seventy-three cities in the US and Canada—voted unanimously to approve the plan at its 2010 annual conference.

SOM is now collaborating with the International Joint Commission to define the next generation of high-priority actions to improve the relationships between cities and the Great Lakes. We are working with the US National Park Service and Parks Canada to imagine a new generation of bi-national parks. SOM continues to collaborate with Great Lakes mayors and cities to identify policies and projects that "do no harm" to the Lakes while improving the quality of life of their citizens. And we are collaborating with the Chicago Architecture Foundation on a bi-national exhibit of SOM's work—with planned opening in summer 2012—to raise public awareness.

The firm's Great Lakes Initiative draws a forward-looking framework for finessing the reality of 150 years of urban and rural pollution into a future of environmental stewardship and jurisdictional collaboration for the region's long-term health and renewed prosperity. It is an agenda-setting gift of civic leadership for the common good, and it is being gratefully accepted throughout the Great Lakes-St. Lawrence basin.

Multiple Jurisdictions

The Great Lakes and St. Lawrence River region is a connected basin created by glacial recession and melting. Today this basin is splintered into thousands of individual jurisdictions. The US-Canada border runs through the middle of the Lakes, effectively splitting the region in two. The US side contains eight states, 213 counties, and fifty-eight Indian reservations; the Canada side comprises two provinces, sixty municipalities, and eighty-seven First Nation reserves. Together they represent over 15,000 towns and cities. The basin is so fragmented by political boundaries that larger comprehensive views are almost inconceivable.

Uncertainty about Climate Change

Managing the effects of global climate change is imperative for a region seeking to leverage its coastal assets. According to a study by the International Joint Commission, climate change is already responsible for a three-and-a-half- to ten-inch drop in water levels since 1962, seventy-five percent of that decline in the past thirteen years. Although the full effects of climate change are not yet completely understood, it may cause shifts in lake levels, agricultural yield, water quality, and forestry production.

Capacity and Congestion

The Great Lakes region is home to North America's highest-volume freight system, handling a majority of the $600 billion annual trade relationship between the US

5 The region is fragmented by over 15,000 separate jurisdictions, complicating planning efforts

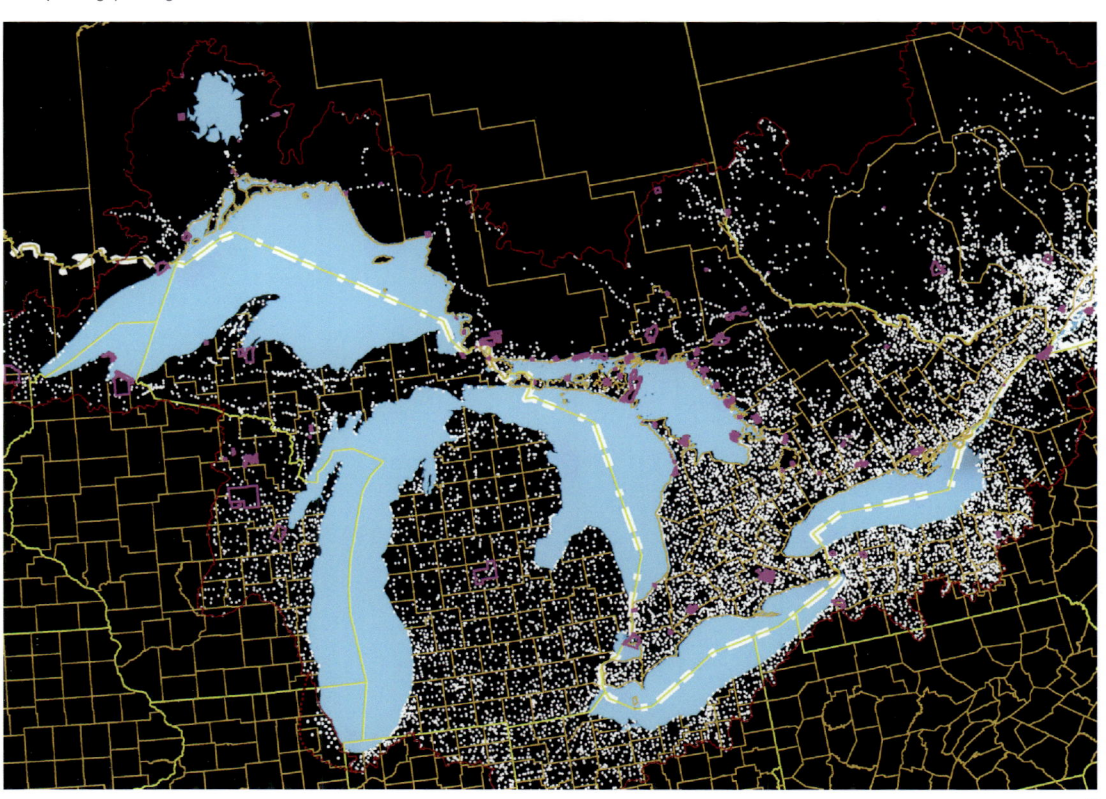

5

6

7

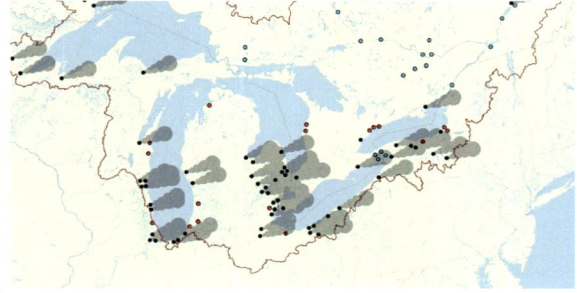

8

9

6 Urban and agricultural runoff in Lake Erie following a storm event
7 The Asian carp poses challenges to local food supplies
8 Coal-fired and nuclear power plants dominate the region
9 Low-density sprawl consumes land and increases impervious surface coverage

and Canada. But this system is approaching capacity while forecasting major increases in volume. Passenger travel—via roads, rail, and air—also faces steadily increasing congestion.

Power Generation
The average power plant in the Midwest was built in 1964 using technology that is nearly obsolete today. Coal burning plants make up the majority of these facilities, which release high levels of CO_2 and deposit mercury into local water sources. Both nuclear and fossil-fuel-burning plants also use enormous amounts of water in the generation process.

Invasive Species
Today, over 180 species of plants, fish, mollusks, and other organisms have entered the Great Lakes ecosystem from other parts of the world, challenging local food supplies and threatening the environmental quality of the Lakes. The most recent challenge is posed by the Asian carp, which migrated up the Mississippi River to the Illinois River, dangerously close to Lake Michigan. These large, prolific fish could disrupt the aquatic food chain and pose significant risk to the entire ecosystem.

Agricultural Runoff
Runoff from agriculture is one of the region's primary sources of pollution. Although pesticide and herbicide pollution remain major issues, phosphorus—found in fertilizer—has become the most critical non-point source pollutant. Phosphorus feeds algae, which depletes oxygen in fresh water and causes eutrophication or "dead zones." Further, a lack of proper erosion controls creates sediment buildups that must be regularly dredged from canals and shipping channels.

Urban Runoff and Sanitary Overflows
Precipitation runoff washes pollutants off our streets, parking lots, construction sites, industrial storage yards, and lawns. Water runoff from impervious surfaces carries a mixture of hydrocarbons, heavy metals like nickel and lead, synthetic organic compounds, nitrates, and phosphorous—all of which end up in the Lakes. During heavy rain events, the capacity of municipal sewer systems can also be overloaded and cause harmful overflows. Untreated or partially-treated sewage can back up into basements, run down streets, or directly enter water bodies. Untreated wastewater contains potentially-dangerous pathogens and high levels of nutrients, organic matter, and solids that can cause algae blooms and spur eutrophication.

Sprawling Cities
Cities are constantly increasing their land areas in the form of low-density sprawl. Sprawling regions turn valuable forests, prairies, and farms into roads, neighborhoods, and shopping malls, drastically increasing impervious surface coverage. Many cities in both the US and Canada are forecast to grow in the decades ahead: Chicago, for example, is projected to increase its footprint by 695 square miles, Detroit by 310 square miles, and Buffalo by 250 square miles.

01 Green Cities and Great Lakes

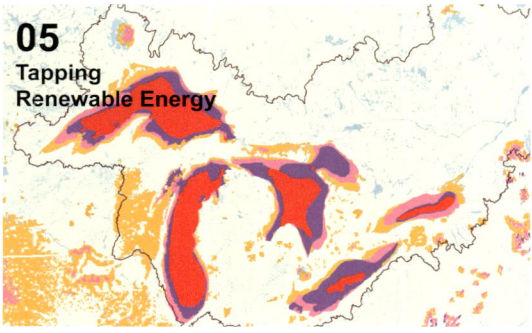
05 Tapping Renewable Energy

02 Bigger than a National Park

06 Achieving Mobility

03 Great Minds and Great Lakes

07 Leaders in a New Economy

04 Blue is the New Green

08 Commitment to Local Food

Pieces of the Vision

01 Green Cities and Great Lakes
Urban Design Best Practices are Clear
- Cities must cause "no damage" to adjacent lake waters
- Make urban ground planes more permeable to replenish the water table
- Purify stormwater and wastewater to remove toxins and pharmaceuticals and return clean water to the lakes
- Accommodate greater urban populations with transit investments, walkable districts, and bicycle systems

02 Bigger Than a National Park
Tourism is the World's Fastest Growing Industry
- Establish an international park defined by the Great Lakes Watershed
- Welcome world travelers to the cities, towns, and natural attractions along an 11,000-mile shoreline
- Designate the basin or key areas as a world heritage biosphere
- Create new ways to tour these Canadian and American waters

03 Great Minds and Great Lakes
Synergizing an Abundance of Research, Talent and Infrastructure
- The basin is home to perhaps the world's greatest concentration of world-class research universities
- Students will help shape the future of the region
- A collective forum to create a greener vision for the region and improved cities
- A "global classroom" focused on our relationship with the Great Lakes

04 Blue is the New Green
Commitment to the Generations to Come
- Adopt water policies that address climate change
- Promote water use awareness and conservation
- Recognize that water is not a free and endless resource
- Make the Great Lakes swimmable, fishable and drinkable

05 Tapping Renewable Energy
Coal and Oil are the Problems, Not the Solution
- Work towards eliminating traditional coal-fired power plants
- Make a regional commitment to renewable energy
- Harvest wind to power urban areas
- Utilize cold waters for urban district cooling and geothermal heat exchange

06 Achieving Mobility
Renewing and Unifying a Regional Economy
- Pioneer carbonless, high-efficiency transportation across the region
- Connect regional urban centers and air hubs with high-speed rail
- Make transit development a priority
- Innovate a post-carbon auto industry
- Take bicycle transportation seriously

07 Leaders in a New Economy
Leveraging the Region's Innovative Heritage
- Fresh water laboratory for the world
- Incubator basin for nanotechnology
- Beyond the cradle of the carbon economy
- A bi-national technology center

08 Commitment to Local Food
Rethinking the Heartland's Agricultural Practices
- Eliminate polluting farmland runoff
- Recognize and develop regional food economies
- Promote smarter farming strategies
- Invest in organic farming
- Incentivize crop diversification

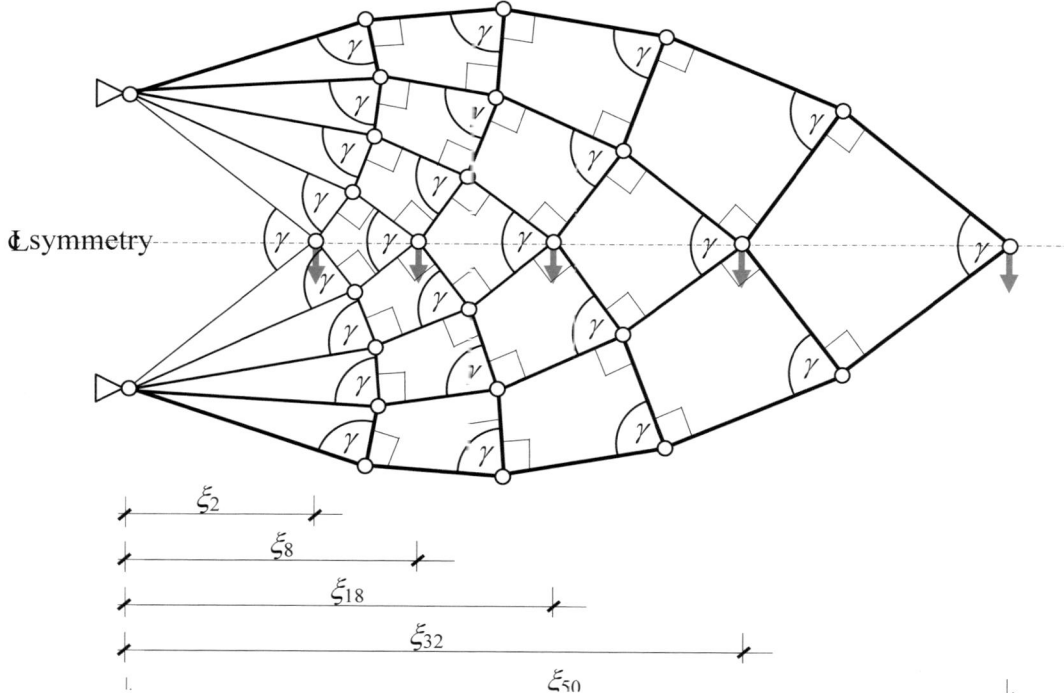

SOM Research

The SOM Research Group is an internal unit of engineers and architects whose interest in innovation has given rise to a seminar-like undertaking in design-related research. Group members develop personal interests in addition to their ongoing design workload in the office. If an individual does not have a specific interest, but still wants to participate in the group, a variety of topics are made available for investigation. The group meets periodically and everyone is welcome to attend.

Members of the group have ongoing collaborative relationships with nearby academic institutions. The outcome of this research is then introduced into the firm's design work, in addition to being published and presented at conferences.

One principal focus of study within the group is the characterization of optimal structural topologies. Topological study is a new frontier in architecture and an evaluative benchmark for the performance of both existing and future structures.

The methodologies described here are a limited sample of the interests of the SOM Research Group. New design tools are continuously explored and only await application in the next project.

Michell Frames

At its inception, the group was inspired by the work of Australian mathematician A. G. M. Michell, especially his seminal paper "The Limits of Economy of Material in Frames-Structures" (published in *Philosophical Magazine,* in 1904). Michell trusses represent a theoretical solution to optimal truss member layout for minimum structural material. Such layouts are highly dependent on the loads applied and the type of supports. The interest in such frames stirred a variety of research activities within the group and the rediscovery of valuable mathematical tools for the design of frame systems.

The research group has rediscovered Maxwell's theorem (in *Scientific Papers),* an important design tool at the foundation of Michell's work. This theorem states that for any plane frame layout with defined support points and location of applied loads, the difference between the product of the volume of the members in tension (Vt), multiplied by the allowable stress in tension (ft), minus the volume of the members in compression (Vc), multiplied by the allowable stress in compression (fc), is a constant. This fundamental theorem indicates that completely different frame layouts for the same structural problem have a mathematical constant in common. Hence, it provides helpful guidance in the comparison of the efficiency of various frame systems in the preliminary design stage of a project.

The research group has been uncovering the mathematics behind Michell frames and searching the literature for the most recent developments on the analytical theory of optimal frames. Among the major contributions, a custom Michell frame generator tool has been developed which enables the engineer to draw the cantilever Michell frame for a variety of parametric conditions: bound/unbound frame, various heights, various grid densities and base angles.

Michell frames are optimum solutions derived mathematically in a continuum. However, structural frame systems are by nature discrete, being made of columns, beams, and braces. Therefore, a legitimate question ensues: are the solutions in the continuum directly applicable to the discrete? The answer is no, as reported by Arkardiusz Mazurek, William F. Baker, Cenk Tort (in "Geometrical Aspects of Optimum Truss-like Structures," published in the *Structural and Multidisciplinary Optimization Journal,* 2010). The paper is another important outcome of the group research activities and describes the graphical rules to construct optimal discrete frames for the three point problem (i.e., frames with two points of support and one point of loading).

An important practical conclusion of the study on Michell's frames for highrise building is that forty-five-degree braces are not the optimal solution for a braced frame system. The optimum is a brace with the working point at the

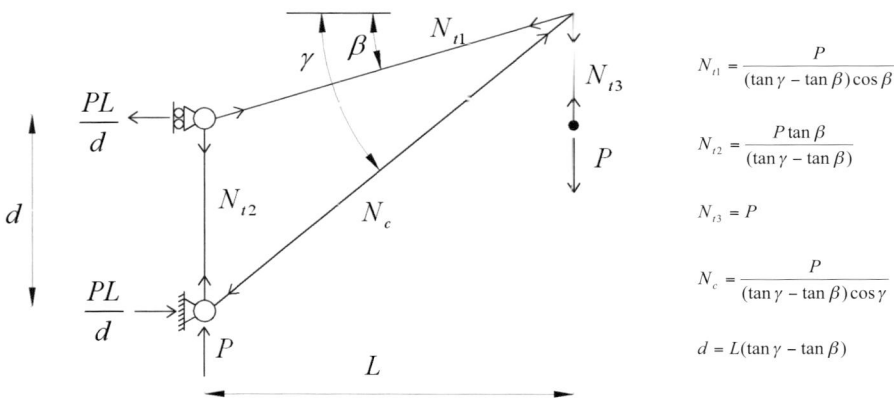

$$\sum \vec{F}_t \bullet \vec{r}_t = -PL(\tan\gamma - \tan\beta) = -Pd$$

$$V_t f_t - V_c f_c = A_t L_t \frac{N_t}{A_t} - A_c L_c \frac{N_c}{A_c} = \frac{L}{\cos\beta}\frac{P}{(\tan\gamma-\tan\beta)\cos\beta} - \frac{L}{\cos\gamma}\frac{P}{(\tan\gamma-\tan\beta)\cos\gamma} + 2PL\tan\beta = -PL(\tan\gamma-\tan\beta) = -Pd$$

$$\longrightarrow \sum \vec{F}_t \bullet \vec{r}_t = V_t f_t - V_c f_c$$

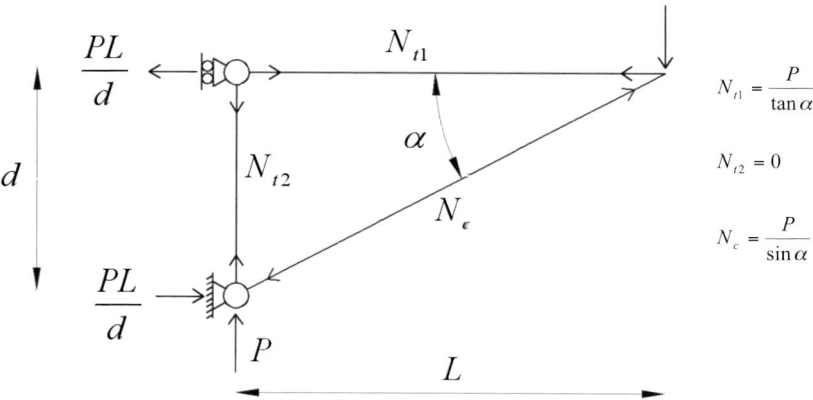

$$\sum \vec{F}_t \bullet \vec{r}_t = -PL\tan\alpha = -Pd$$

$$V_t f_t - V_c f_c = A_t L_t \frac{N_t}{A_t} - A_c L_c \frac{N_c}{A_c} = \frac{PL}{\tan\alpha} - \frac{PL}{\sin\alpha\cos\alpha} = -PL\tan\alpha = -Pd$$

$$\longrightarrow \sum \vec{F}_t \bullet \vec{r}_t = V_t f_t - V_c f_c$$

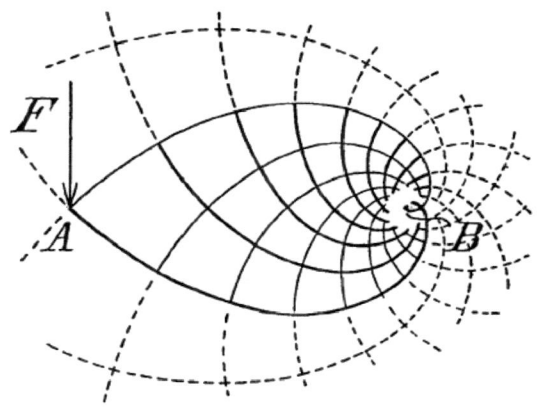

Cantilever beam

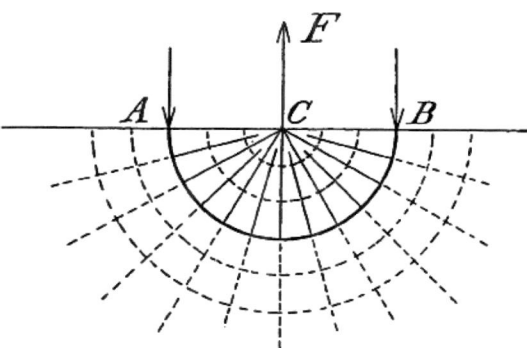

Simply supported beam

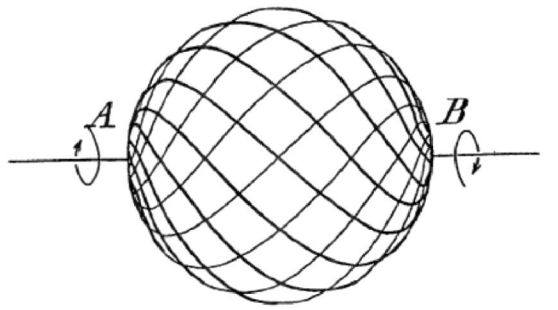

Beam under torsional load

3

< 1 Discrete Michell Truss
 2 Maxwell's Theorem: two completely different frames share the same mathematical constant
 3 Michell frames for various load and boundary conditions

intersection raised above the forty-five-degree solution as shown in the structural system for the concept design of a highrise office building.

Principal Stress Trajectories

Principal stress trajectories represent the natural flow of forces in a continuum. The trajectories are derived analytically by solving the equations governing the stress state in a body. They are then traced on a building surface using a custom script developed in visual basic (VBA) for AutoCAD®. The resulting principal stresses represent streamlines such that the lateral load "enters" the continuum at a certain elevation and flows through the trajectories to the foundation. There is an infinite number of principal stress lines in a continuum solid. However, the transition to a discrete structural system requires the selection of a limited set of lines. Since principal stress trajectories form cascading patterns, the set of lines can be identified by selecting a limited number of starting points at the top of the building (three to four points) and superimposing the resulting geometries. There are two distinct sets of lines traced: the compression lines (in blue) and the tension lines (in red). Notice that the trajectories follow specific geometric rules: the tension lines are orthogonal to the compression lines at each point, the lines intersect at forty-five degrees at the building's center-line, and they are orthogonal or parallel to the building side boundaries.

Topology Optimization

Theoretical (Michell frames) and analytical (principal stress trajectories) methods for optimal members layout

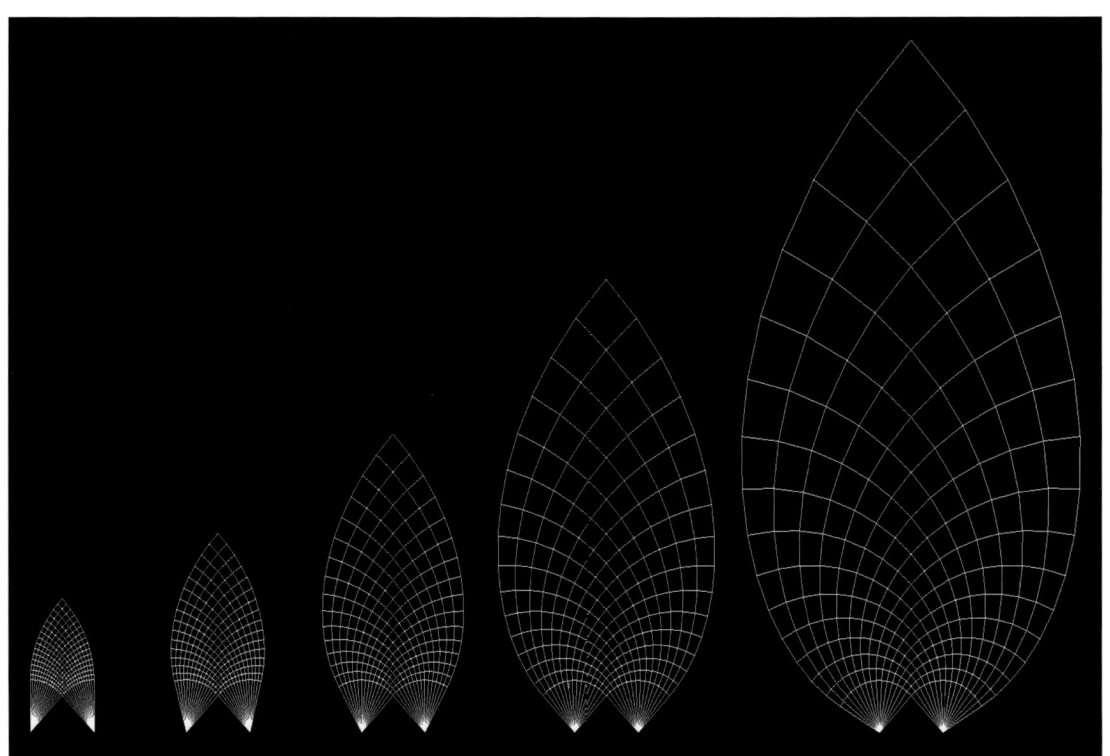

4 Research in discrete Michell frames
5 Michell truss generator
6 Concept design for an office highrise building and mathematical derivation of bracing angles

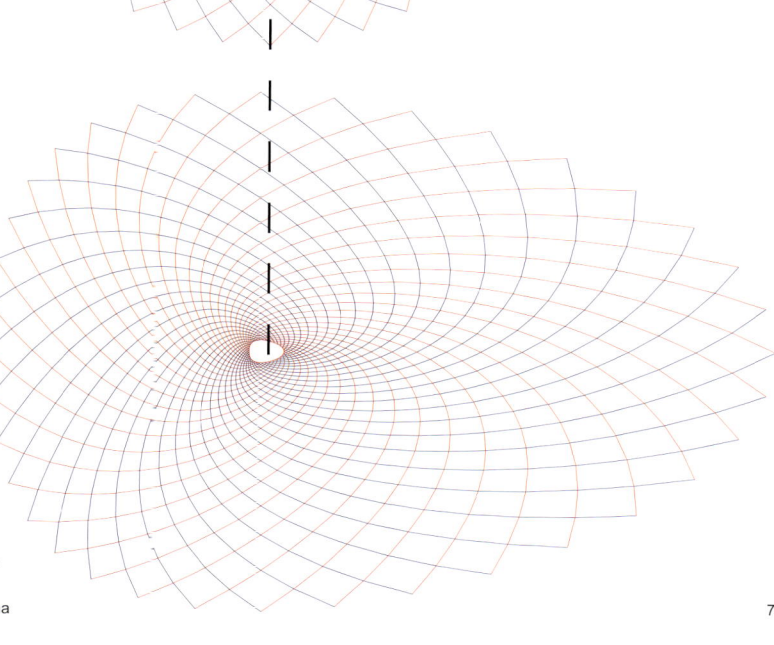

THE STARTING GRID IS THE MICHELL TRUSS FOR A CANTILEVER BEAM

INITIAL GRID IS ROTATED 360 DEGREES

GRID IS MAPPED TO THE SHAPE OF THE SITE

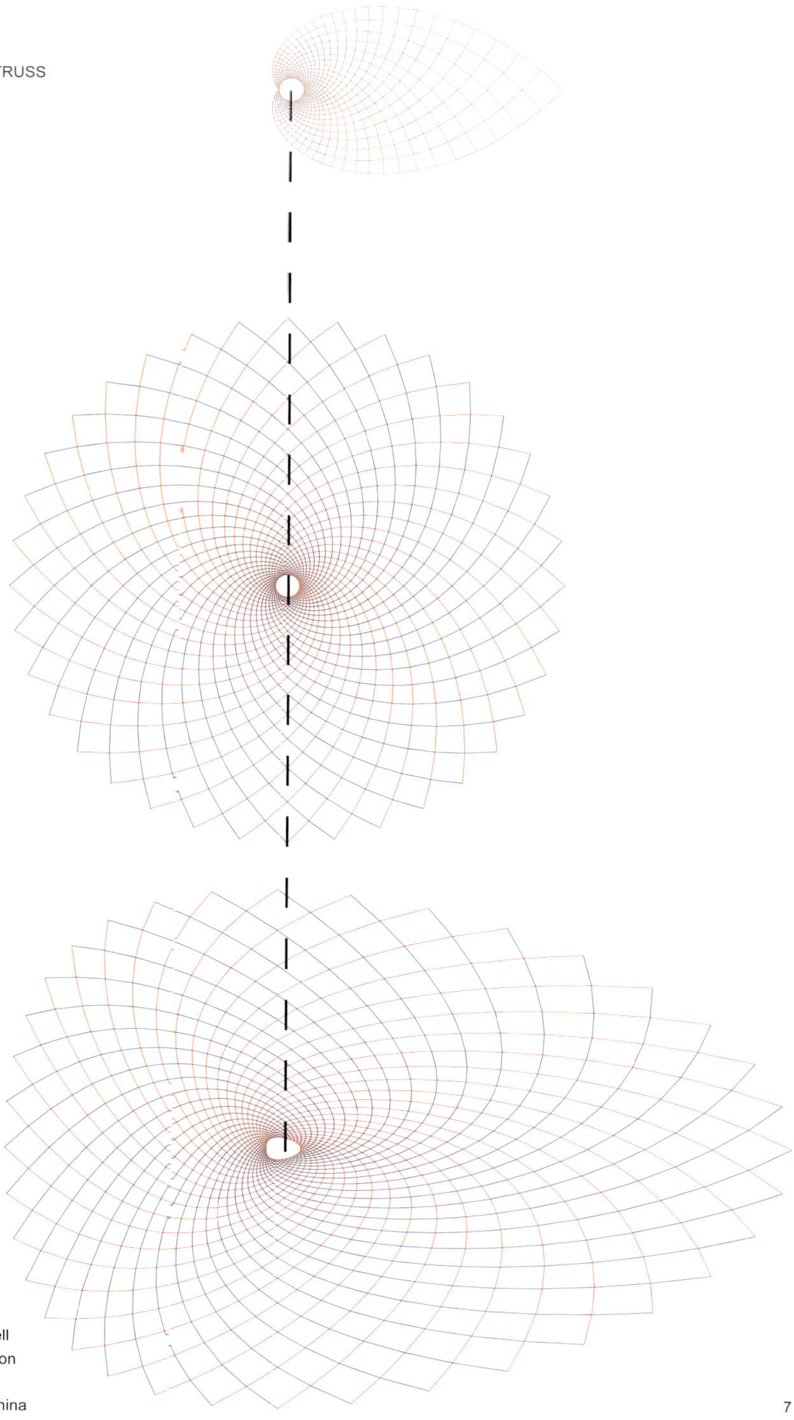

7 The research on Michell's frames also inspired the member layout for a grid shell composed of logarithmic spirals. Derivation of the grid layout
8 Grid shell for train station roof, Tianjin, China

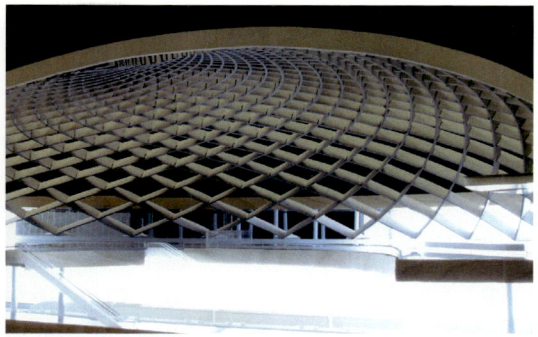

are limited to simple topologies and load conditions. Numerical methods for topology optimization provide a more general framework of solutions. In this approach, the material is iteratively redistributed in the design space so as to optimize the structural target (e.g.: maximize structural stiffness or minimize compliance in this case).

The design space is modeled via finite elements and, during the iterative process, the stiffness of each element at each step is modified according to its contribution to the overall objective function. The element stiffness is related to its density via a power law function such that low stiffness corresponds to low density. The values of density range between zero and one; zero corresponds to the white color in the images, while one corresponds to black. If the element has a major influence on the overall stiffness, its density is high (black areas in the image) and the low contribution elements have low density (white areas in the image). In the process, the volume of material available to maximize the objective

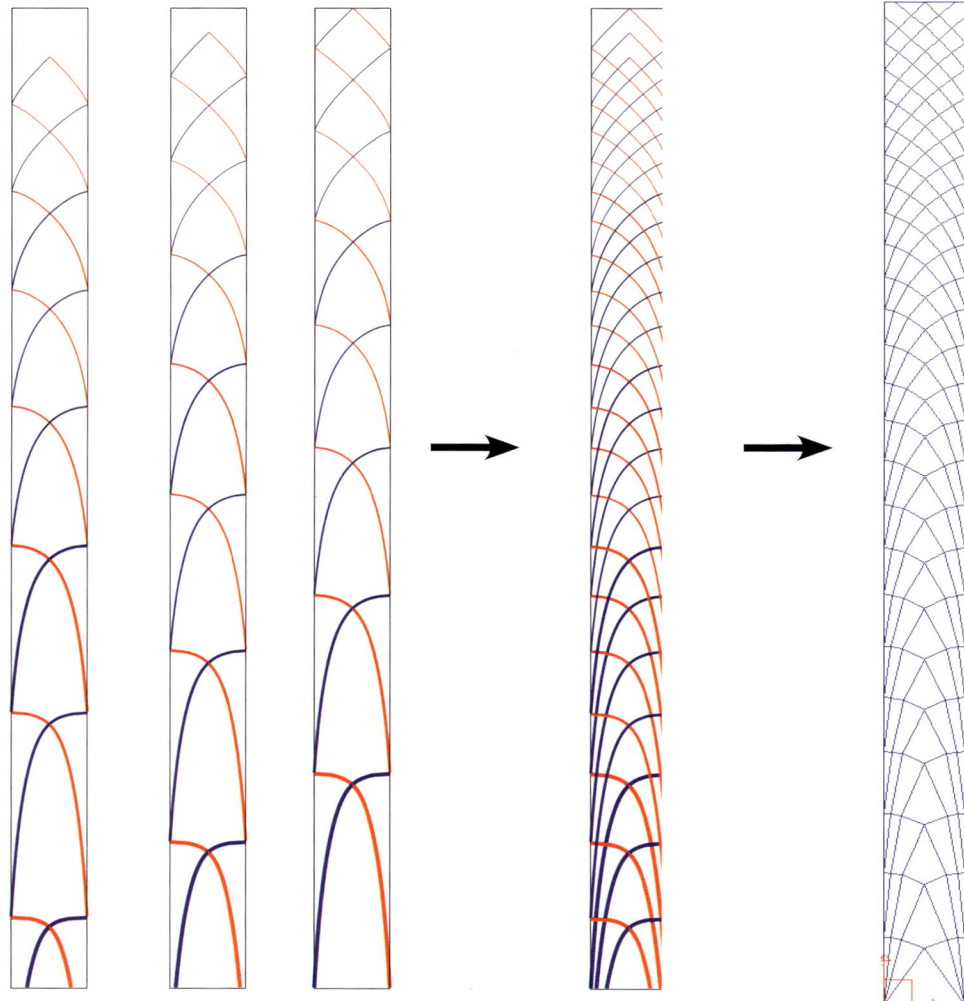

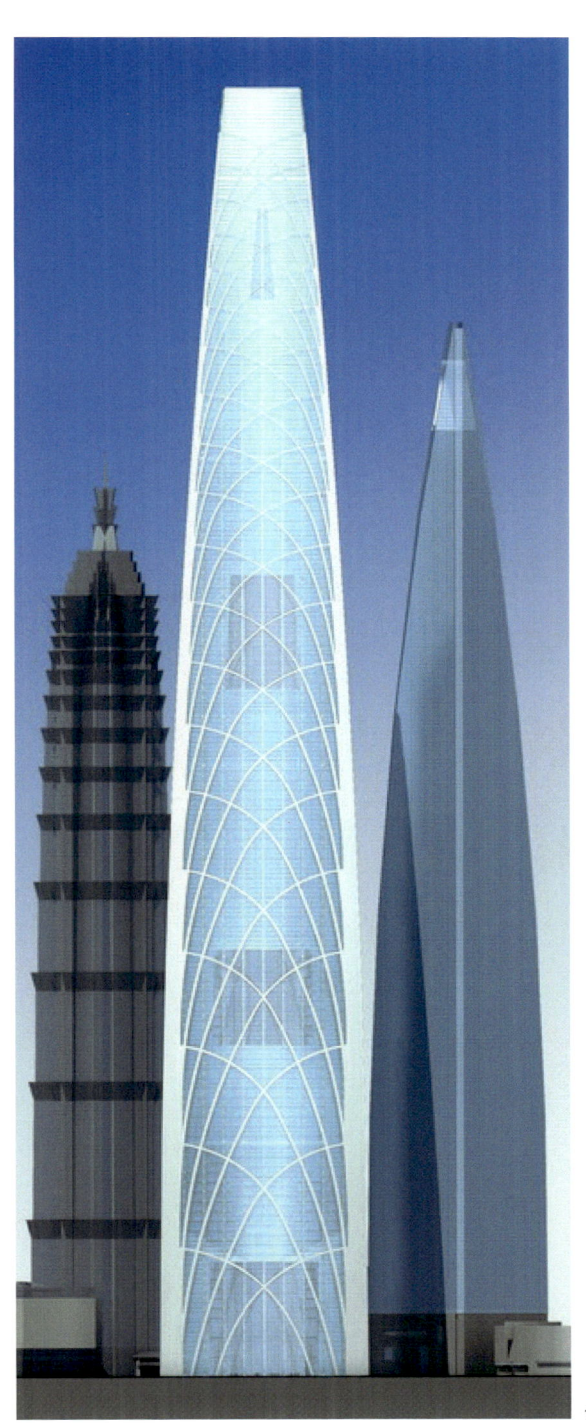

9 Principal stress trajectories form cascading patterns which can be superposed to generate the final optimal bracing geometry
10 Competition entry for a 580-meter-tall highrise building, Shanghai, China

function is constrained to a fraction of the material which can fill the design space (typically twenty to fifty percent volume fraction). Therefore, material is progressively "moved" to regions which guarantee the best performance of the structure in terms of the target.

Topology optimization has been applied extensively for the conceptual design of structural systems and substructures. Shown here is the result for the optimal steel braced frame layout for gravity loading in a bridge structure connecting three mid-rise buildings in Shanghai, China. The target of the optimization was to maximize the overall stiffness.

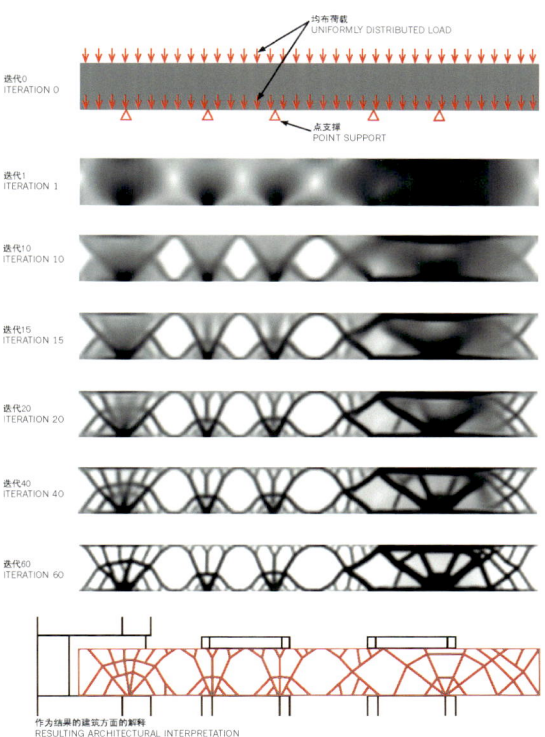

11 Iteratively distributed material designed to optimize the structural stiffness
12 Optimal steel braced frame layout for gravity loading in a bridge structure connecting three mid-rise buildings, Shanghai, China

Genetic Algorithms

Genetic algorithms are searching procedures mimicking the process of natural selection (survival of the fittest). In structural engineering terms, this means that the best, or "fittest," solution is the one which satisfies a target structural goal (maximum stiffness, for instance) for a certain volume of material (as a constraint). The analysis is always based on a parametric model of the structure where the controlling parameters are grouped together to form a "genome." An initial random population of genomes is evaluated for structural "fitness." The best performing genomes move to the next generation while the poor performing genomes are replaced by new ones. The new genomes are partly generated randomly and partly by a variety of basic operations on the previous generation of genomes. These operations include combining two well-performing parent genomes (crossover) and slightly modifying a well-performing genome (mutation). The optimum solution is the one which results from the evolutions of several generations of genomes. The process ends when additional iterations bring minor changes to the structural performance.

The computational procedure used in the example shown here is a combination of a custom-written genetic algorithm search engine and a commercial finite element software. The genetic algorithm code, written in visual basic .NET, has a very flexible architecture, thus allowing interfacing with several types of software to solve a variety of problems. The genetic algorithm communicates with the finite element software via custom-written codes in the Application Programming Interface (API). At each iteration of the analysis, the finite element model is modified according to the parameters determined by the genetic algorithm, and a structural analysis is run. The calculated structural response based on the structural objective is then returned to the genetic algorithm for genome fitness evaluation. Depending upon its performance, a genome may or may not survive at the next generation.

The topology optimization has been carried out with a custom written program developed in collaboration with the University of Illinois at Urbana Champaign (UIUC).*

* Some results of the ongoing collaboration with UIUC on topology optimization for highrise buildings are documented in the 2010 paper "Application of Layout and Topology Optimization Using Pattern Gradation for the Conceptual Design of Buildings," by L. L. Stromberg, A. Beghini, W. F. Baker, and G. H. Paulino.

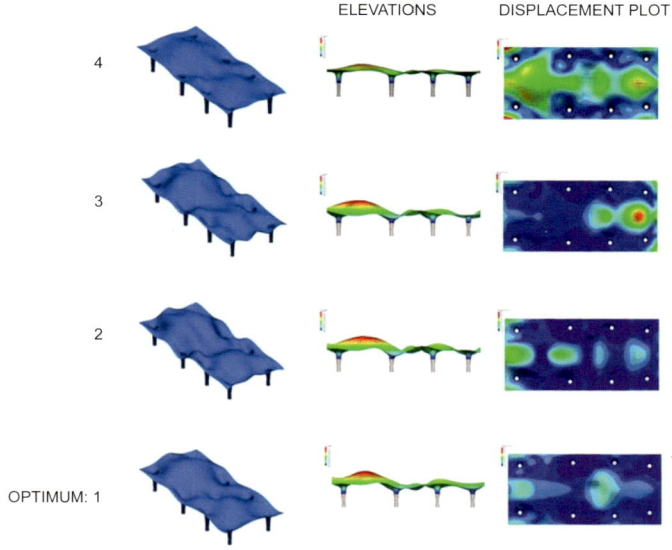

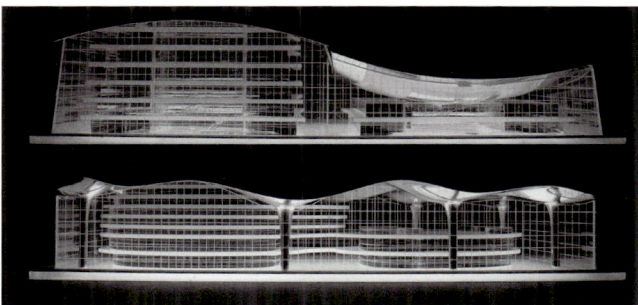

13 Computational procedure showing generational phases of a population of genomes
14 Application of genetic algorithms to the problem of roof curvature in a convention center, Tianjin, China
15 Aerial rendering of convention center

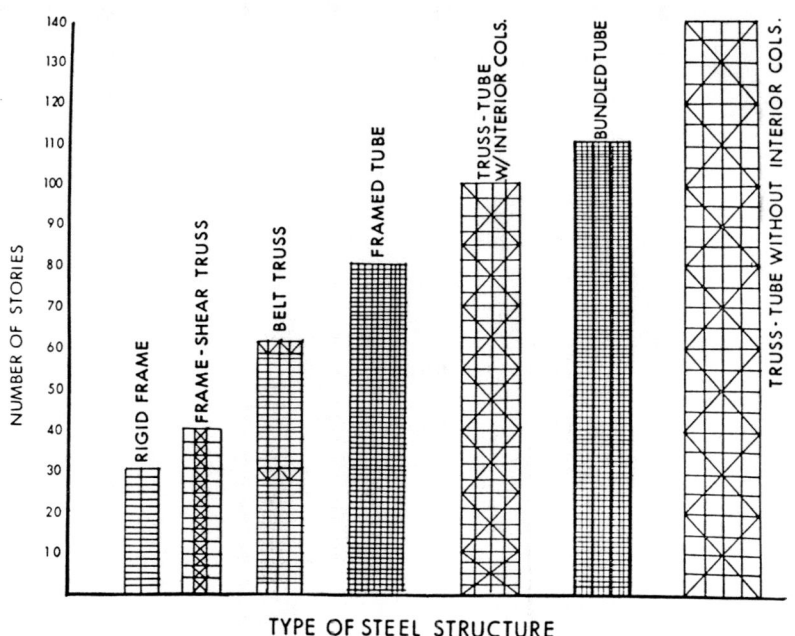
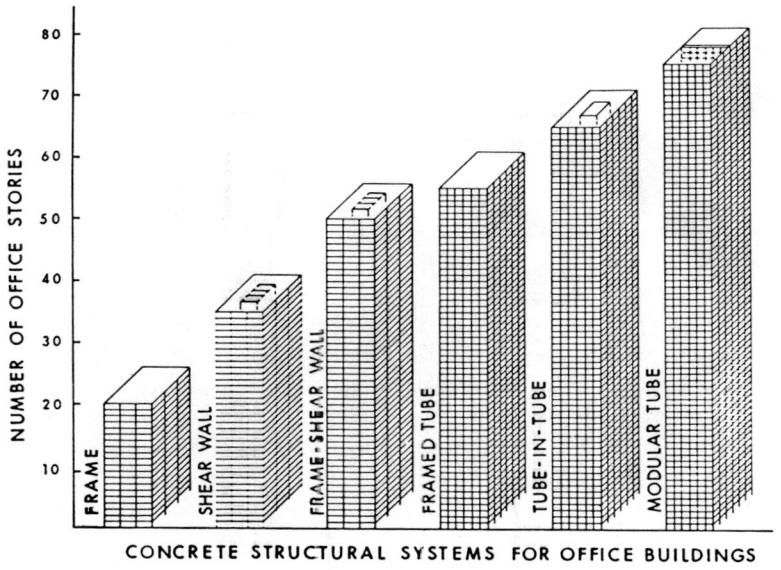

Fig. 1 Kahn's catalogue of structural steel systems and concrete structural systems based on height from "Evolution of Structural Systems For High Rise Buildings in Steel and Concrete" Proceedings of Regional Conference on Tall Buildings, Bratislava, Czechoslovakia, April 9–13, 1973

Beyond Tall: Issues of Scale and the Evolution of Tall Buildings at SOM
William F. Baker

Introduction

Throughout SOM's history, the evolving size and scale of tall buildings has fostered a need to invent new structural systems to enable the firm's architecture. Stemming from his time as both a student and employee of Mies van der Rohe, and continuing throughout his tenure as a structural engineer and architect at SOM, Myron Goldsmith studied issues of scale. He understood that nature and economy will not permit systems to extend beyond their appropriate range and breadth. Fazlur Khan (often in collaboration with Goldsmith) extended Goldsmith's work, developing a series of structural systems appropriate for the buildings of his time. Today, SOM has ushered in the modern era of the super-tall building. The essay will explore the issues of scale confronted by each new generation and how this study, along with the creation of emergent technology and construction methods, is essential to current tall building design at SOM.

Issues of Scale—The Initial Work

In 1987 Myron Goldsmith published an essay entitled "The Effects of Scale" in the monograph on his work by Werner Blaser. This essay was a refinement of Goldsmith's master's thesis of 1953, written under the supervision of Mies van der Rohe at the Illinois Institute of Technology. During his career, Goldsmith grappled with the essay's theme and republished his evolving understanding of it several times.[1] For Goldsmith, issues of scale were quite profound. In his ensuing essays, he discusses the manner in which issues of scale dictate the appropriate systems for structures such as bridges and domes. This is a man who, as an architect, produced some of the most eloquently proportioned buildings of the modern era. And yet, in the essay, he does not discuss the aesthetic qualities of the suspension bridge over the arch bridge. Instead, he evaluates the appropriate system for a given span. Goldsmith believed that the scale of a problem would lead to a solution that was both natural and appropriate. One can easily imagine Goldsmith taking any of these systems and making extensive studies of the proportions of this hanger to that beam, in order to produce a design of sublime elegance. In the essay, Goldsmith refers to the book *On Growth and Form*, by D'Arcy Thompson. Thompson was a biologist with a fundamental understanding of engineering mechanics, a branch of engineering and physics that studies how materials (solids, fluids, and gases) respond to stresses and strains. In each example, Thompson demonstrated how the forms of living things correspond to the physics of their existence. Simply stated, the engineering mechanics of scale differentiate the form of a microbe from that of a fly, and that of a mouse from an elephant. Although creatures may be willful, nature is not. Each form only exists within an appropriate range. For example, elephants pass through various forms as they grow from tiny cells to their final size. However, they do not extend beyond the bounds of their given scale, as determined by nature.

Thompson first published his brilliant work during World War I and revised it during World War II. A few years after the second edition (1942), Goldsmith returned from military service and was back in Chicago with Mies. Goldsmith extrapolated Thompson's themes, recognizing the truths of nature and seeking them in the works of man. Using built examples, he proved that engineered structures also have appropriate scales. However, in the man-made realm, available solutions are limited to those that have been invented. Consequently, as new systems are invented, the appropriate ranges are adjusted.

In his thesis, Goldsmith created structural solutions for an eighty-story building. Although these proposed designs were never realized, he later collaborated with Fazlur Khan to create many new structural solutions for tall buildings. Working both together and independently, they discovered that structures have an innately viable range; outside of this range, buildings require alternate solutions. Some of these systems would later be realized in the most iconic structures of the period; others remain unbuilt. Many of these systems were first explored at IIT, where Goldsmith and Khan both assisted graduate architecture students in developing their theses.

If Goldsmith set the stage and framed the problem, it was Khan who published the solutions. In a series of articles, Khan proposed systems applicable for buildings of different heights and, occasionally, different uses. His initial work concerned buildings that were either all concrete or all steel, although he later developed composite systems that used both steel and concrete.

The catalogue of systems reproduced here (fig. 1) represent a compilation of Khan's findings. The systems progress from simple frames for shorter towers to the unrealized superframe for towers up to 600 meters tall.

Issues of Scale—The Tall Building Problem

In order to have a better understanding of Khan's systems, as well as those developed thereafter, it is necessary to understand the tall building problem.

The tall building is in many ways the simplest of all structures. It cantilevers out of the ground like a tree. There is only one direction in which gravity and wind loads can go, and that is from the sky to the ground. With almost Calvinistic clarity, the global forces and final behavior are generally known before design begins. This clarity is not available in most other structures, such as bridges, where there are two or more locations where the structure reaches the ground and the nature of the connection to the support can change the manner in which the loads are distributed. However, if one were to create what engineers call a "free body diagram," or an isolated portion of a building, one generally knows the total forces on the building. Depending on whether the structure is steel, concrete, or composite, within reasonable limits the total weight of the tower is known prior to design. The same is true for the lateral loads of wind and seismic forces. Not only are the forces known in a global sense, but the behavior is generally known as well; the amount of the tower's movement will be limited to values determined by building codes or good practice. And yet, although the total forces and movements of the tower are generally known prior to beginning the design, the detailed solution to achieve these predetermined results is not. This is where the understanding and creativity of the design team comes into play.

In order to understand the solutions outlined in Khan's charts, it is necessary to address the loads that the structure must resist. The most important loads are gravity loads and lateral loads. The lateral loads include wind and seismic, with seismic being of greatest concern for shorter buildings and wind the most important for taller buildings. If there were not lateral loads or stability issues, the structure would be defined by transmitting gravity loads directly to the ground. The arrangement of the structure would thus be set by the considerations of gravity. For shorter structures, interconnected gravity framing with small enhancements can resist the lateral forces. For taller structures, however, it is the resistance of the lateral forces that dominates the structural system; the gravity framing then adapts to the lateral system.

Issues of scale—Beyond Tall

Slenderness is a major factor in tall buildings. The slenderness ratio of a tower is the height divided by the smallest base dimension. In general, the taller the building, the wider the base must be. For example, think of a person spreading his feet to avoid toppling in the wind: the wider the stance, the more stable he is. In the era of Goldsmith and Khan, slenderness was limited by issues of economy, material, and practice. In 1980, the five tallest buildings in the world were made of steel, and had a slenderness range between 6.0:1 to 6.7:1. The economic slenderness range would increase as concrete became more prevalent. (Recent concrete or composite towers are often as slender as 8:1.) The limit on slenderness became the limit of the practical height of the towers. As a building becomes taller, the base becomes proportionally bigger. The Willis (née Sears) Tower has a base that is sixty-nine meters by sixty-nine meters. The distance from the glass to the core is twenty-three meters. This system is at the limits of its scale. If the roof of this steel tower were to be rescaled to 610 meters, the base would grow to ninety-five meters and the total area in the building would increase from a very large 410,000 square meters to an astronomical 1,100,000 square meters. The steel-framed tube of the Willis Tower is currently at its upper limit at 442 meters. If one were to propose a taller solution, a new system must be used. Converting the steel elements to concrete vertical elements would allow additional height. Assuming the same total building area, a system that can have a slenderness of 8:1 could achieve a height of 550 meters, but the distance from the glass to the core is still very large and the total floor area would increase by twenty-four percent in an already huge building.

What are the limits of scale that require a creation of new systems? Some important limits are evident in the preceding discussion. For instance, there are practical limits concerning the distance from the core to the window to allow light to enter the interior space. One could argue that the Willis Tower is already beyond that limit. The amount of total built area is also a concern. There are practical limits on the total floor area in one tower. In addition to the huge cost for finishing and fitting out such enormous building areas, there are also limits on the economic ability of a given urban real estate market to absorb this much area. Also, extreme building areas consequently lead to extremes in elevator and mechanical systems. The massive size is inherently at its practical limit. Many of today's proposed super-tall towers succumb to the problem of excessive floor area. Other issues that must be addressed include vertical transportation, the magnitude of wind forces, motion, and the climatic changes that accompany great height. Construction time is also an important consideration; long construction times can have major economic implications.

All of these issues are in addition to the fundamental concerns for tall towers:

- The shape of a tower and how it interacts with the wind is probably the single most important structural parameter. A building with a "bad" shape can lead to forces that are so large as to render the project unfeasible. Even small changes in the shape of a tower can dramatically affect the wind forces and change the economic viability of a design.
- The management of gravity forces is also critical to all tall towers. Gravity is reliable. Using gravity forces and gravity framing to help resist the wind and other lateral forces greatly improves the economics of the tower. Failure to do so can render the structure economically unviable.

To go "beyond tall" in issues of scale, it is necessary to develop systems that do not require excesses in depth, area, or time. One must develop structural armatures of reasonable cost that can accommodate appropriate building areas with highly useable lease spans and can be constructed within a reasonable time frame.

The Burj Khalifa is a first step in this direction. The creation of its new structural system, the "buttressed core," addresses each of these aforementioned issues for a building up to a height of one kilometer. The Buttressed Core System consists of a central hexagonal system of core walls providing torsional stiffness to the tower. Too slender to reach great heights alone, the core is in turn buttressed by the three wings of the building. The walls along the corridor act like the web of an I-beam, with the cross wall and columns acting like flanges; in-fill walls at the mechanical floors tie all the vertical elements together at approximately thirty-floor intervals. With a total building area of 286,000 square meters, the Burj Khalifa has lease spans only eleven meters in depth, and was built like a vertical factory. However, if one refers back to Goldsmith's principles of scale, this structural system is not appropriate for structures shorter than 200 meters, and other systems should be employed. In the range of 200 to 600 meters, existing systems aside from the Buttressed Core may also be considered.

Point towers such as the Willis Tower, Taipei 101, Shanghai World Financial Tower, and most of the other existing super-tall buildings scale geometrically by the cube. If a point tower building were to be built taller, its base must be wider and thicker. If the Willis Tower were to double in height, the floor area would grow cubically (2^3) and increase by a factor of eight. With a similar vertical expansion, the Burj Khalifa would only grow by a factor of four (2^2). This is because if it were twice as tall, it would be twice as wide but no thicker. The lease span would not change. The buttressed core system has a practical limit of around 1,100 meters, and the floor area would increase to its practical limit. This could be partially offset by higher floor-to-floor height or with a taller spire, but these are just refinements on a basic system.

Frank Lloyd Wright's 1956 proposal for a mile-high tower, called The Illinois, is an interesting study in the implementation of a super-tall building design. The structure may not have worked due to the lack of torsional stiffness (the importance of torsional stiffness was not generally recognized in the 1950s), but the concept for the building's lateral system contains the essence of a reasonable idea. The shape was also likely to have worked well with wind forces on the tower. In the end, in my opinion, Frank Lloyd Wright's tower was not a viable proposal because it failed to recognize the issues outlined above. Rather, it has too much floor area (1,672,254 square meters), too many floors (528), and would likely take ten years to top out. (Early occupancy of the lower floors during construction, such as was done on the Trump Tower in Chicago, could have partially ameliorated this problem.)

One solution to the problem is to decouple issues of slenderness ratio from issues of lease span. The overall structural proportions are set by the economics of structure. Depending on the overall shape of the tower and the speed of the wind, the base dimensions of a tower with steel vertical elements should be in the range of 5:1 to 8:1, while a tower with concrete vertical elements should be in the range of 6:1 to 10:1. However, the depth of the floor plate should match the function of the space. Office space is usually nine to eighteen meters deep with twelve meters being a common value. A residential unit can also vary quite a bit, but nine meters from the corridor is common.

The Burj Khalifa achieves this goal by using the Buttressed Core structural system. The lease span for the unit can be any reasonable value and varies from 7.4 meters to 11.7 meters along the length of the wing. It is important to note, however, that there are several other potential solutions besides the buttressed core. One approach might be to decouple the issues of height from the lease span. A common restraint is that each floor is supported on the one below. If this relationship is broken, the floor areas can be customized to match the practical limitations of the market. There are ways this can be done. The Stayed Mast scheme proposed for the 7 South Dearborn Tower has floors that cantilever from a central shaft. The design has three gaps that reduce the lateral wind forces by twenty-five percent and give the tower its iconic shape. With the help of specialized formwork that can be hung from the core, the gaps can be much larger and allow a precise customization of the floor area. As designed, the tower only had 180,000 square meters, which was the maximum permitted by zoning regulations. The 7 South Dearborn project demonstrates one way in which a structural system for a point tower can be created in a way that allows for customization of the floor area.

An example of a tower that could exceed one kilometer is the system used on the proposal for the aSpire (fig. 2). The building proposed to divorce the occupied floor area from its conventional dependency on ground supported columns, allowing the building to soar with as much or little floor area as necessary. This super-tall solution is based on a super-core structural system. Like a giant redwood, the structure is rooted in the ground with an appropriately sized base for the height, and with the floors cantilevering like branches from the shaft. The building tapers to the top to confuse the wind, avoid correlated vortex shedding, and reduce the wind sail. The floor area is as large or as small as the market can bear. The interior of the super-core can be either utilized or left empty (air is cheap).

Scale as a Basis of Conceptual Creation

Myron Goldsmith laid the foundation. His early and sustained recognition of the importance of indentifying, creating and using the appropriate structural system for a building has become the basis of over fifty years of structural and architectural creation. Fazlur Khan, along with Goldsmith, distilled the tall building problem down to its essence; he was able to extend the vocabulary of architecture with a series of sharply defined, paired adjectives and nouns: framed-tube, braced-tube, bundled-tube and super-frame. The succinct use of language mirrored the purity of the structural system. The brevity of the description leads to an understanding of the essentials and sets up a hierarchy of importance. Architects such as Myron Goldsmith and Bruce Graham would use these systems to create architecture that respected, expressed, and refined these structural concepts. Too often, one sees lesser designers applying structure as if it was an exercise in graphics, without understanding the concise nature of these fundamental structural principles.

As buildings continued to grow ever taller, the structural vocabulary of architecture needed to be expanded. The issues of scale that led to the development of Goldsmith/Khan's systems also limited their use beyond their appropriate range. The creation of concepts such as the stayed mast, buttressed core or the super-core will allow further upward growth.

In nature, evolution leads to the creation of new creatures of different scales using tools of cross breeding and

Programming

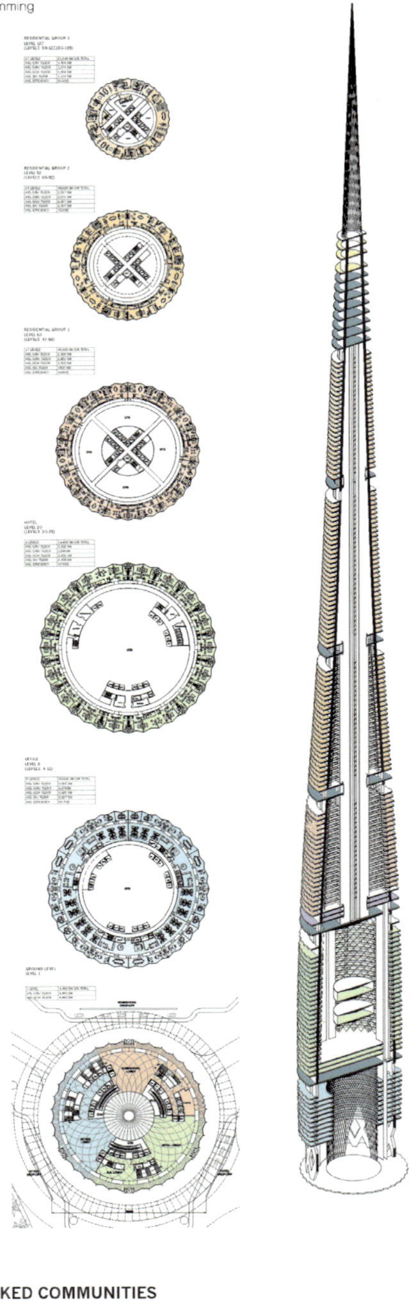

STACKED COMMUNITIES

The compact footprint and density with common amenity functions creates a city within a tower.

Fig. 2 aSpire plan and section showing stacked communities. The compact footprint and density with common amenity functions creates a city within a tower.

mutation. Within the discipline of architecture, we must rely on creativity to invent new structural systems. The solutions share similar objective values of efficiency and appropriateness. Their validity is neutral with respect to aesthetics, but each appropriate system has its own aesthetic potential. It is the art of the designer to find the aesthetic potential in the concept and refine the structure to create a work of architecture.

In tall buildings, this is the ultimate contribution of the collaborative practice that is SOM: architecture emerging from the solutions to the problems of scale.

1 "The Tall Building" originally appeared as Myron Goldsmith's thesis; *The Effects of Scale* (Master's thesis, Illinois Institute of Technology, 1953). It was revised, republished, and presented as a lecture numerous times, as follows:
"The Tall Building—The Effects of Scale," *Quarterly Column* 6 (April 1963), pp. 38–48.
"Tall Buildings—The Effects of Scale," lecture, National Accelerator Laboratory, Batavia, IL, (November 1974).
"The Effects of Scale," lecture, National Convention of the American Society of Civil Engineers, Dallas, TX (April 25, 1977).
"The Effects of Scale," lecture, University of California, Berkeley (March 1, 1978).
"The Effects of Scale," *AIA Journal* (Oct 1980), pp. 60–62.
"Effects of Scale," in *A Graphic Survey of Perception and Behavior for the Design Professions,* ed. Forrest Wilson (New York, 1984), pp. 126–37.
"Effects of Scale on Long-Span Roofs," lecture, Third International Symposium on Long-Span Structures, University of Stuttgart, Germany (March 18–22, 1985).
"The Effects of Scale on Tall Buildings," Goldsmith's lecture delivered by Joseph G. Burns, American Society of Civil Engineers Convention, Denver, CO (May 2, 1985).
In addition, eleven of Goldsmith's thesis drawings, three drawings of Borovay House, and a bridge model entered the permanent collection of the Art Institute of Chicago in 1982.

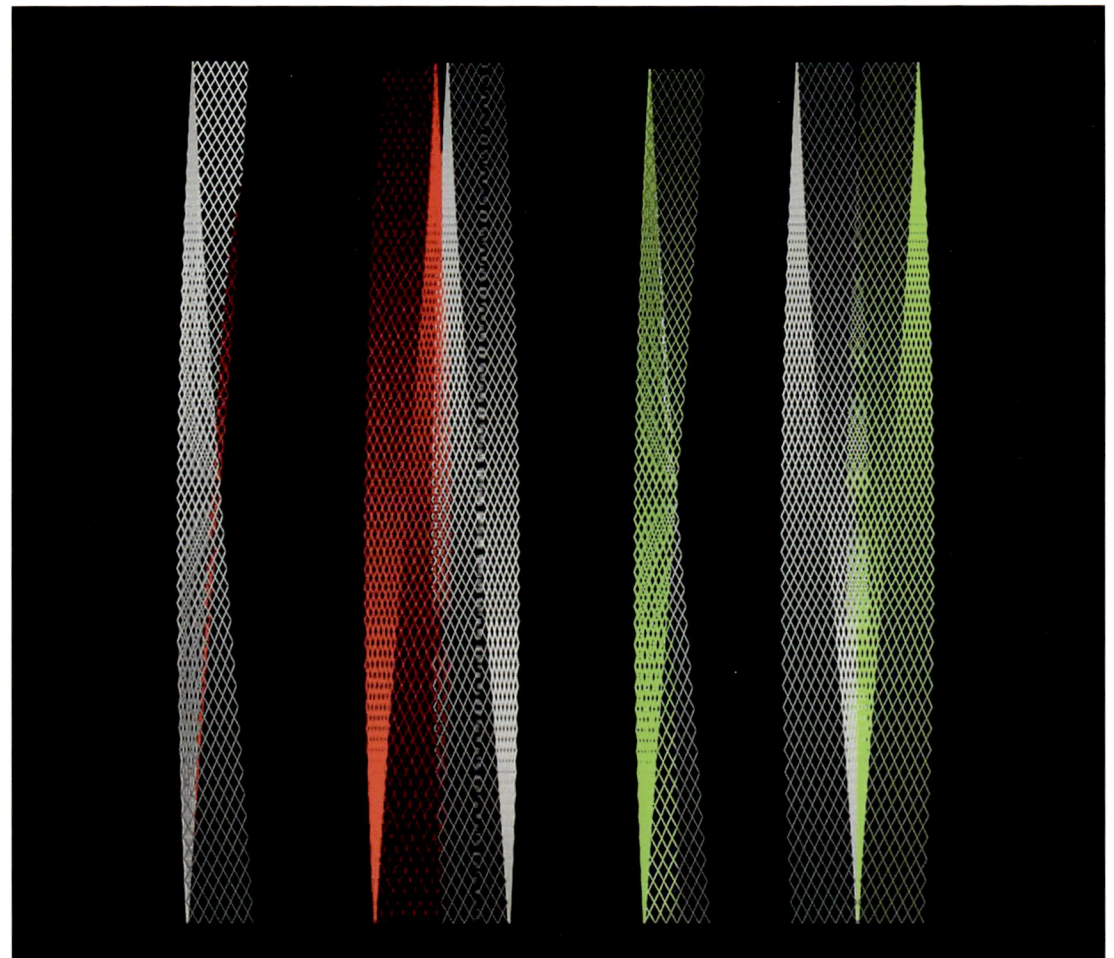

Fig. 1 Jinling Tower Competition

The Integration of Emergence and Flow: Combining Forces from the Ground Up
Mark Sarkisian

What if structures in the future could be designed for basic sustained forces by using internally flowing material in response to transient loading, increasing in density in areas where necessary? What if this behavior was three-dimensional, considering the volume of a structure rather that just its perimeter? What if the behavior emerged through a central controlling force of collective intelligence?

According to Joke Brouwer and Arjen Mulder in their book *Interact or Die!*, random behavior in networks can create strong but flexible structures and forms without a central designing coordinator or code that pushes the process in a definitive direction. Instead it considers interaction that selects effective, functioning parts of networks and leaves the non-effective parts to die. The idea is to create as much variation as possible and then let the parts of the network that function and interact select themselves and let the non-working parts degenerate. This interaction may proceed messily, but in an exploratory, flexible way that allows the most efficient parts of the design emerge.

Emergence or self-organization is the interaction between simple common elements having singular and common characteristics, each functioning according to its own simple rules, resulting in complex behavior, without an obvious central controlling force. Emergent organisms respond to constraints using basic components related by intrinsic rules to create and reach a state of equilibrium. Most consider emergence as a random act of organization, but perhaps a collective intelligence is at work assembling a natural and involuntary response given particular environmental and boundary limit conditions. The properties of an emergent system cannot be inferred from its components and are more than simply the sum of its parts: one element repeated and collected into a complex interaction results in emergence. When applied to light, space, and structure, it can lead not only to efficiency in structures, but also create a symbiotic relationship between structure, architecture, and buildings systems: design solutions that could be fluid—interactive and transient without permanence.

Termite colonies are a good example of emergence theory—complex forms emerge from a large number of termites following what appear to be simple rules for each participant. Horizontal passages are intermittently braced with vertical diaphragms to prevent the "tubes" from collapsing. What emerges from this structure is a control of temperature, humidity, and air flow in hot climates that is achieved through these horizontal passages, and that with very little variation, interconnect vertically—something we have yet to achieve in manmade structures.

The most efficient structure is one that emerges from individual elements absent of internal bending—the greatest resistance with least material. For instance, the natural behavior of a fixed-base cantilever subjected to lateral loads is to bend. If, however, this bending could be resolved into a mesh of individual axial "strings" capable of only resisting tension and compression, the most effective structure would emerge. At a small scale, these "strings" would transform larger forms into a smaller single element repeated throughout (fig. 1). The structure is one that is self-healing if violated naturally or unnaturally. Neighboring elements within the structure assume newly imposed loads if violated in a seismic event or a manmade explosive attack. The structure would remain stable through its inherent redundancy.

It is particularly useful to consider emergence theory concepts for structured forms with fluid definitions. A topographic strain density analysis can be performed with imposed boundary conditions and external loadings. Iterative computer analysis programs using finite element techniques such as OptiStruct result in a natural response by placing material density only where it is required (fig. 2). The analysis is started by placing a uniform thickness of material over the entire structure. The analysis looks for areas where material is not required and moves that material to areas of higher demand.

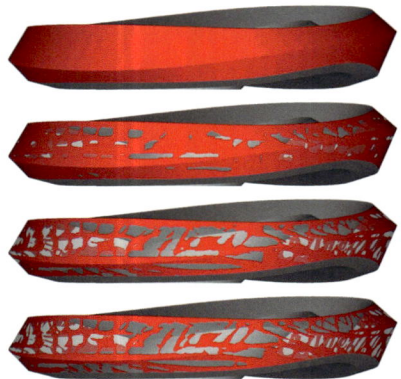

Fig. 2 Material replacement responding to load demands

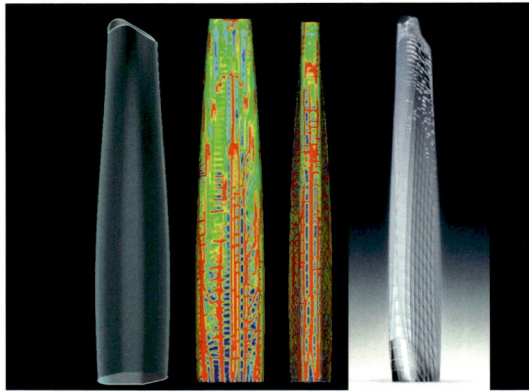

Fig. 3 Exterior transformational elevations

A solution is not obtained after the first analysis; most frequently the results do not converge on an optimal solution until several hundred analyses are performed. The internal structured forms that emerge are intuitive. The final response to the internal forces may be discrete placement of material or variations of material thickness along a membrane form.

A tall building form analyzed with similar emergent principles illustrates the sensitivity to support conditions (fig. 3). Forces and corresponding materials flow throughout the building elevation converging on best use of materials: one portion of common matter assembled and repeated. Response to this flow needs to be rational and buildable; the form line space that emerges efficient and beautiful (fig. 4).

Exterior wall systems for structures represent the single greatest opportunity to consider flow and interaction between structure and building service systems. Hundreds of millions of square feet of occupied area are enclosed each year by a system that essentially provides protection from the elements and internal comfort. A closed loop structural system integrated with the exterior wall system that includes liquid-filled structural elements such as pipes could provide a thermal radiator that when heated during the day could be used for building service systems such as hot water supply or heat for occupied spaces, especially during the evening hours. A solar collection system could be integrated into the network and this system could be integrated into double wall systems where it is important to heat the internal cavity to provide warming in cold climates. Transparent photovoltaic cells could be introduced into the glass and spandrel areas to further capture the energy of the sun. When storing in structural systems of great height, pressures within the networked vessel become very large. With this level of pressure, water supply systems to the structure or to neighboring structures of lesser height could easily be supplied without requiring additional energy to move the water. Constant low flow through these systems would prevent the liquid from freezing.

Liquid within the networked system could act to control motion with fluid flow acting to dampen the structure when it is subjected to lateral loads from wind and earthquakes. In addition, liquids at high pressure could add significantly to the axial stiffness and stability of members subjected to compression, increasing capacities without increasing structural material by creating capped compartments. Combining ultra-high strength tensile materials such as carbon fiber fabricated into closed circular forms where loads are primarily resisted by hoop stress with the liquids under ultra-high compressive stress would likely result in the greatest efficiency.

The concept of flow can be further developed into structures that are interactively monitored for movement. Through the measurement of imposed accelerations due to ground motions or wind, structures could respond by changing the state of the liquid within the system. For instance, the structure could use endothermic reactions

Fig. 4 View looking through center of structure

to change liquids to solids within the closed network. Sensor devices could inform structural elements of imminent demand and initiate a state change in liquids that would be subjected to high compressive loads where buckling could occur. In the simplest sense, water within the system could be frozen for additional structural rigidity.

In a more sophisticated application, when imminent demand from ground motions is sensed, electromagnetic flow could be used to create a separation of the superstructure from its foundations. Temporary levitation created by electromagnetism provides frictionless seismic isolation.

In cases where base isolation is not practical, pneumatic dampers that incorporate flow of compressed air could be strategically placed within frames to increase damping and consequently reduce the forces attracted from the ground.

The study of these emerging forms as they interact with the architecture (overtly or covertly) will only yield further opportunities to explore light, space, structure, and a new relationship that combines them all in an ephemeral solution. The investigation into the flow of material that can be manipulated to adhere to a seismic, temperature, or safety condition can only inform us of new ways to design and build. The combination of these two studies, emergence theory and flow, can give us the basis for new structures that will no longer limit themselves by being static. They can organically emerge as a singular system that from the ground up provides efficiency in material, intelligence in response to unknown forces, and a form that is derived from nothing but from the purest and most absolute function.

Fig. 1 Louis Sullivan, Guaranty Building, Buffalo (1896)

Notes on the Articulation of Highrise Form, 1896–2003

Kenneth Frampton

Above the City

You know our office on the 18th
floor of the Salmon Tower looks
right out on the

Empire State and it just happened
we were there finishing up some
late invoices on

a new book that Saturday morning
when a bomber roared through the
mist and crashed

flames poured from the windows
into the drifting clouds and sirens
screamed down in

the streets below it was unearthly
but you know the strangest thing
we realized that

none of us were much surprised because we'd always known that those
two paragons of

progress sooner or later would perform before our eyes this demon-
stration of their
true relationship.

—James Laughlin

The American Invention 1896–1961

It is arguable that the aesthetics of modern highrise construction begins with Louis Sullivan's seminal essay of 1896, "The Tall Office Building Artistically Considered," wherein he differentiates between the base and the shaft of his thirteen-story Guaranty Building, completed in Buffalo in the same year; a work which, by today's standards, would hardly qualify as a highrise at all. Nevertheless the format of the Guaranty represents a significant conceptual advance over what was then the received idea of handling a high building, namely, to divide it into bottom, middle, and top; a formula naïvely predicated on the subdivision of a classical column into base, shaft, and capital. In the Guaranty Building Sullivan emphasized the verticality of the shaft by suppressing the floors through recessed spandrel panels and by doubling up the mullions at twice the interval of a standard span in steel frame construction; that is to say, behind every other mullion there was no actual frame. This aesthetic subterfuge was implicitly revealed through the direct expression of the steel frame through fat, cylindrical, fireproofed columns on the lower two floors while simultaneously rendering the blocky podium as a four-square monumental form (fig. 1). Most of Sullivan's medium to highrise commercial structures after 1896 adopted and expressed the standard bay spacing of a steel frame thereby tending to stress the horizontality as well as the verticality of the structure. Nevertheless, in New York's Bayard Building (1899), a sense of height was still conveyed by alternating the thickness and depth of the vertical piers, clad in terracotta. The tectonic probity of the frame was most directly expressed perhaps in Sullivan's Schlesinger and Mayer Store, completed in Chicago in 1903, with the large, plate glass display windows of its two-story base being echoed above by the typical tripartite Chicago window, the primary motif determining the (typically) horizontal proportion of the building (fig. 2).

The expression of the steel frame *in se* was totally abandoned a decade later in the fifty-five-story, neo-Gothic Woolworth Building designed by Cass Gilbert and realized in downtown Manhattan in 1913. With considerable prescience, Gilbert opted for reiterating the piers of a neo-Gothic terracotta skin whereby the vertical proportions of a Gothic stone shaft could be infinitely extended to emphasize the height of the building while suppress-

Fig. 2 Louis Sullivan, Carson Pirie Scott, Chicago (1899)

Fig. 3 Cass Gilbert, Woolworth Building, New York (1910)

Fig. 4 Eliel Saarinen Chicago Tribune Competition Entry (1922)

ing the floors (fig. 3). A further refinement of this historicizing neo-Gothic syntax was arrived at in the winning entry of the Chicago Tribune Competition of 1922, which may now be seen as the cultural breakpoint in which the scholarly neo-Gothic manner of Hood and Howells's design for the thirty-four-story newspaper building was countered by Eliel Saarinen's second prize design which stressed the profile of the shaft through monumental corners and neo-Gothic piers culminating in a rhythmic series of setbacks and a shallow-pitched roof (fig. 4).

This inspired design, plus the setback requirements of New York's 1917 zoning code, jointly serve to crystallize the format of the Art Deco skyscraper as this mode was variously elaborated in the rival seventy-five and eighty-five-story Chrysler and Empire State Buildings, respectively designed by William Van Alen and by Shreve, Lamb, and Harmon (both completed in 1930). The Saarinen highrise format of 1922 was perhaps most finely resolved in the seventy-story RCA Building (1936), erected as the centerpiece of Rockefeller Center which was at the heart of a much larger complex, of some fourteen buildings of varying height, erected on the eight block site in the center of Manhattan between 1930 and 1940 (fig. 5). The picturesque potential for a city made of comparable developments became evident in the neo-Aztec, Piranesian imagery of Hugh Ferris's phantasmagoric perspectives that illustrated his book *The Metropolis of Tomorrow* of 1929 (fig. 6). While this highly romantic vision was hardly a realistic proposition, the idea of planned cluster development, involving more than one highrise at a time would resurface, from time to time, throughout the century.

The two structures, which recast the aesthetic ground rules for highrise steel frame construction after World War II were Mies van der Rohe's twin ten-story apartment towers built at 860 and 880 Lake Shore Drive, in Chicago, and SOM's twenty-three-story Lever House in New York designed by Gordon Bunshaft, both works being completed in 1951 (figs. 7 and 8). In retrospect it is hard to imagine two works that were more categorically opposed in aesthetic terms despite the fact that they were both predicated on standard steel frame construction. Where Lever House consisted of a hermetic glass wall projected in front of the frame, and subdivided by thin metal mullions to yield a floating orthogonal slab form, Mies's twin towers on Lake Shore Drive were of a

Fig. 5 Amalgamated Architects, Rockefeller Center, Manhattan, New York (1930)

Fig. 6 Hugh Ferris, *The Metropolis of Tomorrow* (1929)

Fig. 7 Mies van der Rohe, 860–880 Lake Shore Drive, Chicago (1951)

Fig. 8 SOM, Lever House, Manhattan, New York (1951)

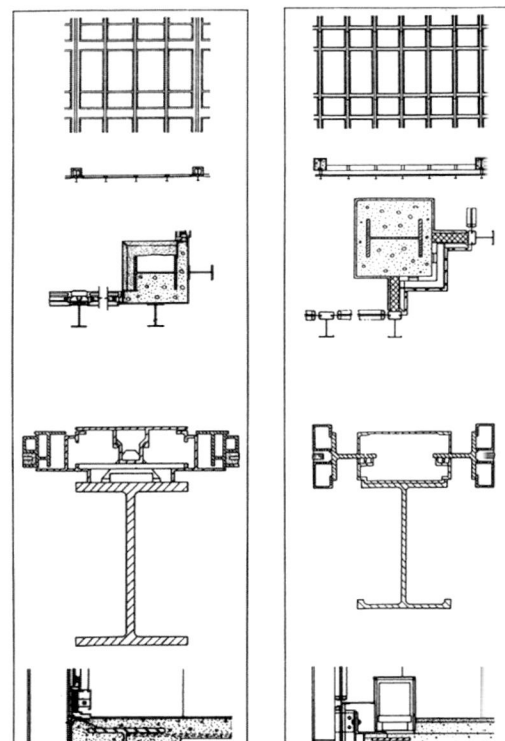

Fig. 9 Mies van der Rohe, comparitive study of elevations and sections of 860–880 Lake Shore Drive (left) and the Seagram Building

Fig. 10 Mies van der Rohe, Seagram Building, New York (1959); all-metal model of the building

more nuanced expression in which standard, steel frame construction was brought into a syncopated relationship with the H-sectioned steel mullions spanning from the floor to ceiling. This syncopation was achieved by covering the fireproofed structural columns and the edge beams steel face plates that were made integral with the prefabricated steel fenestration. Conversely, by totally suppressing the structural frame, Lever House presented its twenty-story abstract form as a skin tight, glistening green prism suspended above a two-story, plate glass podium upon which it would ostensibly depend for its support. The overall figure of Lever House was very ambiguous since its form remained uneasily suspended between the repetitive horizontality of the green spandrel panels at every floor and the overall verticality of the slab, covered in a seamless glass skin. In contrast, the mullion versus structural frame counterpoint in Mies's Lake Shore Drive apartments was a tectonic solution of exceptional sophistication. By hoisting pre-welded sections of the steel curtain wall into position on top of the fireproofed steel frame, Mies was able to express both the repetitive rhythm of the vertical mullions and the regular bay spacing of a standard steel frame, creating a kind of dematerialized neo-suprematist relief, comparable in its overall plastic density to the stone *modenature* of an Art Deco skyscraper.

While Mies would ring the changes on this format in one highrise after another, he would never again attain the tectonic rigor of his twin towers on Lake Shore Drive, not even with his magisterial, sixty-story Seagram Building realized in New York, in 1959. In this last work, Mies would employ bronze, anodized, rolled steel mullions in

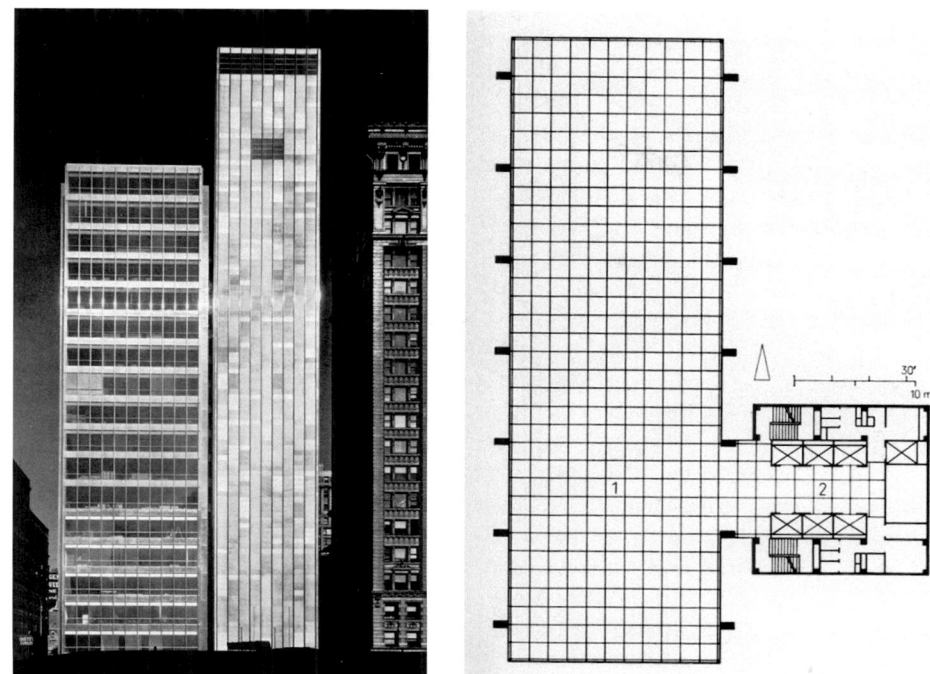

Figs. 11 and 12 SOM, Inland Steel Building, Chicago (1965), general view and plan

Fig. 13 William Lescaze, PSFS Building, Philadelphia (1931)

Fig. 14 SOM, Pepsi Cola Building, New York (1959)

Fig. 15 SOM, Chase Manhattan Bank, New York (1961)

Fig. 16 Mies van der Rohe, Glass Skyscraper (1920)

Fig. 17 Auguste Perret, Villes Tours, (1915–23)

a particularly consistent manner in as much as the curtain wall was projected *in front* of the steel frame (fig. 9). However, unlike Lever House, the mullions, in this instance, established the unequivocal verticality of the form by emphasizing the re-entrant steel corners of the vertical shaft as the whole mass-form was set back to accommodate a monumental plaza opening onto Park Avenue. It is significant that Mies built a large, all-metal model of the Seagram so as to simulate the way in which the bronze anodized steel components would fuse with the brown tinted glass of the curtain wall to yield a megalith that was as homogenous in its overall character, as the stone-faced, bronze-plated façade of Hood's RCA Building of 1936 (fig. 10).

Fig. 18 Le Corbusier, Plan Voisin, Paris (1925)

Of the eight major highrise structures that were designed and realized by SOM in the space of three intense years between 1958 and 1961, the most tectonically innovative was the nineteen-story Inland Steel Building, in Chicago, that was finally completed in 1965 (Figs. 11 and 12). The most radical aspect of this design was the sixty-foot clear span, steel girders, connected by welds to the seven pairs of composite steel columns set on either side of the slab, thereby producing some 10,200-square-feet of column-free office space on each floor, with a separate, free-standing twenty-story service tower positioned to the rear of the slab. Seemingly inspired by the pioneering exo-skeletal structure of the PSFS office slab, built in Philadelphia to the designs of Howe and Lescaze in 1931 (fig. 13). Inland Steel, unlike either Mies's 860–880 Lake Shore Drive or Bunshaft's Lever House, differentiated absolutely between the framing interval of the vertical structure and the recessed spandrels of the curtain wall. This expressive tension between the structural frame and the curtain wall will be obviated in SOM's eleven-story Pepsi-Cola Building, erected on Park Avenue in the same year as the Seagram (fig. 14). In this instance, five pairs of fire-proofed steel columns carry a concrete floor plate, with a thirty-nine-foot mid-span and thirteen-foot cantilevers to either side. The street elevation of this proto-"minimalist" work consisted of five spandrels, framed by aluminum mullions carrying single panes of clear glass, measuring nine feet by thirteen feet, a proportion which approximated the classic golden section. SOM will return to the format of Inland Steel in their last major highrise of the late nineteen-fifties, above all in their sixty-story Chase Manhattan Bank built in downtown Manhattan in 1961 (fig. 15). The much larger footprint of this building necessitated four lines of columns at eighteen-foot centers with the articulated columns assuming the form of an exoskeleton. As in Inland Steel this expression was emphasized by short, cantilevered overruns at the ends of the slab. Meanwhile, the virtually mullion-less, Pepsi-Cola Building will be taken a step further, in the twenty-story Hartford Insurance Company Building, realized in Chicago in 1961. This was an atypical, exposed reinforced concrete structure, in which the structure predominated while the floor to ceiling glazing was recessed behind the box frame on all floors. Here, an unusual balance between horizontal and vertical elements recalled the equitable proportions of the Schlesinger and Mayer store of sixty years before.

The European Interregnum, 1914–1965

The idea and image of the skyscraper would virtually haunt Europe from the time of Antonio San't Elia's setback skyscrapers featured in his Futurist Città Nuova series of drawings (1914) until the outbreak of World War II, in 1939. The image of an all glass highrise first appears in Mies's sheer glass curtain wall highrise proposals of somewhat unspecified height and structure, dating from 1920 (fig. 16). These were preceded by Auguste Perret's proposition for a city of towers dating from around 1915, as depicted in a remarkable aerial perspective, drawn by Jacques Imbert and published in the magazine *Wendingen* in 1923. Perret envisaged an avenue of seventy-story towers, spaced out at intervals on

Fig. 19 Arnest Rogers, Torre Velasca, Milan (1958)

Fig. 21 Le Corbusier, Paris Plan, (1937). Four Cartesian Skyscrapers rise to the same height to establish a new datum

Fig. 20 Le Corbusier, Cartesian Skyscraper (1936)

either side of a high-speed traffic route which was wider and longer than the Champs Elysée. The highrises that made up this futuristic vision, published around the same time as Le Corbusier's Ville Contemporaine of 1922, were to have been executed in a Beaux Arts Neoclassical manner closer to the work of McKim, Mead, and White than to the classical rationalism of Perret in his prime. They exemplified an early, transatlantic Romanticism which will be entirely absent from Mies's glass skyscraper projects of virtually the same date (fig. 17).

Other than the fifteen-story Unité d'Habitation at Marseille of 1952 and four other variations of the same type built between 1952 and his death in 1965, Le Corbusier never realized a highrise building. However, his sixty-story so-called Cartesian skyscraper, first projected in the drawings for his Ville Contemporaine and later elaborated in his Plan Voisin of 1925 (fig. 18), was predicated on a Hennebique concrete framing system in which a reinforced concrete structure was cantilevered out on all four sides. This proposition that provided for a continuous, uninterrupted curtain wall membrane was close to Mies's highrise, curtain wall aesthetic as we find this in his Friedrichstrasse office block competition project of 1922. Some three decades later at the end of the nineteen-fifties, Ernesto Roger's Torre Velasca built in the center of Milan in 1958, interject, overnight as it were, an entirely postmodern, twenty-eight-story, steel-framed tower that overtly mimicked the profile of a fortified tower (fig. 19). At the same tower, the structure was more overtly expressed than in Le Corbusier's Cartesian Visions.

Fig. 22 Le Corbusier, Quartier de la Marine, Algiers (1938)

160

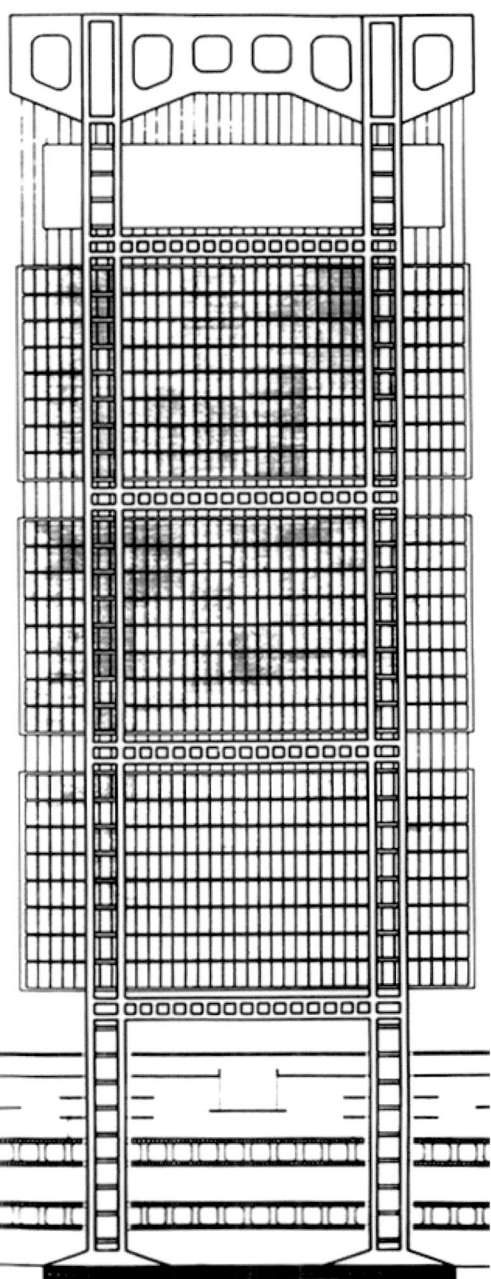

Fig. 23 Amancio Williams, twenty-eight-story prototypical highrise (1948)

Perhaps the most radical aspect of Le Corbusier's so called Cartesian skyscraper of the early nineteen-twenties was the clustering of its form as into twenty-four glistening glass towers conceived as the administrative core of the Ville Contemporaine. In this instance, each tower with the same cruciform serrated plan, rose to the same height so as to establish a new horizontal datum some sixty stories in the air. He will continue to assert this strategy throughout his ambitious urban proposals of the next two decades, as these will be eventually assembled into his book *La Ville Radieuse* of 1934. The type-form of the Cartesian skyscraper will be modified in the nineteen-thirties around this time from a cruciform plan with a serrated perimeter to a smooth-surfaced, Y-shaped plan, providing exceptionally well-lighted office space of relatively shallow depth, illuminated from both sides (fig. 20). While this variation would have been a rather uneconomic form of development in terms of square footage on each floor, it will play an important, iconic role in the four towers that make up Le Corbusier's plan for Paris of 1937 (fig. 21). One should also note that the aesthetics of Le Corbusier's Cartesian type, irrespective of whether its plan was cruciform or Y-shaped, was equally concerned with the horizontal spread of the form as with its height and with the clustering of such forms, having the same height so as to create a new urban datum. It is to be regretted that this concept should only have been realized on one or two occasions during the twentieth century; most notably in the ministerial slabs lining both sides of the monumental axis in Brasilia, and in the four slabs rising to the same height that make up the Segelgatan development in the center of Stockholm, realized between 1955 and 1965.

Le Corbusier first confronted the aesthetic challenge of a skin-tight undifferentiated curtain wall in the one-off skyscraper that he projected for the Quartier de la Marine, in Algiers, in 1938. Here in a project for a free-standing, fifty-story office slab with a lozenge-shaped plan he divided the height into three equal sections above an initial six-story base (fig. 22). Each of these sections were to have been separated one from another by interstitial floors that were to have been treated as single-story bands with pierced windows, ostensibly assigned to accommodate archives, although they could just as easily have been service floors. It is striking that he found it necessary to give this prototypical, free-standing slab a central focus, which took the form of a recessed opening in the center of the main façade. In a later highrise building projected for Algiers, this focus was extended over the entire middle section of a tripartite façade to form a syncopated relief through the manipulation of *brise soleil* in front of the glass. In fact, through the rhythmic application of such sunbreakers, the two manipulations were envisaged as operating together; the first was a vertical, counter-changing *brise soleil* running up for the full height of the building, the second was a horizontal elaboration of the central third of the form which falsely suggested a modification of the program within. This subterfuge may be accounted for as a *horror vacuii* which is inherent in highrise structures, made up of nothing but the repetition of anonymous floors.

The Late Modern Skyscraper, 1948–1997

The idea that a work of great height could be modified by a giant structural frame lying outside the body of the building is first fully formulated by Amancio Williams in his 1948 proposal for a twenty-eight-story highrise structure for an unspecified site in Argentina (fig. 23). In this instance the floors are hung on steel cables from four gigantic vierendeel beams in reinforced concrete construction, with the load of all four spans being brought down on four box columns in concrete. It is an interesting fact that the main mass of the highrise was subdivided by service floors into three parts. From 1966 to 1973, Louis Kahn and his engineer Auguste Kommedant collaborated on the design of a thirty-five-story highrise for Kansas City with the floors being suspended on wire cables from four inverted, reinforced concrete, bow-string trusses and compressive loads being carried down to the ground on four cluster columns, one at each corner of the plan (fig. 24).

Norman Foster's forty-one-story Hong Kong and Shanghai Bank (fig. 25), under construction on a prominent site in Hong Kong from 1979 to 1985, would seem to have been inspired by William's unrealized exo-skeleton highrise proposal of 1948. Foster's Hong Kong bank integrated two ideas which had been at issue in the evolution of highrise office buildings for some time; first how to modulate the height of a building through its structure,

and, second, how to introduce semi-public uses with which to alleviate the all too repetitive stacking of bureaucratic space. The second of these aims had already been achieved, on a small scale, in Frank Lloyd Wright's six-story Larkin Building, in Buffalo, New York, of 1904. Although hardly a highrise, this canonical work was nonetheless a multi-level office building in which the anonymity of the repetitive floors was offset by a full height, semi-public space in the center of the building. It is just this precedent that Foster will apply to the inner core of his HSBC headquarters in Hong Kong (fig. 26). At the same time, the multi-layered highrise, comprising three separate slabs rising to twenty-eight, thirty-five, and for-

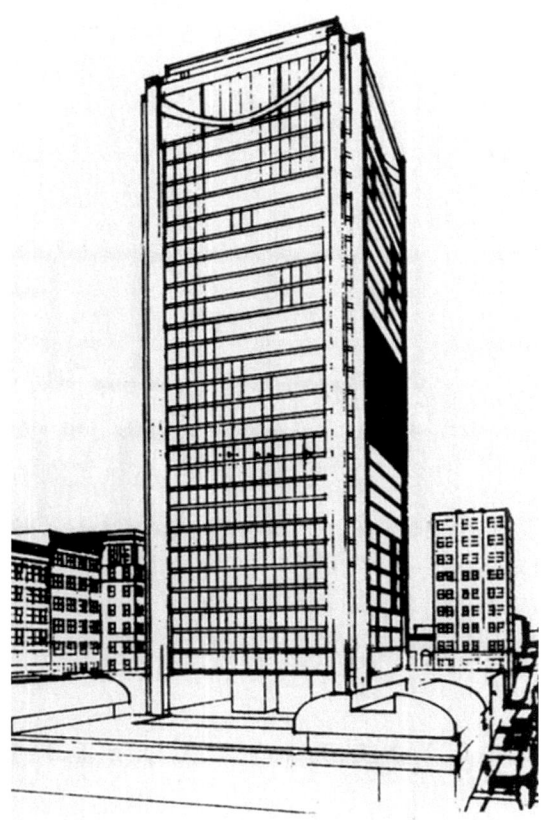

Fig. 24 Louis Kahn and August E. Komendant, thirty-five-story office building, Kansas City (1966–73)

ty-one stories respectively, will be modulated in terms of its overall height by tubular steel, triangulated trusses, each spanning thirty-eight meters and carrying the floors beneath on wire cables. This structural system enabled the building to span over a venerable civic space in downtown Hong Kong. This space will be linked by escalators to the atrium volume running up inside the core of the building.

Foster will return to the same highrise, composite theme, in his forty-five-story Commerzbank built in downtown Frankfurt in 1997 (fig. 27). This last is a multi-story office building predicated on a triangular plan, in which the office floors make up three sides of an equilateral triangle, enclosing a void running up throughout the full height of the building. The service cores, in this instance, are relegated to the points of the triangle while the void consists

Fig. 26 Norman Foster, Hong Kong Shanghai Bank, Hong Kong Interior of atrium fed by escalators rising from the public square beneath

Fig. 25 Norman Foster, Hong Kong Shanghai Bank, Hong Kong (1979–85)

Fig. 27 Norman Foster, Commerzbank Frankfurt, Germany; general view

Fig. 28 Norman Foster, Commerzbank Frankfurt, Germany; section and perspective showing the position of the garden terrace, and a general view across the atrium of the building

of a forty-five-story public atrium covered by a glass roof. While the actual structure supporting the floors is of conventional construction, the height of the building is broken up by seven, two-story, "sky gardens" alternating from one side of the building to the other, thereby affording semi-public, garden terraces for the benefit of the bank employees (fig. 28). These "hanging" gardens break up the height of the Commerzbank in such a way as to enable it to relate the remaining six-story stacks of office floors between the terraces, back to the average height of the surrounding residential fabric. In this way the Commerzbank was tentatively reconciled to the continuity of the city.

More recently, two different stratagems seem to have arisen for the mediation of highrise structures in relation to a pre-existing fabric. The first of these stems from the notion that large highrise curtain-walled structures may be handled as though they were abstract sculptural forms at a gigantic scale, while the second depends on the idea that the excessive over-development of highrise form may be compensated for by enriching the base of such as structure with public amenities. This second option, has perhaps been most convincingly formulated of recent date in Renzo Piano's fifty-two-story New York Times Building, completed in midtown Manhattan, in 2007. It may be said that this highrise benefits from a

Fig. 29 RPBW, New York Times tower

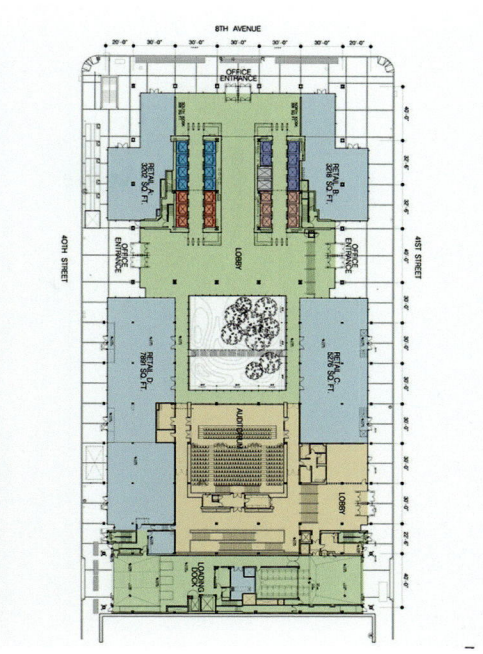

Fig. 30 RPBW, New York Times tower plan showing the combination at grade of commercial space, garden court, and public auditorium

three-part mediation of its bureaucratic form. In the first instance the mass of the shaft is broken up by four louvered planes that project beyond the structural frame and weather-proof curtain-wall so as to render the overall of the mass dematerialized spatial/planar cluster. This ephemeral verticality is countered by the horizontality of the louvers themselves as they open up at every floor to permit clear views out. Like Foster's HSBC building, Piano's New York Times tower, with its sun screening of ceramic tubes, inserts itself into the agitated skyline of Manhattan as an articulate, ephemeral image which responds in a hypersensitive way to the varying luminosity of the light (fig. 29).

The public appointment of the New York Times tower is most evident during the rise of its first four floors above ground where commercial space, flanking the entry on three sides, is indented so as to permit direct access into the ground floor foyer and elevator lobbies from each street (fig. 30). This space is visually linked to a green patio open to the sky and beyond that to a public auditorium, which is served by a separate entry hall in the depth of the block. This complex is capped by the New York Times newsroom that occupies the top three floors of the podium above the auditorium. A third mediatory aspect is evident in direct stair access between floors at the corners of the tower. All these amenities make the New York Times tower into the most civic highrise to be erected in Manhattan since the completion of Rockefeller Center in 1938.

As to the first option of treating highrise structures as though they were nothing more than giant, sculptural forms, one of the earliest precedents was unquestionably Luis Barragan and Mathias Goeritz's Satellite City Towers, realized outside Mexico City, in 1957 (fig. 31). Although these forms were not buildings nor, for that matter, of excessive size, they demonstrated nonetheless the possibility of treating a cluster of vertical elements, rightly called towers in this instance, as if the assembly was of artistic significance in and of itself.

Fig. 31 Luis Barragan and Mario Goeritz, Satellite City Towers, Mexico City (1957)

Fig. 32 Fumihiko Maki, World Trade Center Tower No. 4, New York (2010), upper and lower office floor plates

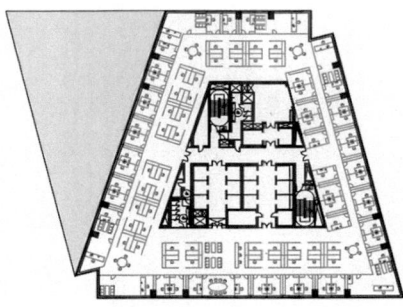

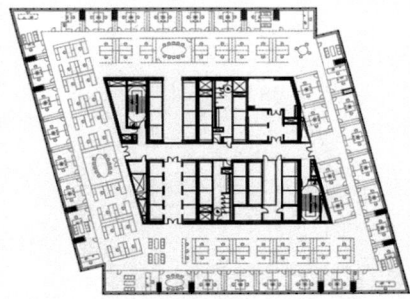

Fig. 33 Fumihiko Maki, World Trade Center Tower No. 4, New York (2010), general view

Fig. 34 Fumihiko Maki, Gate Tower, Taipei Station (2008)

One of the most exemplary works in this genre of recent date is the sixty-four-story World Trade Center Tower No. 4, in lower Manhattan, designed by Fumihiko Maki (fig. 32). In this instance, the sharp plasticity of a single highrise form is achieved by accommodating the office space in two distinctly different floor plates; the floor plate of the mid-rise section, covering floors four to forty-seven, assuming a parallelogram shape echoing the configuration of site, and floors forty-eight to sixty-four being based on a shifted, trapezoidal floor plate (fig. 33). The overall combination of these forms was alternately fluted and articulated at the corners of the prism so as to create a particularly sharp profile. In 2008, Maki will adopt a similar ploy in the design of two adjacent highrise slabs, the so-called Gate Towers, rising to eighty and sixty floors respectively, in his design for the reconstruction of Taipei Central Station. In this instance, there is a comparable sculptural shift in which the towers are carefully modulated in height so as to establish precise lateral relationships between their respective forms (fig. 34). Each slab is treated as megalith divided programmatically between offices beneath and skewed hotel accommodation above. The hotel accommodation on the top of each slab is inflected towards the north while the office slabs are aligned with Mount Chi-Shing in the distance. The form and counterform in this instance corresponds to the landscape inflections of a triangular park at the foot of the slabs along with a commercial development encompassing the newly formulated station at grade.

As for other options, one might conclude, as Tadao Ando is supposed to have opined, that over a certain height, architecture is no longer possible.

Fig. 1 Adolf Loos, Chicago Tribune Competition design (1922)

The Skyscraper Problem
Thomas A. P. van Leeuwen

The skyscraper "problem" was expounded on in two articles written by critic Montgomery Schuyler: "The 'Skyscraper' Up To Date," for *The Architectural Record* in 1899, and "The Skyscraper Problem," for *Scribner's* magazine in 1903 (his concern was limited to aesthetics and had nothing to do with the legal and social discord the skyscraper caused later on).[1] By the time these critiques were published the skyscraper had achieved the status of a distinct architectural type, and had even been acknowledged as characteristic of American civilization.[2] Its height had stabilized somewhere between twenty and forty stories and its construction was invariably of the steel cage or skeleton type.[3]

Attempts to provide the skyscraper with some respectable and aesthetically satisfying order developed along the lines of the Aristotelian *taxis,* the tripartite system (also called "the columnar analogy") by which the three elements of the classical column—base, shaft, and capital—were transferred to the façade. This principle was applied with considerable success by men like George B. Post in the design of his Union Trust (1899–90) and New York Times Buildings (1888–89), and Bruce Price in his unexecuted design for the New York Sun (1890) and the American Surety Building (1894–95).[4]

Another suggestion was put forward by Louis Sullivan in his "midwestern" tall buildings such as the Wainwright Building in St. Louis (1891), the Chicago Stock Exchange (1893–94), the Guaranty Building in Buffalo, NY (1895), and New York City's Bayard Building (1898). In Sullivan's design of the façade, the tripartite organization was maintained throughout, but he treated the "shaft" in strict classical terms, by giving it fluting similar to that of the Doric columns of the Parthenon (as Adolf Loos was later to shape the "shaft" of celebrated design of 1922 for the Chicago Tribune Building; fig.1). Schuyler admired Sullivan's solution greatly, although he interpreted it differently. About the Bayard Building he wrote: "There is nothing capricious in the general treatment of this structure. It is an attempt, and a very serious attempt, to found the architecture of a tall building upon the facts of the case. The actual structure is left, or rather, is helped to tell its own story, this is the thing itself."[5]

Schuyler's praise is remarkable for insisting upon the organic analog. A comparison with the Doric column is avoided; instead there is a direct reference to the skeleton construction—"the actual structure"—upon which "the case" is to be based. It is typical of the rhetorical power of the organic analogy that it blends the moral and aesthetic components of the argument; because of its similarity to the human skeleton, the structure of the frame is elevated to a higher status. Moreover, to exhibit the structure is regarded as an act of honesty in the moral sense, as it is, in the scientific sense, a revelation of the truth. Every now and then architectural theory is enlivened by a proclamation of the necessity to strip architecture of its superfluous dress and to emphasize the structure. As a corollary, structure is equated with truth, and truth, in turn (*Le beau c'est le vrai*), is equated with beauty.

To Schuyler and his contemporaries the conviction that nature is never capricious, always truthful, and therefore always beautiful, must have seemed self-evident, nor did they ever question the assumption that architectural structure can be equated with that of natural organisms. Thus Schuyler's conclusion that architecture is beautiful as long as it is allowed "to tell its own, providing structural, story," could count on enthusiastic support from American progressivist, and even patriotic, thinking.[6]

This theory, which has been *de rigueur* for about a century, is generally associated with Louis Sullivan, but its full scope and deeper consequences were in fact realized by Claude Bragdon and translated into architectural form by Eliel Saarinen. The three men were contemporaries but, owing to Sullivan's lack of commissions and his untimely death, it was left to the two survivors to bring the raw idea to perfection.

Sullivan's Problem

In his essay "The Tall Office Building Artistically Considered" (1896), Sullivan started off with this dramatic question: "Problem: How shall we impart to this sterile pile, this crude, harsh, brutal agglomeration, this stark exclamation of eternal strife, the graciousness of those higher forms of sensibility and culture that rest on the lower and fiercer passions."[7]

How Sullivan dealt with this problem is well known, and even better known is his famous maxim "form follows function." It has been said that this maxim was abused by many, mostly the proponents of modernism, whose interpretation of function was dangerously close to Sullivan's. So close even, that Sullivan was designated "the father of modern architecture."[8] This, however, led to an increasing number of other misunderstandings, of which architectural historian and critic Siegfried Giedion's emerging realization that the father of his own ideology was suffering from an artistic "split personality" was certainly the most tragic.[9]

For modernists, Sullivan's lifelong interest in the metaphysics of architecture and artistic creation was, though slightly off the track, mildly acceptable. The boxy shapes of his Chicago-style tall buildings and the neutral treatment of their fenestration were hailed as clear prophecies of modernity, but the naturalistic ornament he applied to the surface caused the deepest estrangement.[10] The reasons for this confusion were complex, a complexity due to differences in theoretical training, religion, and attitudes toward the question of creation; and to a fundamentally antagonistic notion of the term "function."

In European modernism the term "function" pertained to socially determined activities, such as they are—to have a place to live, to work, to recreate, to move. Function in this sense is understood as an externally organized activity, performed by the members of society as well as by their respective tools, the CIAM (International Congresses of Modern Architecture) manifestoes often interpreted in the sociological sense, and the corollaries for architectural and urban planning were essentially of an economizing and ergonomic nature. A functional house, for example, was interpreted as a house that enabled the maximum number of actions to be performed in the minimum number of movements. The kitchen of such a house was above all a study in ergonomics.[11]

If Sullivan's maxim is applied to this frame of thinking, the "form" of the kitchen must be determined by the "functions" performed in it, in other words the ergonomics of that kitchen. No such thing is to be found in Sullivan's writing; on the contrary, he was not in the least interested in the technical requirements nor in the economics of movement. His fascination with motion was entirely directed at its expression, not its economics.

The Function of Function

Having summarized the main conditions of the tall office building, Sullivan went on to say that, "As to the necessary arrangements for light courts, these are not germane to the problem, and as will become soon evident. I trust need not be considered here. These things and such others as the arrangements of elevators, for example, have to do strictly with the economics of the buildings, and I assume them to have been fully considered and disposed of to the satisfaction of purely utilitarian and pecuniary demands."[12]

That Sullivan regarded "the arrangements of elevators" as "not germane to the problem" only goes to show how profoundly the two approaches differed. For Sullivan the problem was not the social or external function, but the biological-internal, or organic, function. Architectural form was dependent not on internal evolution. A building is like an organism, and it should grow as if coming from a seed planted in the ground. Sullivan wrote, in his *System of Architectural Ornament* (1924): "The germ is the real thing. Within its delicate mechanism lies the will to power; the function is to seek and eventually to find its expression in form" (fig. 2).[13] In other words, the qualities of the plant are contained in the germ; the form of the plant is but the realization of those qualities. Or, as Sullivan put it: "The pressure we call Function; the resultant, Form."[14]

The transition from organic to inorganic was a matter of conviction. Sullivan explained:

> By the word inorganic is commonly understood that which is lifeless, or appears to be so; as stone, the metals, and seasoned wood, clay, or the like. But nothing is really inorganic to the will of man. His spiritual power masters the inorganic and causes it to live in forms which his imagination brings forth from the lifeless, the amorphous . . . . For man is power, and this power is native in nature with the power of the germ of the seed. Thus he commands at will the realm of the organic or living, and therein again he

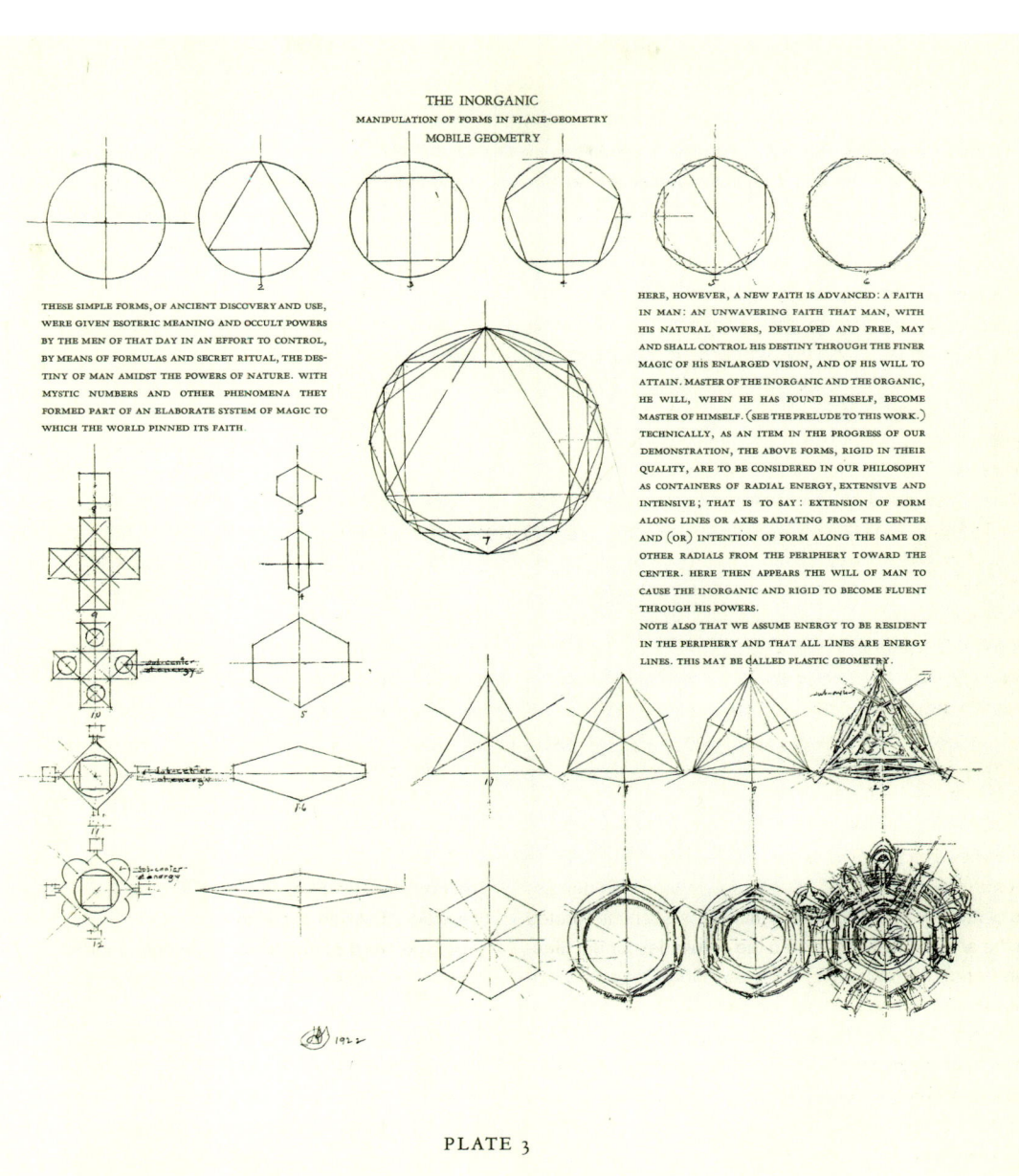

Fig. 2 Louis Sullivan, *System of Architectural Ornament*

creates as he will; for he has the power to will . . . Hence, for the germ of the typical plantseed with its resident powers, he may substitute, in thought, his own will as the seat of vital power."[15]

It is quite evident that Sullivan's organic theory went far beyond the scope of European functionalism, and recent research by Narciso Menocal and Philip Steadman, for example, has made this clear enough.[16] What has not been sufficiently acknowledged, though, is that Sullivan's interest in traditional biological analogies was not as profound as it might seem, particularly compared to his quest for demiurgical creation and the importing of life to lifeless matter.

Claude Bragdon singled out this particular aspect of his intellectual and spiritual curiosity. "The core of his philosophy was his belief in the essential divinity of man: 'For man is godlike enough did he but know it, did he but choose, did he but remove his wrappings and his blunders, and say good-bye to his superstitions and his fears.'" These quotations from *The Autobiography of an Idea,* Bragdon continued, "may aid in an understanding of the following letter, written after the reading of my manuscript" [from December 1903, which he had submitted to Sullivan for approval]. Upon which followed, on January 2, 1904, a letter from Sullivan to Bragdon, in which he wrote: "These principles have as their prototype the Great-God of the Universe. This divinely-human and humanly-divine creative element and power it was my purpose to show forth, to the receptive mind, in 'Kindergarten Chats.'"[17] Sullivan's conception of the "divinely-human" creator is directly dependent on the idea of the demiurge as revealed in the Pimander chapter of *The Corpus Hermeticum.*[18]

A reconstruction of the possible sources of Sullivan's thinking has yielded a rather mixed bag. French and Anglo-American evolutionism predominates, blended with mostly German nineteenth-century idealism. The influence of Herbert Spencer as well as that of Hegel, Schelling, and, as may be deduced from the above, Schopenhauer, has been proposed.[19] Menocal has pointed to Emanuel Swedenborg's cosmology and the theory of opposite forces as a possible source for Sullivan's ideas on ornament and decoration, as well as the theories of the Prague-born American architect Leopold Eidlitz concerning artistic creation and the notion of anthropomorphism.[20] Eidlitz must have been a major influence indeed. After all it was he who first expounded the form-follows-function formula—not in the same succinct form, but nevertheless with the same purport: "In nature forms are the outcome of environment. Environment determines function, and forms are the result of function."[21] In the passage which follows the tendency toward evolutionism is strongly present, as is the Hegelian notion of artistic creation:

> This energy of function is expressed in nature in visible form. As art is re-creation, and the forms of architecture are entirely ideal, the problem to be solved may be stated thus: We know the methods by which nature arrives at her forms: shall the architect presume to create his forms at once full-fledged, complete as it were, in their final shape; or, in other words, shall he attempt to tell a story before he has analyzed the facts to be related? Can this be done? No; what he must do is to study the condition, analyze the environment, yield to it everywhere, respond to it always, until the functions, resulting from all this are fully expressed in the organism; and while he is thinking of all this, forms will grown under his hands . . .[22]

The solution Eidlitz suggested must have held a strong appeal for Sullivan, and they may have inspired his definitive statement in *A System of Architectural Ornament:* "A work of Art, like a work of nature, is a realized idea," Eidlitz wrote echoing the words of Hegel, "and the ideal is the essence of architecture. It is the godlike attempt to create a new organism, which because it is new, cannot be an imitation of any work of nature, and, because it is an organism, must be developed according to the methods of nature."[23] Eidlitz's thoughts on anthropomorphism, architectural empathy, and the animation of the artifact were, apparently, quite compatible with American transcendentalism, or at least with Sullivan's thinking, which eventually developed into a unique and interesting bricolage enabling him to penetrate the question of creation. From "The Tall Office Building" to *A System of Architectural Ornament,* a progression toward a radical Hermetic belief in the demiurgical powers of man becomes apparent.[24] In "The Tall Office Building Artistically Considered," Sullivan expounded the idea of the "active" skyscraper:

painful solidity soars like an arrow to heaven apprizes us in an unusual manner of that law of gravitation . . ."[26]

Architectural Alchemy

In his *Autobiography of an Idea* (an enigmatic title which becomes less enigmatic if read with Hegel's terminology in mind), Sullivan again takes up this image, referring to it as "the element of loftiness, in the suggestion of slenderness and aspiration, the soaring quality of a thing rising from the earth as a unitary utterance."[27] If there be a dominant idea that could be distilled from Sullivan's writings on the form of skyscraper, it should be his insistence upon movement and life: the skyscraper should look like its action. Since this action was originally integrated in a collective performance, the task of the designer, following the Aristotelian principles of organic entity, was to find a form for the part that would harmonize with the whole and would reflect its quality.[28]

The tragedy of Sullivan was that his theories were not followed by a successful application, and that, despite what most of the critics thought, he did not find an adequate way "to impart life to the sterile pile." Nevertheless, there were others who were adept in this bizarre branch of architectural alchemy, and they came amazingly close, both in theory and practice, to fulfilling Sullivan's ideal.

Fig. 3 Alfred C. Bossom, *Building to the Skies, the Romance of the Skyscraper* (1934). Illustrations of the pre-determined "packing case" office building

We must now heed the imperative voice of emotion. It demands of us, what is the chief characteristic of the tall office building? And at once we answer, it is lofty. This loftiness is to the artist-nature its thrilling aspect. It is the very organ-tone in its appeal. It must be in turn the dominant chord in his expression of it, the true excitant of his imagination. It must be tall, every inch of it tall. The force and power of altitude must be in it, the glory and pride of exaltation must be in it. It must be every inch a proud and soaring thing, rising in sheer exultation . . .[25]

There is something of Emerson here, in the combination of loftiness and movement, or rather in his description of the relation between architecture and the law of gravity. Emerson wrote: "In architecture, height and mass have a wonderful effect because they suggest immediately a relation to the sphere on which the structure stands, and so to the gravitating system. The tower which with such

"Life and the form," Sullivan wrote, "were absolutely one and inseparable, whether it be the sweeping eagle in his flight or the open apple blossom, the toiling work horse, the blithe swan, the branching oak, the winding stream at its base, the drifting clouds, over all the coursing sun."[29] For Sullivan the essence of life resided more in their doings than in their being, thus it was the "sweeping" that made the eagle an eagle, distinct from, say, the sparrow, which would merely flutter. Correspondingly, a skyscraper was a skyscraper by virtue of its "soaring" quality and not the number of floors, elevators, or steel beams. But how might this quality be imparted to the sterility of the steel cage? The steel frame of a tall building is essentially comprised of horizontal units—the beams must be longer than the columns are tall. Sullivan's solution was to subdivide the distance between the two verticals by means of intermediate, non-load-bearing columns, and he used it successfully in the Bayard and Wainwright Buildings, the Chicago Stock Exchange and, best of all,

173

Fig. 4 Louis Sullivan, Bayard Building, New York

in the Guaranty Building, which was erected almost simultaneously to the publication of "The Tall Office Building" (fig. 3).[30] By eliminating horizontal divisions and by articulating the vertical elements, Sullivan created a calm, uninterrupted, uprising quality which was new to the skyscraper. For this he was rightly praised, but it would be unwise to believe that the problem had been solved for good.[31] "Lofty" and "proud" his buildings were, but their ability to soar was severely limited. The Guaranty Building clearly illustrates this. Darkly looming over St. Paul's Church, it has a depressing effect rather than one of rising upward, the vertical movement of the piers, which Sullivan has so diligently achieved, is abruptly curtailed by a heavy cornice and darkly shaded attic. With its cantilevered roof it resembles the flattened top of a pile driven down by a steamhammer, sinking deeper into the ground with every other blow. It looks like the Palazzo Strozzi, jammed by some freak accident into the heart of the city. Sullivan no doubt perceived the obvious contradiction, but this is perhaps the best he could do with the type of Chicago office building ("the packing case type of building," as the English-born skyscraper architect Alfred C. Bossom called it), in the structural shape of which he had no say in.[32] Sullivan made the following comment in "The Tall Office Building": "This brings us to the attic which . . . gives us the power to show by means of its broad expanse of wall, and its dominating weight and character, that which is the fact—namely, that the series of office tiers has come definitely to an end. This may perhaps seem a bald result and a heartless, pessimistic way of stating it, but even so we certainly have advanced a most characteristic stage beyond the imagined sinister building of the speculator-engineer-builder combination."[33]

The architect-artist had no choice but to cooperate with this "speculator-engineer-builder" alliance, and he grudgingly acquiesced. On the other hand, he was dominated by Hegel's conviction that architecture is essentially a system of post-and-lintel, and he must have found it impossible to think in any other forms than the block. The Guaranty and Bayard Buildings were his last skyscraper commissions. Unable to exert any influence on the shape of the building, and stranded in the periphery of the architectural profession as "a mere decorator" (which in all honesty he was), Sullivan had, by 1900, reached the end of his career, and he died in 1924. The few charming commissions that he realized in the Midwest were but proof of his lack of success, and therefore not charming at all, but merely tragic.[34] This tragedy was summed up by Claude Bragdon, when he wrote: "Sullivan failed to write himself in an arresting way on the skyline of any of our cities."[35]

To call Sullivan "the prophet of modern architecture," as so many historians have, is not only a flagrant misjudgement of modernity, but also a merciless denial of a great man's right to choose his own company.[36]

1 Montgomery Schuyler, "The Skyscraper Problem," originally in *Scribner's* 34 (August 1903), pp. 253–56, reprinted in, William H. Jordy and Ralph Coe, eds., *American Architecture and Other Writings by Montgomery Schuyler* (Cambridge, MA, 1961), vol. II, pp. 442–49.
2 Montgomery Schuyler, "The 'Sky-scraper' Up to Date," *The Architectural Record* VIII (Jan–March 1899), p. 231.
3 By 1899 the average height of the tall buildings was twenty-one stories. Bruce Price and George B. Post designed, in 1890 and 1899 respectively, a thirty-story tower for the New York *Sun* and—for the Prudential Life Insurance Co.—a tower of more than forty stories (see Winston Weisman, "A New View of Skyscraper History," in *The Rise of an American Architecture*, Edgar Kaufmann, Jr., ed. [New York, 1970], p. 145). The tallest office tower in the world, until the advent of the forty-seven-story Singer Building, in 1908, was the thirty-story Park Row Building built in 1899 by R. H. Robertson, both in New York.
4 Weisman 1970, see note 3, p. 115, fig. 3-1 and p. 116, fig. 3-2.
5 Schuyler 1899 (see note 2), pp. 231–57.
6 Ibid., pp. 3–4.
7 Louis Sullivan, "The Tall Office Building Artistically Considered," originally in *Lippincott's* 57 (March 1896), pp. 403–09; reproduced in *Kindergarten Chats and Other Writings* (New York, 1979), pp. 202–13.
8 Hugh Morrison, *Louis Sullivan, Prophet of Modern Architecture* (New York, 1935); Philip Johnson, "Is Sullivan the Father of Functionalism?", *Writings* (New York, 1979), pp. 183–86; Leland McRoth, *A Concise History of American Architecture* (New York, 1979), pp. 183–84: "Sullivan was both creator and prophet of the modern commercial skyscraper, and is rightly lauded as the father of modern architecture," van Leeuwen, "The Skyward Trend of Thought" (Cambridge, 1988), pp. 20ff.
9 van Leeuwen 1988 (see note 8), p. 25.
10 Ibid., pp. 25ff.
11 See Reyner Banham, *Theory and Design in the First Machine Age* (London, 1972), p. 320ff. Jurgen Joedicke, "Anmerkungen zur Theorie des Funktionalismus in der modernen Architektur," *Jahrbuch fur Asthetik und allgemeine Kunstwissenschaft* (Cologne, 1965), pp. 14–24.
12 Sullivan 1896, p. 203 (see note 7).
13 Louis Sullivan, *A System of Architectural Ornament* (New York, 1967), n. p.
14 Louis Sullivan, *Kindergarten Chats* (New York, 1979), p. 48. See also Donald Drew Egbert, "The Idea of Organic Expression and American Architecture," in *Evolutionary Thought in America*, Stow Persons, ed. (New Haven, 1950), pp. 344–66.
15 Sullivan 1967, n.p (see note 13).
16 Narciso Menocal, *Architecture as Nature: The Transcendentalist Idea of Louis Sullivan* (Madison, WI, 1981); Philip Steadman, *The Evolution of Designs, Biological Analogy in Architecture and the Applied Arts* (Cambridge, 1979).
17 Claude Bragdon, *The Secret Springs: An Autobiography* (London, 1938), pp. 158–59.
18 *Corpus Hermeticum*, A. D. Nock, ed. (Paris, 1945). The books *Pimander* and *Asclepios*, attributed to Hermes Trismegistos, represent the story of creation in the dualistic-gnostic sense, in which man, as a fallen angel, is gifted with the same powers of creation as his original creator. The demiurge is the god that God created after himself. The demiurge is known from Plato's *Timaeus* in which he is represented as the agent who brings order to the physical world. I am grateful to Dr. Oosterbaan, who introduced me to hermetic thought.
19 Menocal 1979 (see note 16), pp. 10ff.
20 Ibid., pp. 24–25. Leopold Eidlitz, *The Nature and Function of Art, More Especially of Architecture* (New York, 1881).
21 Ibid., p. 358.
22 Ibid.
23 Ibid., p. 57.
24 Nock 1945 (see Note 18).
25 Sullivan 1896, p. 206 (see note 7).
26 Vivian C. Hopkins, *Spires of Form: A Study of Emerson's Aesthetic Theory* (Cambridge, MA, 1951), p. 83. The source is manuscript Journal B., 1835–36, II, Comments on aesthetic form, etc.
27 Louis Sullivan, *The Autobiography of an Idea* (New York, 1956), pp. 313–14.
28 The Aristotelian, or tri-partite columnar principle of ordering architectonic elevations was proposed by Schuyler, in Schuyler 1899 (see note 2). Sullivan referred to it in Sullivan 1896, p. 206 (see note 7). See also Steadman 1979 (see note 16), pp. 9ff.
29 Sullivan 1896, p. 208 (see note 7). In his essay "Ornament in Architecture," for *The Engineering Magazine* (August 1892), reprinted in Sullivan 1979, p. 18 (see note 14). Sullivan wrote: "That is to say, a building which is truly a work of art (and I consider none other) is in its nature, essence and being an emotional expression. This being so . . . , it must have, almost literally, a life." This is a paraphrase of Eidlitz's dictum that "every structure, like the human body, that assumes to be a work of art, must also be possessed of a soul" Eidlitz, 1881 (see note 20), p. 92.
30 "The Tall Office Building" was published in 1896, whereas the Guaranty (later Prudential) Building was begun in 1894 and finished in 1895.
31 James Marston Fitch, *American Building: The Historical Forces that Shaped It* (New York, 1987): " . . . in the Wainwright and Guaranty buildings he (Sullivan) produced the prototype, which . . . was materially not to be approved upon for half a century" (p. 201). Claude Bragdon, on the other hand, being unconvinced that the line of evolution would run straight to the post-World War II steel-and-glass slab pointed to the interregnum of the Woolworth Building type: "In Sullivan's day the skyscraper as a sky-piercing obelisk, like the Woolworth Tower and the Empire State Building, did not exist, and Sullivan's buildings must look stunted and old-fashioned by comparison." Bragdon, however, admitted: "but he nevertheless gave vertical building its true dramatic expression" (Bragdon 1938, p. 149 [see note 17]). In the modernist vision, however, the Sullivan model remained sacrosanct, his tall buildings "a milestone in the evolution of the Modern Movement" (Nikolaus Pevsner, *Pioneers of Modern Design* (Harmondsworth, 1975), p. 141.
32 Alfred C. Bossom, *Building to the Skies, The Romance of the Skyscraper* (London and New York, 1934), p. 62. See also Bossom's *American Architecture, 1903–1926*, Dennis Sharp, ed. (London, 1984).
33 Sullivan 1896, p. 205 (see note 7).
34 See William H. Jordy, *American Buildings and their Architects* (Garden City, NY, 1976), p. 174, n. 76.
35 Claude Bragdon, *Merely Players* (New York, 1929), p. 92.
36 Hopkins 1952 (see note 26).

Fig. 1 The Sky Ride at the Century of Progress Exposition, Chicago (1933) was an aerial tramway designed by Robinson & Steinman, an engineering firm better known for the design of bridges such as the Hudson River Bridge over Spuyten Duvil (1936)

How the Leopard Got Its Spots: Lever House as a Skyscraper
Nicholas Adams

Introduction
Lever House in New York (1950–52) is Skidmore, Owings & Merrill's great success story. The building brought light and air into the center of the city and demonstrated the new modern style of the American corporation. But by the nineteen-seventies the building had retreated from favor. In the early flush of postmodernist sarcasm the critic Charles Jencks dismissed Lever House as "background wallpaper and businessman's vernacular."[1] The proliferation of faceless glass boxes in the heart of the American city had become a problem, sourced in the popular mind, with Lever House. The brilliant restoration of Lever House (2002) by SOM suggests yet another ending. To uncover the narratives underlying Lever House we need to look at how it became the iconic building we know today.

The Skyscraper and SOM
Skidmore, Owings & Merrill is famous for its skyscrapers: twice over it has built the world's tallest building, and from Johannesburg to Genoa, from São Paolo to Calgary, one finds that if SOM was not the first firm to erect a tall building in a city, at one point or another they erected the tallest building in the city, or just a significant number of that city's tall buildings.[2] But tall buildings were not always the firm's core business. Louis Skidmore and Nathaniel Owings started their firm in the winter of 1937–38, building residential housing. Over the next decade, although they built many buildings, none were over three stories. Then, all of a sudden, there is one tall building after another. At twenty stories, Terrace Plaza, in Cincinnati (1945–48), was the first of these taller buildings, but the critical work from which all else develops is Lever House in New York (1950–52), the "miniature skyscraper," built in association with the structural engineers, Weiskopf & Pickworth. In making this foray into the "big time," Owings and Skidmore knew they had the chance to enhance the firm's reputation decisively and they played this opportunity for all it was worth. Both Terrace Plaza and Lever House were extensively "glamorized," one of Owings's favorite words; treated as if they were Christmas trees draped with novelties and surprises. Glamorization bought column inches in newspapers and magazines and good publicity produced ample advertising that put around the name of the firm.[3] But how did Lever House become glamorized as a "skyscraper"? Using a purely empirical definition, the architectural historian Henry-Russell Hitchcock used to say that a skyscraper needed, at least, to scrape the sky and at twenty-four stories (ninety-two meters) and as a square top slab, Lever House might be disqualified on two counts. But somehow the term stuck to Lever House.[4] Terms and labels are a convenience for historians, critics, and the public at large, and not to be confused with buildings. Seeking to understand how Lever House found its place as a skyscraper without actually being one, therefore, requires unpacking the mechanics of glamorization.

The Beginnings
Owings served his architectural apprenticeship in Chicago under Louis Skidmore at the Century of Progress Exhibition in 1933–34. Skidmore was head of design and Owings took charge of the rides and concessions. Among the public relations techniques Owings learned there was how to embellish projects with gimmicks and tricks to draw in repeat customers and entice new ones: it required, as he said, "a little hokum." His most prominent achievement was the Sky Ride, a daring cable car system that led out toward Lake Michigan (fig. 1). Owings arranged for it to have its own song, "Let's Take a Ride on the Sky Ride," written by Nelson Shawn, later noted as the author of "Ridin' the Range," for the Gene Autry film *Boots and Saddles* (1937). He staged a Sky Ride photography competition, "to add to your enjoyment and to perpetuate your memory of one of its greatest attractions." And alongside the Sky Ride he organized a skydive that ended in disaster when one of the parachutists (dressed as Uncle Sam) committed suicide. One of his

Fig. 2 Terrace Plaza Hotel, Cincinnati (1948). Both Gourmet Restaurant (above) and the Skyline Dining Room (at the lower level) are visible (Ezra Stoller ESTO).

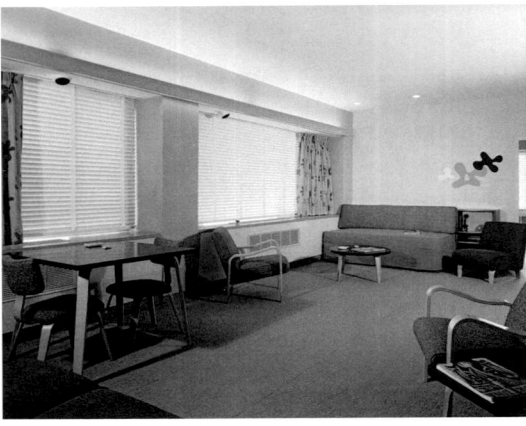

Fig. 3 Terrace Plaza Hotel in Cincinnati (1948). Motor-driven sofa beds and sliding partitions were common in the hotel suites (Ezra Stoller ESTO).

greatest coups was a historic transportation pageant from the covered wagon to the airplane called Wings of the Century.[5] If nothing else, success at the Century of Progress proved the power of advertising. A little hokum could go a long way.

In some of the projects undertaken by the firm in the late nineteen-thirties and early nineteen-forties one can see Owings (and Skidmore) using the skills of salesmanship they had developed at the Century of Progress. One early job was arranging the exhibitions at the Chicago Museum of Science and Industry, and they opened their New York office in 1938 on the basis of the commission for a bathroom display for American Standard at Raymond Hood's Radiator Building (1923–24). For the decoration of the Toffenetti Restaurant ("Famous for Ham and Sweets") at 43rd Street and Broadway, Owings contacted the artist and practical joker Hugh C. Troy (1906–1964), who in turn contacted the photographer Barrett Gallagher (1913–1994). Together they decorated a fifteen-by-sixty-foot wall with a mixture of paintings and sepia photographs. "Madness" was the subject of the mural, according to the artists. "Thus," as reported in *The New Yorker,* "lambs turn eerily into peas, a bass viol into crockery, musical notation into baked potatoes, a parasol into Winged Victory, melons into a talking machine, a cow into a fish, and a tree into fireworks . . ."[6] Owings was merely warming up!

The first large-scale exploitation of glamorization in architecture came with the construction of the Terrace Plaza Hotel, in Cincinnati (fig. 2). Begun in 1945 when Gordon Bunshaft was in the army, the project involved both the Chicago and New York offices with Owings, Skidmore, and their staffs contributing ideas. The program for the competition was open and SOM won the commission with a thoroughly glamorized proposal combining skyscraper hotel with apartments, office space, and a pair of department stores. The hotel was designed and decorated by SOM; the retail areas were left to be completed by their tenants. In the hotel the rooms had motor-driven sofa beds and they were painted in different colors to reflect the direction of the view: rooms to the south had cool colors (gray, white, dark green); rooms to the north had warmer colors (gray, white, and terracotta) (fig. 3).[7] Some rooms could be interconnected by a mechanized sliding partition to make suites, and some two-and-three room suites had "electric kitchenettes" for permanent guests. Magazine writers for the hotel trade admiringly described "a make-up mirror . . . at the proper height . . . an adjustable shower spray . . . [and] the full-length mirror" in the bathrooms.[8] Dining rooms of different types were available for visitors: a simple cafeteria on the ground level; an exclusive circular restaurant called, with clarion precision, Gourmet Restaurant, at the penthouse level, had been the work of Louis Skidmore; and

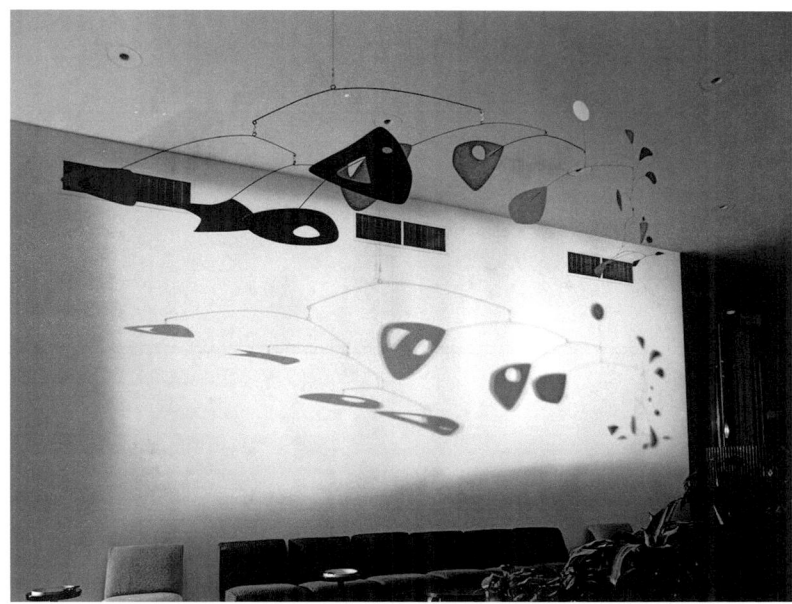

Fig. 4 Terrace Plaza Hotel in Cincinnati (1948). Alexander Calder mobile in the eighth-floor lobby (Ezra Stoller ESTO).

in between, a skyline restaurant on the eighth floor (where you could sit out in the summer and ice skate in the winter) and in front of the main entrance to the hotel, the sidewalks were heated to keep snow from accumulating. Modern art also made a significant (and glamorizing) appearance: a mobile by Alexander Calder in the eighth-floor lobby; a lighthearted mural on life in Cincinnati in the Skyline Dining Room, by Saul Steinberg; and a mural by Joan Miró in the Gourmet Restaurant (fig. 4).[9]

Coverage was local and national, in professional and popular magazines. *Architectural Forum* dedicated much of an entire issue to Terrace Plaza in December 1948, and, in addition, devoted four articles to the building (in February 1946, December 1946, April 1948, July 1948).[10] Terrace Plaza was on the cover of the magazine in December 1948 with interior color illustrations (they cost more) throughout and there were eight well-coordinated full pages of advertising by the suppliers. And it wasn't just the major architectural magazines that wrote about Terrace Plaza, but *Chain Store Age* (for the Bonds and J. C. Penney stores), *Hotel Monthly* and *Hotel Management* (described the hotel facilities), *The Magazine of Light* (described the range of interior lighting), *Engineering News-Record* (on construction techniques), and the *Official Bulletin of Heating, Piping, and Air Conditioning Contractors* (described the HVAC). And then there was *Fortune, Life, Harper's, Time,* and *Newsweek*.[11] And the local Cincinnati newspapers all wrote articles about the articles in the national magazines—one by one, and then, as publicity coverage grew, collectively. Thus the headline in the *Cincinnati Enquirer* "New Hotel Scores National Publicity Smash." It was a truly synergistic effort proving that "glamorization" worked to market both the building and the architects. For the opening Gordon Bunshaft, back from the war, turned up, and as the *Cincinnati Post* announced: "Nearly 10,000 Crowd in at Terrace Plaza Debut."

Lever House

Lever House, though less spectacular in the variety of its amenities—it was only an office building, after all—was equally well glamorized. In fact, it began life as Nathaniel

Owings's glamorized marketing idea. The idea itself was relatively simple: a two- or three-story block to occupy the footprint of the site could be complemented by a vertical office slab at right angles to the major street. The result would hold the street line, provide vertical rental space, and bring light and air into the heart of the city. First expounded in a lecture to the Building Managers' Association in Chicago, Owings thought his concept so winning that starting in 1947, two years before the Lever commission was a glint in his eye, he published his "ideal office tower" three times over: in *Skyscraper Management* (1947), in *National Real Estate and Building Journal* (1948), and in *Architectural Forum* (1949).[12]

Owings conceived of a glamorized building thick with novelties—it was, he wrote in 1947, first and foremost, a solution to the "dark, grimy, dismal canyons of stone" of the American city (fig. 5). He recounted its special selling points with breathless enthusiasm. It would be completely air conditioned; it would take advantage of prefabrication throughout; it would have parking underground and on the second and third story; an outdoor park "with real grass, pools, and restaurants" on the horizontal block; and automatic window washing for the slab. And all these advantages, Owings argued, would mean that it might rent for $5 a square foot more than other offices. Owings proposed to set up a "planning and research office [on site] where the needs of each tenant are studied in order to utilize the space to its maximum efficiency." (This was not unlike an office he and Skidmore had run at the Century of Progress Exhibition to help exhibitors plan their pavilions.) And he promised to "cut space requirements as much as twenty-five percent," thus reducing rental costs significantly. It would, wrote Owings, "throw into obsolescence our present standards in the field of multi-storied building design." He had a salesman's faith. "We Americans are going to eat tender juicy steaks, no matter what they cost us because we like them. We are going to keep on buying big fat, sleek automobiles as fast as they roll out of the black market at twice pre-war prices because we want automobiles. I firmly believe that the American will pay for whatever he wants but he has got to want it and want it badly. This takes glamorizing, takes a keen knowledge of human passions, takes courage, brains to produce."[13] But his building was far from an economic proposition, as the

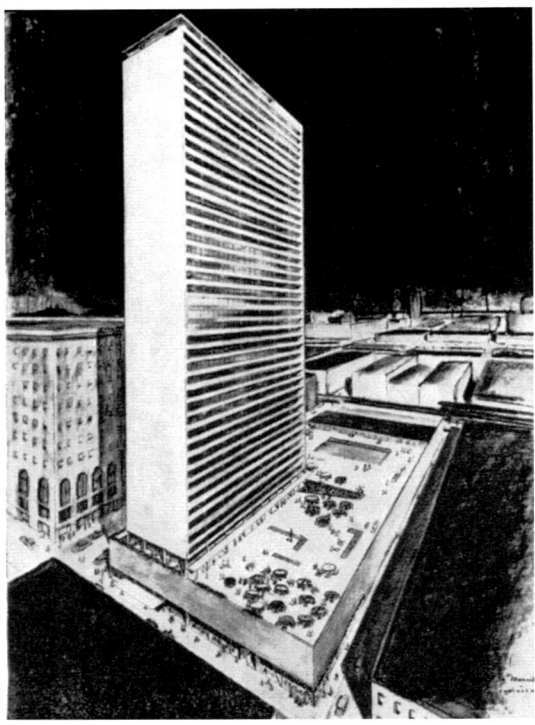

Fig. 5 Nathaniel A. Owings (1947). The original design planned by Owings had forty-seven stories. Owings reproduced it in 1949 in *Architectural Forum* in an article entitled "The Ideal Office Building—A Dream Boat Speech by Architect Owings."

developer George R. Bailey (then with the real estate firm of Albert H. Wetten) and later president of the Chicago Buildings Owners & Managers Association, pointed out in the next issue of the same magazine. His article, entitled "I Am Going to Build This Building," actually argued the reverse: that the building proposed by Owings was too costly for a Chicago center city site.[14] Owings persisted. In 1949 he even had a client for the Lever-like glass-covered slab connected to a new Greyhound Bus Terminal in Chicago.[15] The idea was to have buses descend to an underground entry area, keeping high-value retail stores at sidewalk level. The glass slab could then float above and behind the block. Ambrose Richardson (1917–1995), who worked on the project, commented: "With few exceptions, that's exactly what happened in Lever House, except at Lever House they went even further. They opened up the ground floor at Lever House to make a garden-like open atmosphere out of it with a tower coming out."[16] Richardson recalls that Lever even thought of moving to Chicago at this time and with this in mind a Chicago team under Charles Wiley was working on a scheme, at Michigan and Oak, just to the north of the Drake Hotel, with a plinth and a glass-faced slab.[17] In the end, of course, Lever moved to New York and the job fell to Gordon Bunshaft. Two unpublished accounts leading up to construction stress the importance of public relations and advertising for Lever House. The first was a lecture by J. E. Drew, the Public Relations director for Lever Brothers, which was delivered to a session on the Economic Values of Design at the AIA Annual Convention in New Orleans in June 1959.[18] In it Drew described the public relations strategy adopted by Lever and SOM prior to the inauguration of Lever House and during its first years. The second is a report on the background to the Lever House commission prepared for Owings, in 1970, by George A. Fry (1901–1973), the management consultant who handled the Lever Brothers move from Cambridge to New York.[19] Both make clear how important glamorization was to the success of the building.

The first task was selling the clients. Owings presented the design concept to Unilever (where the architect Charles Luckman, president of the American office, well understood the potential power of architecture and, indeed, later claimed the entire design as his own in a highly fictionalized account in his autobiography) as well as to the rather conservative lawyers of the real estate firm responsible for negotiating the lease.[20] "Nat Owings was on a hot seat. Nat's performance was masterful but he had a hard time convincing the lawyer as to the design of the building. The attorney said he didn't want it [the building] to look like the United Nations building and he was very definite in his position in this matter. Nat countered by saying that in his opinion the design of the New York Daily News building and Rockefeller Center were desirable so far as basic designs were concerned. When Nat mentioned Rockefeller Center as a possible guideline, this seemed to satisfy the attorney."[21] The architects' ability to tailor their message, perhaps slightly stretching the truth, was of critical importance.

Drew makes a similar point. The success of the publicity program at Lever House, he wrote, "was due in no small measure to the assistance of our architects. Through their understanding of our problems, their patience, efforts, and most important, their ability to convert technical language into laymen's terms, they were able to provide an abundance of highly usable material." The narrative line advanced by Owings in his lecture on the ideal office tower even found its way into the architectural press. In 1947 (and repeated in slightly different forms in 1948 and 1949) Owings had his building speak: "Our environment is established. We are self-contained. Because of our size we are clearly identifiable as a single important unit. We have *individuality!* We have *character!* Our office building is a clear simple rectangular shaft rising from a pedestal, or base, free of obstruction on all sides, permitting in perpetuity, light air and view."[22] The editors of *Architectural Forum* took Owings's description and ran it through Louis Sullivan's description of H. H. Richardson's Marshall Field Warehouse and produced one of the most memorable statements about American corporate architecture:

> Here I stand in complete clarity, without mystery. Look, here are my structural columns, my office space, my circulation system—all visible, evident, and obvious. It's easy to see I am completely expressive of this industrial age. Look at me and I'll reflect back your image, darkly—but no more dramatically than you would like really to be. My personality is the image of yourself you see in my shining walls, as you stand before me in a luxurious suit made in Rochester and wonderful shoes made in St. Louis, with an airline ticket to California in your pocket. I'm you. I'll be standing here when you're gone, to say what you were like. I'm you, but I'm bigger than you.[23]

Owings's narrative tool had been magnificently glamorized! (Consultants are still trying to drive home the need for architects to develop a winning narrative.)

Effective salesmanship also meant using the language of modernity (efficiency, rationality, cost saving, cleanliness) rather than the language of architectural modernism. As Drew told his audience: "Design was geared to function. It was not something that was separate and apart either as an exercise in architectural fantasy or a client's personal whim. It is a solid, working, efficient, economical office building." This theme, in fact, became the dominant narrative for the presentation of Lever

House. John Duncan Miller (an English architect, journalist, and financier), a friend of Owings and Skidmore from the Century of Progress, described Lever House for the Unilever Magazine *Progress*. "The innovations are not extravagant whimsies but are exactly suited to the most efficient development of the site." Lever House offered the virtues of light, air, and space. Even the exterior of the building, the tight skinned "blue glass and stainless steel," was a solution to cleanliness and saved money. As was the air conditioning: here was a building that was not an "open target for city soot . . . both for those who work in Lever House and for those who must keep it clean."[24]

What was more, the new building presented Lever as a good corporate citizen. The open courtyard ("an eye-stopper and a source of endless curiosity," Drew called it) demonstrated the public-spirited generosity of the corporation. Jervis J. Babb, who succeeded Luckman as Lever's president told the *New York World-Telegram and Sun*, using a folksy turn of phrase, hoped that New Yorkers would look on the building as theirs and that they would find "our front yard a friendly a pleasant place to pause now and then during the busy day."[25] Drew noted that "the straight clear lines of Lever House, with its shimmering glass tower, suggests cleanliness, and being a soap company, cleanliness is Lever's business. The daring design of the building itself implies that the company that built it is a progressive organization which has imagination, vision, and courage." Marketing the building to clients and to the public meant marketing Lever products. Or, as the developer Percy Uris noted somewhat grumpily in a letter to *Architectural Forum*, the cost per square foot of Lever House was immaterial. "Lever Brothers," he wrote, "are building a permanent advertisement for their merchandise."[26] It was an advertising coup worth between $7 and $25 million according to Drew.[27]

SOM also marketed Lever House to the Rockefellers. In June 1950 Louis Skidmore sent photographs of the model of Lever House to Nelson A. Rockefeller (not yet governor of New York) who responded: "thanks—design fascinating." And shortly thereafter plans were laid for an exhibition of the work of Skidmore, Owings & Merrill at the Museum of Modern Art, an exhibition (September 26 to November 5, 1950) in which the Lever House model

Fig. 6 "Skidmore, Owings & Merrill Architects, U.S.A.," Museum of Modern Art Bulletin. The cover has the qualities of a Miesian collage.

had pride of place. One might well imagine that Philip Johnson, as director of the Department of Architecture and Design, had something of a hand in selecting the illustrations for the *Museum of Modern Art Bulletin*: never again did SOM look more Miesian (fig. 6).[28] It was, as an anonymous writer in *Architectural Forum* noted, "the world of Mies can be said to have come into a second generation."[29] Yet from SOM (and Lever Brothers) there were no such claims: this was useful architecture, like the Museum of Modern Art's exhibition of useful objects.

Success was instantaneous: according to Drew, over 750 publications covered the inauguration by Major Vincent R. Impellitteri and publicity followed the pattern set by Terrace Plaza.[30] *Fortune, Time, Life, Newsweek, Business Week, Saturday Review,* and *The New Yorker* provided the national image reflected in the local New York press; professional magazines also covered a specialized variety of glamorized elements just as with Terrace Plaza, thus: *Chemical and Engineering News, Chemurgic Digest, Engineering News-Record, General*

Fig. 7 Lever House employed as an advertisement by Pittsburgh Glass (1952). The image shows the pre-existing buildings to the north of Lever House and conveniently obliterates those to the west. Lever House appears to be surprisingly monumental

Contractors Association Newsletter, General Electric Review, National Safety News, Plats Power, Refrigerating Engineering, Steel Construction Digest, as well as the major architectural periodicals.³¹ In *Techniques of Plant Maintenance and Engineering,* Lever House was described as "a sort of maintenance Utopia."³² As in the case of Terrace Plaza advertising was coordinated for maximum effect (fig. 7).³³ But so far, at least, the word "skyscraper" had yet to be invoked. And with good reason, for as everyone knows, in a city of tall buildings, Lever House is not that tall. In 1952 it was not even the tallest building on Park Avenue above 42nd Street.³⁴ In Nathaniel Owings's lecture on the ideal office building the word "skyscraper" was never used. Even in the Museum of Modern Art exhibition, the Lever model was not called a skyscraper.³⁵

The first connection of Lever House to the word "skyscraper," is an article in *Architectural Forum* in June 1950.³⁶ The cover photograph shows the model from an aerial perspective, looking down on the façade to the garden (fig. 8). Inside, the article was entitled "Miniature Skyscraper of Blue Glass and Metal Challenges Postwar Craze for Over-Building City Lots," and the magazine reproduced the cover, but this time in color, and began with the article with the noted lines from Genesis (11:4) about "a tower whose top may reach unto Heaven, and let us make us a name . . . ." And, lest the point be missed, the first words of the article sent readers back to their Old Testament. "Ever since the Tower of Babel . . . ." And the common description of Lever House thereafter is as a "skyscraper."³⁷ Even the children's book *Let's Take a Trip to a Skyscraper,* while noting that Lever House was small for a skyscraper, included it to demonstrate many of the qualities of the skyscraper.³⁸ Why should that have been?

It cannot possibly be the case that just because one magazine in the specialized architectural press called Lever House a skyscraper that everyone else fell in line. More likely, the intuition of the *Forum* editors corresponded to what emerged as a popular description. It is looking more closely, a somewhat surprising label for a building whose paneled glass curtain wall exerts no special vertical propulsion—rather the reverse. The curtain wall hides the vertical structural piers from the viewer and even at night the building seems more like a series of horizontal planes piled one above the other and linked by thin mullions rather than a series of thrusting verticals. Photographed *di sotto in su* (and vice versa) might persuade one to give emphasis to its height but these are unnatural views, either in reality or photographically. Characteristic views, from 53rd Street looking up towards Lever House, as in the advertisement and framed effectively to fill the page, do give the building a monumental presence but only when one is directly to the east of the tower (a highly unfavorable viewing point) does one get the giddy balance of a skyscraper. *Architectural Forum* published that view from the model; in reality it is much harder to capture (fig. 8).

In the end one may never be able to pin down an answer to why one label sticks and another falls off like leaves from a tree in autumn. What seems the most compelling condition for the acceptance of this label on this building is that as the most modern expression of corporate architecture it naturally linked itself to the pre-war office skyscraper, not because it looked like them but rather because it didn't. It was an anti-skyscraper: low not high, rural not urban, slab-like not needle-like. Its modernity offered an experimental alternative, an improvement in terms of space, light, and cleanliness over the traditional wedding cake or the total occupation of the zoning envelope. This was, in fact, the narrative advanced by *Architectural Forum* in 1950, the first article to link Lever to the tradition of the skyscraper. Rockefeller, Chrysler, and Woolworth had laid the foundations for the modern skyscraper and now New York would be "getting a fine office building that carries on from Rockefeller Center, a tower built on pride and the desire to build a name than the chance for a quick profit." Its importance rested not on its height but on it being "the only imaginative contribution of private enterprise to the architecture of a more livable metropolis."³⁹ Lever House, the German art historian Will Grohmann wrote in 1955, was "a turning point" for the history of the skyscraper, not because it was tall, but because it wasn't; not because its bulk occupied ground-level space, but because it didn't.⁴⁰ It was an opinion voiced by *Architectural Forum* in 1950 and echoed in the press elsewhere.⁴¹

Lever House opened the way for SOM to build more skyscrapers. When Inland Steel (1955–57) went in search of an architect to build the first new office building in

Fig. 8 This image, based on a photograph of the model of Lever House, appeared on the cover of Architectural Forum (in black and white) and on the interior in color.

Chicago within the Loop since the war, they went to Bunshaft in New York. In San Francisco, Owings took a hand in the erection of the Crown-Zellerbach Building (1957–59), the city's first curtain wall building.[42] In New York, David Rockefeller soon sought out Owings and Bunshaft to build One Chase Manhattan Plaza (1958–61), the tallest of SOM's buildings—sixty stories and 248 meters.[43] All had ambitions similar to Lever House: to bring light and air into the city—and these modest postwar modernist tall buildings were soon dwarfed by the buildings of the next generation of skyscrapers, buildings like that built for Pan Am (1963) with 3.1 million square feet.[44] Twenty years after Lever House opened, Owings the glamorizer was troubled by what his vision had produced. In 1973, when interviewed by Richard Threlkeld for CBS News, Owings stumbled when describing Lever House. It was a "skyscraper, so to speak," almost if he knew it wasn't or now regretted that everyone thought it was. What was truly significant about Lever House in his opinion was that at "twenty-two stories high, it occupied one third of the site on Park Avenue and it was a lovely bringing the country to the city" [sic]. Moreover, when completed it was "surrounded by beautiful buildings like the Marguery, the Racquet Club, and St. Bartholomew's church." Architecture didn't take the aesthetic lesson that Owings thought SOM was teaching when it built Lever House; it followed the path George Bailey had laid out when he had contested Owings's plan. "Suddenly," Owings continues, "that seemed to have opened a Pandora's Box and look at the place now. Park Avenue is a bunch of blockbusters! Well something happened. What was it? So as our firm has succeeded we have wondered and I particularly have been concerned with what that success means? It seems to mean perhaps worse than no success at all for it leads into things that are creating termite conditions . . . for people with hundred-story buildings."[45]

Glamorization succeeded in the short term. SOM built a building that real estate experts thought could never be built. It was an advertisement for the firms that built it—both Unilever and SOM. Understood as a skyscraper, though that was not its architects' intention, it became the model for (almost) every thin-skinned glass and steel box in America (and abroad), not least its cheesy northern neighbor, the General Reinsurance Building at 400 Park Avenue (Emery Roth, 1957): a tragic piece of mimicry.[46] Tom Wolfe called Lever House "the mother of all glass boxes. She was as fecund as a shad."[47] The market thus took the architectural path of the tall building in a direction neither Owings nor Bunshaft, foresaw. The narrative that seemed to end in romance with the hero's triumph over evil ends in satire, with the hero's vision undercut by a market system that had been all too briefly tamed. Faithful to the vision of Owings and Bunshaft, the restoration (2002) and the care of its new owners RFR Reality, is cause for celebration providing a moment in which economic and human interests coincide.[48]

Acknowledgement: I am grateful for research support from brilliant students, current and former: Nicola McElroy, Miranda Kimball, and Kristine Olson. I delivered a version of this paper at the Society of Architectural Historians Meeting, in Pittsburgh, PA, in 2009, and am grateful to David Smiley for the invitation to speak there.

1 Charles Jencks, *Modern Movements in Architecture* (Garden City, NY, 1973), p. 200; Jencks, *The Language of Post-Modern Architecture* (New York, 1977), pp. 19–20.
2 At the time of writing the tallest building in the world is Burj Khalifa, Dubai (completed 2010). In its time the Willis (Sears) Tower, Chicago (completed 1974) was the tallest building in the world.
3 The American Institute of Architects banned direct advertising by architectural firms (starting 1909); in its place firms relied on—and stimulated—advertising by suppliers that pictured their buildings. The advertising around Terrace Plaza and Lever House was so extensive that it is hard not to believe that these were not organized campaigns.
4 Judith Dupré, *Skyscrapers* (New York, 2001). "In terms of size, Lever House barely qualifies as a skyscraper," p. 43.
5 See Nathaniel A. Owings, *The Spaces in Between: An Architect's Journey* (Boston, 1973), chapter 4.
6 Talk of the Town, *The New Yorker* (August 17, 1940), p. 10.
7 "Everything's Up to Date in Cincinnati," *Harper's* (1948), p. 575.
8 A full account of the novelties in the hotel can be found in Voegele, "New Ideas in Hotel Design," *Hotel Management* 54, 3 (September 1948), pp. 46–64.
9 Henry-Russell Hitchcock compared the murals favorably with the work of Le Corbusier at the Pavilion Suisse and Ronchamp. (See Hitchcock, Introduction, *Architecture of Skidmore, Owings & Merrill, 1950-1962* (New York, 1963), p. 13. Miró, when he visited the city for the first time, successfully confounded local taste. As a *Cincinnati Times Star* headline reported (June 11, 1952): "What Does Hotel Mural Show: Nothing says Spanish Artist." Connections with Miró had probably been facilitated by the client, John J. Emery (1898–1976), who was also a trustee of the Cincinnati Art Museum. Although not an expert in art he took advice from the museum's director, Philip Adams.
10 "Penthouse Hotel for Cincinnati is Built on Two Big Stores," *Architectural Forum* 84 (February 1946), pp. 1–10; "Terrace Plaza Hotel, Cincinnati," *Architectural Forum* 85 (December 1946), pp. 101–08; "Barroom Art in the Modern Manner," *Architectural Forum* 88 (April 1948), pp. 148–150; "The Walls Have Laughs," *Architectural Forum* 89 (July 1948), pp. 114–17.
11 "Steel Erection for the Terrace Plaza Hotel," *Engineering News-Record*, September 4, 1947, pp. 104–07; "Penney's Most Modern Store," *Chain Store Age* 24 (May 1948), pp. 20–21; "When they built Cincinnati's New Terrace Plaza hotel . . . they dared to be different," *The Hotel Monthly* (August 1948), pp. 22–39; "Ten Story Terrace Plaza Hotel Set Atop Store Seven Stories High," *Engineering-News-Record*, August 7, 1948, pp. 84–87; Walter O. Voegele, "New Ideas in Hotel Design," *Hotel Management* 54, 3 (September 1948), pp. 46–64; "Cincinnati's New J. C. Penney Store in the Terrace Plaza Building," *The Magazine of Light* 17, no. 4 (1948), pp. 28–31;"Terrace Hotel in Cincinnati," Building (November 1950), pp. 430–32; "Cincinnati's Combination Building," *Official Bulletin of Heating, Piping, and Air* Conditioning Contractors (March 1953), pp. 27–28; "Miro's Mural," *Harper's Bazaar* (June 1948), pp. 92–3; "Everything's Up to Date in Cincinnati," *Harper's* 1177 (June 1948), pp. 574–76; "Storetop Hotel," *Life* (September 20, 1948), pp. 171–72; "Arrival in Cincinnati: Prototype of the Mid-Century Hotel is a Triumphant Marriage of Art and Economics," *Fortune* 38 (October 1948), pp. 113–17; 156–58, 160.
12 Nathaniel A. Owings, "The Office Building of Tomorrow," *Skyscraper Management* 32 (November 1947), pp. 10–11; 24–27; "A Radically New Conception of Tomorrow's Office Building," *National Real Estate and Building Journal* (January 1948), pp. 28–29; "The Ideal Office Building—A Dream Boat Speech by Architect Owings," *Architectural Forum,* August 1949, pp. 75, 164, 165. The first discussion of "Lever House," occurred June 1949 (see the report of George A. Fry, discussed below).
13 Owings, 1947 (see note 12),"The Office Building of Tomorrow," p. 11.

14 George R. Bailey, "I Am Going to Build This Building," *Skyscraper Management* 32 (December 1947), pp. 6–8; 30–32. Bailey is associated with the demolition of Adler & Sullivan's Garrick Theater and Burnham and Root's Women's Temple. As neither a preservationist or a trustworthy predictor of the future Bailey has, as yet, a rather clouded reputation.
15 "Pickaback Office Building," *Architectural Forum* (August 1949), pp. 70–75.
16 *Oral History of Ambrose M. Richardson*, interviewed by Betty J. Blum (Chicago, 1990), p. 201.
17 *Oral History of Ambrose M. Richardson*, p. 204. The possible location is noted in Abercrombie, "25-Year Award Goes to Lever House," *AIA Journal* (1980), p. 77, as well as in Owings's own account. According to Owings, the Chicago office made "a jewel-like Plexiglas model, beautifully set in a velvet lined box" to show Luckman. This account is in a typed draft of *The Spaces in Between* in the Library of Congress, Nathaniel A. Owings Papers, container 49. SOM later built the bus terminal incorporating some of characteristics of Owings's ideal office, see "Greyhound's New Chicago Terminal," *Architectural Record* 115, 4 (April 1957), pp. 167–73.
18 A copy is preserved at Skidmore, Owings & Merrill, New York, Marketing Division files.
19 Fry's report, written in the form of a letter to Owings, dated March 6, 1970 is found in the Library of Congress, Nathaniel A. Owings Papers, Container 49, Correspondence and Contracts.
20 See Charles Luckman, *Twice in a Lifetime: From Soap to Skyscrapers* (New York, 1988), pp. 233–44. Luckman later presented Samuel Bronfman with a proposal for the Seagram Building that looked like a whiskey bottle!
21 Fry, March 6, 1970, pp. 10–11. Library of Congress, Nathaniel A. Owings Papers.
22 Owings, "The Office Building of Tomorrow," p. 11.
23 "Lever House," *Architectural Forum* (1952), p. 106. Was the writer consciously echoing the famous lines written by Louis Sullivan about the Marshall Field Warehouse in Chicago?
24 John Duncan Miller, "Lever House, New York," *Progress: The Magazine of Unilever* 42, 235 (Summer 1952), pp. 21–29.
25 Lever Brothers was also careful to alert Park Avenue residents about construction progress. Neighbors received a letter concluding: "When Lever House is completed in the fall of next year, it will take its place as a good neighbor in the Park Avenue." This letter was published in chapter "Sales Letters that Sell," in James F. Bender, *Make Your Business Letters Make Friends* (New York, 1952), p. 228.
26 Percy Uris, Letter to the Editor," *Architectural Forum* 93 (September 1950), p. 34.
27 Drew noted that this had repercussions throughout Lever. The personnel department had 782 applicants for jobs on the first day after opening, meaning that Lever could be "highly selective in choosing its new employees . . . . Ask any personnel manager," wrote Drew, "if he doesn't consider this a kind of dream world." By 1960 Lever estimated that the advertising value had "shrunk" to $1 million a year and they noted the loss of $200,000 a year in rent. See "Today's Outstanding Contemporary Buildings Reflect the Corporate Image," New York *Times*, August 7, 1960, pp. 1, 6.
28 Thanks to Joseph Siry, Wesleyan University, for this point.
29 "Our New Crystal Towers," *Architectural Forum* 98 (February 1953), p. 153.
30 Vincent R. Impellitteri, the Mayor of New York City, inaugurated Lever House on April 29, 1952, echoing the optimistic vision of the New York World's Fair. Here was "the building of tomorrow which promises to set the pattern for the city of tomorrow. " See, "New Lever Glass House Dazzles New Yorkers," *New York World-Telegram and Sun*, April 29, 1952; "New Silhouette on City's Skyline," *New York Times Magazine* (April 27, 1952), pp. 20–21. Lever House continued to draw visitors through the year as reported in *American Business* 23 (1953), p. 23: "New Building Draws 50,000 Visitors."

31 See "On the Frontier," *Fortune* 45 (January–March 1952), p. 78; "Art: Ready to Soar," *Time* 59 (April 28, 1952); "Shiny new Light: Soapmaker's Washable Building is World's Glassiest," *Life* 32 (June 2, 1952); "Glass House . . . On Park Avenue," *Newsweek* 39 (May 5, 1952), pp. 82–83; "Lever House: Spacious, Efficient, and Washable," *Business Week* (May 3, 1952), pp. 76–77; Bennett Cerf, "Trade Winds: Lever House, New York," *Saturday Review* 35 (May 31, 1952), p. 6; *The New Yorker* had a review by Lewis Mumford in his Skyline column (August 9, 1952), as well as in The Talk of the Town section, 27 (April 26, 1952), pp. 27–28; (May 26, 1952), pp. 20–22. See *New York World-Telegram,* April 25, 1952; *New York Herald Tribune,* April 30, 1952. Among the technical magazines to cover Lever House, see *Chemical and Engineering News* 28 (1950); *Chemurgic Digest* 10-11 (1951); *Engineering News-Record* 150 (1953); *General Contractors Association Newsletter* 423 (1952); *General Electric Review,* 56 (1953); "Largest Noise Reduction Unity at Lever House," *National Safety News* 69 (1954), p. 84; *Plats Power* 96 (1952), p. 145; *Refrigerating Engineering* 62 (1954), p. 64; *Steel Construction Digest* 6–13 (1949), pp. 20, 35. In addition to articles in *Architectural Record, Architectural Forum, Interiors, Progressive Architecture,* and *the Magazine of Building* there were articles in *Werk* 41 (February 1954), pp. 49–54; *Architecture aujourd'hui* 24 (December 1953), pp. 34–38; *Der Monat* 73–76 (1954), p. 76; *Nuestro Tiempo* 1–6 (1954), p. 8.
32 *Techniques of Plant Maintenance and Engineering* 11 (1960), p. 60.
33 For example, *Architectural Record* ran twenty-one advertisements between May 1952 and November 1953 that featured Lever House. *Architectural Forum* ran a similar number in the same period. Advertising also appeared in suppliers' magazines such as *Glass Digest* (between September and December 1952) culminating in an article on Lever House ("An All-Glass Office Home," *Glass Digest* 31, 12 (December 1952), pp. 14–16.
34 Warren & Wetmore's New York General Building (1928–1929) is thirty-five stories and even Schultze & Weaver's Waldorf Astoria (1931) is forty-seven stories.
35 Skidmore, Owings & Merrill, *Bulletin of the Museum of Modern Art,* 18, 1 (Autumn 1950).
36 "Miniature Skyscraper of blue glass and metal challenges postwar craze for over-building city lots," *Architectural Forum* 94 (June 1950), pp. 84–89.
37 See also *Harpers* vol. 207:1241 (October 1953), p. 92; *Newsweek* (May 5, 1952); *Billboard,*November 14, 1953, p. 6; *American Heritage* 14 (1953), p. 45; *Buildings* 53 (1953), p. 29. Albert Christ-Janer, *Modern Church Architecture: A Guide to the Form and Spirit of 20th-Century Religious Buildings* (New York, 1952), p. 154.
38 Sarah R. Riedman, *Let's Take a Trip to a Skyscraper* (New York, 1955).
39 "Miniature Skyscraper," *Architectural Forum,* p. 86.
40 Will Grohmann and Matilda V. Pfeiffer, "The Great Architects," *College Art Journal* 15, 1 (Autumn 1955), p. 49. pp. 46–50. See also the article of Eugene Raskin, "A Square Foot of Sky . . ." *The Nation,* September 6, 1958, pp. 112–13. Raskin makes a similar point at a later moment by which time new buildings had begun to look at "undistinguishable and replaceable as the stacks of cereal boxes in the supermarket." Lever and Seagram he argues, were in the tradition of Rockefeller Center.
41 For example, *American Heritage* 14 (1953), p, 45. This was also the opinion of Robert Jungk, see "The Church and the Skyscraper," in *Tomorrow is Already Here* (New York, 1954), pp. 155–70.
42 See the commentary of Allan Temko, "San Francisco Buildings Again," *Harper's Magazine* 220: 1319 (April 1960), pp. 51–59. Temko describes the state of inertia in architecture prior to the arrival of SOM. "At this point Nathaniel A. Owings . . . exuberantly entered the local scene. He is probably the most successful salesman of serious design in the history of modern architecture. Corporation after corporation has yielded to his argument that maximum expenditure for aesthetic and human purposes—which of course means the renunciation of giant size and the sacrifice of quick investment returns, as at Lever House—is the wisest way of achieving prestige," p. 56.
43 One could also add Ford Motor Company Headquarters, Dearborn, Michigan (1953–56) to the list of buildings influenced by Lever House.
44 Meredith Clausen, *The Pan Am Building and the Shattering of the Modernist Dream* (Cambridge, 1974).
45 Vital History Cassettes, Encyclopedia Americana CBS News Audio Resource Library, Grolier Educational Corporation (August 1973), the interview was broadcast July 25, 1973.
46 See, for example, "The Disciplines of Fenestration," *Architectural Record* 117 (April 1955), pp, 198–216.
47 Tom Wolfe, *From Bauhaus to Our House* (New York, 1981), p. 68. For a more closely situated discussion of Park Avenue, see Vincent Scully "The Death of the Street," in *Modern Architecture and Other Essays* (Princeton, 2003), pp. 120–27.
48 The terms "satire" and "romance," are drawn from Hayden White, *The Historical Imagination in Nineteenth-Century Europe* (Baltimore, 1973).

Gottscho-Schleisner, Park Avenue and 54th Street with Seagram Building under construction, January 23, 1957 (Gottscho-Schleisner Collection, Library of Congress Prints and Photographs Division Washington, DC)

The Seagram Building: Thoughts on Context
Nicholas Adams

On March 22, 1811 the Commissioners of Street and Roads in the City of New York presented their survey of the island of Manhattan creating the great grid plan with which we still live. In a memorandum sent to the State Legislature in Albany in 1807, the City Council set forth its goal to lay out the streets "in such a manner as to unite regularity and order with the public convenience and benefit and in particular to promote the health of the City . . . ." One further reason why the Commissioners selected the grid plan is revealed in their report: "In considering that subject they could not but bear in mind that a city is to be composed principally of the habitations of men, and that straight-sided and right-angled houses are the most cheap to build and the most convenient to live in." Manhattan received its grid plan. On the occasion of the bicentennial of the Commissioners' Plan it seems fitting to think about Mies van der Rohe's Seagram Building (1954–57) and its site in the context of the city's grid plan. Although one of New York City's most expensive office towers, it is also one of the buildings that sits most comfortably within the grid.

Seagram is a marvel of simplicity: just a raised plaza and a rectangular tower. Abstraction is its interpretative identity. It is frequently described as an abstract grid, a work of high architectural idealism, cut off from the world, and immune from conventional sources. Mies agreed. To a question posed by Katherine Kuh about the effect of the Chicago School on his work he answered in the negative: "As to your question, no: living in Chicago has had no effect on me." William Jordy was doubtful that Mies could have held himself so thoroughly aloof from his surroundings, offering the absurd picture of the architect driving through Chicago in a taxi cab with the blinds drawn. But if Mies eschewed modern schools and building trends in the abstract, he was not aloof to place. The great skyscraper designs for Friedrichstrasse are rich with contextual consciousness (1921–22), as are the designs for the Brick Country House (1923) and his designs for the bank and department store on Hindenburgplatz, Stuttgart (1928). Phyllis Lambert, who served as director of planning for Joseph E. Seagram, described the effect that the Seagram Building was intended to have in a letter to a friend written in 1954. "This solution for the building has promise for terrific things—set back you hardly see it from the street coming up or down the Avenue but now what an impression—when you arrive there—almost Baroque, you don't know what is there then you come upon IT . . . ." That effect was quickly lost when the apartment building to the north across 53rd Street was demolished as Seagram reached completion. Already in 1958 Paul Rudolph anticipated the results. "Its [Seagram's] relationship to Park Avenue will be largely ruined by its forthcoming northern neighbor, which will also be set back, thus producing not a break in the wall lining Park Avenue, but merely a widening of the road." Shortly thereafter, Vincent Scully commented on the results. "Seagram's," he wrote, "has perhaps not lost in intrinsic quality, but it has disastrously lost its urban point and its setting." If site was truly unimportant to Mies we could ignore the changes that have taken place. It could be, however, that reconsidering the setting actually helps us recapture something about the building that we may sometimes overlook.

No views of the Seagram Building are more telling than those across Park Avenue between it and McKim, Mead & White's Racquet and Tennis Club (design partner, William Symmes Richardson, 1916–18) or the view from the tower out to the grid of Manhattan. Mies's study model of Park Avenue included all of the buildings between 46th Street and 57th Street, and Phyllis Lambert reports that using the model Mies would peer for hours down his Park Avenue and that when he was on site he would walk along Park Avenue noting how "the buildings relentlessly lined the sidewalk." Since Mies could not be certain of the form of the buildings that would replace those slated for destruction north and later to the south, he used simple ten-story volumes running to the property line to suggest their lines. The Racquet and Tennis Club was the most proximate anchor for the design. It is "dignified and urbane," as Joan Ockman noted of the Racquet Club's Tuscan order façade, and it was an appropriate façade to face Seagram: the rugged Tuscan order the classical equivalent of the bronze anodized frame and wide-flange H-beams used by Mies. The blind arcade on the third level of the Racquet Club—typically left open on the Renaissance façade, reflects the interior placement of the tennis courts; a common Renaissance practice adjusted for modern functionalist reasons. As more than one commentator has noted, the center of the façade of the Racquet Club aligns perfectly with the center of the Seagram Building. "Curiously enough," wrote Peter Blake, "it was only the . . . Racquet Club . . . that could look the new bronze tower straight in the eye without flinching." They share an axis on the same datum line as well as the same rhythmic proportion.

The force fields of Seagram and the Racquet Club their plastic character and intuitive order, create a cross-axial bond across Park Avenue. In early studies for the Seagram plaza, Mies proposed to use sculpture as a point of reference on the empty plaza, and only after the impossibility of finding a satisfactory work for the site did he proceed to build the reflecting pools. Any specific focus or permanent installation on the plaza, destroys the natural linkage between city and building. As William Whyte, observed: "You can't tell where the social life of the street and the plaza leaves off. They are inextricable." In a letter to a friend, April 20, 1969, Lambert wrote: "The wonderful living quality about the Seagram plaza is that is changes all the time, the people are the sculpture. It looks wonderful when it is empty, then it changes as people go in and out of the building or just wander on the plaza. When people sit on the benches and the walls, it again has another character." The space, as has often been noted, combines the casual and the formal: hard (the stone), soft (the ivy), and liquid (the water).

The plaza also opened new views to Skidmore, Owings & Merrill's Lever House (1950–52), and standing on its atrium or looking out from the tenth floor provides ideal locations from which to see Seagram. Mies's design was mindful of this neighbor, too. The swirling patterns on the green Tinian marble benches, the green ivy, and the reflective sparkle of the pools recall the colors and textures

View east along 52nd Street showing the south side of the Racquet and Tennis Club with the Seagram Building across Park Avenue to the east

of Lever House. Even the dull green finish of Seagram as the afternoon sun strikes it surface recalls Lever. Mies and Gordon Bunshaft maintained a cordial friendship. On release from hospital, Mies wrote to Bunshaft on August 12, 1958, thanking him for his letter and the "two bottles of 'cheer' water." Unfortunately, Mies was "on a diet which bans cheer water of all kinds." But, he continued playfully, "every once and a while I make an exception and always think of you."

Postmodernism trivialized the precious concept of context by suggesting that buildings need do no more than repeat the formal character of their neighbors to be considered contextual. The Seagram Building transformed the grammar of the Racquet Club for the new epoch and it echoed the color and surface of Lever House. The plaza fully remediates the weakness of the grid plan allowing us the chance to look at Seagram, it also offers the best views of Lever House and the Racquet Club. As

McKim, Mead & White's Racquet and Tennis Club (design partner, William Symmes Richardson), 1916–18

Vincent Scully commented " . . . if visual chaos rather than the arches of the Racquet Club had been mirrored in [Seagram's] entrance doors, it would have been a much less successful building." No tall building in New York City has better sight lines and few interact with comparable sympathy for their neighbors. It was an issue about which Mies felt strongly. Listening to Mies, Myron Goldsmith took notes on just this point:

> Question of putting a modern building in center of old group—can it be done?
> Mies: Yes but it should be done with tact. Question always came up in Europe when something was to be built in surroundings of really fine buildings.

And in isolated note on this topic Goldsmith added:

> . . . unity from same principles rather than same forms.

By way of contrast, Lever House is unrelated to the Racquet Club; the lines of the atrium do not meet McKim Mead & White's entablatures; the shiny surfaces are flat and reflective compared to the matte surfaces of its neighbor.

So is the grid of the plaza solely the place of the present or a means of "crowding out the dimensions of the real and replacing them with . . . aesthetic decree," to quote Rosalind Krauss? Or a "diagram of capitalist rationality" and the aesthetic and technological extension of the post-World War II military-industrial complex, to quote Reinhold Martin? These descriptions may also be true, but Seagram's grids inhibit no one's movement and the summer crowd lounging on the marble benches, amply studied by Whyte, suggest that in the city of the grid, facing a neo-Renaissance building, nothing could be more contextual than a grid. The grid at Seagram does not overcome history and change the rational organization of reality, it incorporate it. In 1959 Alan Temko thought Seagram a work of "ruthless predictability," but so too is the street pattern of the city where it is located.

A Gottscho-Schleisner photograph in the Library of Congress dated January 23, 1957, gives a sense of the surprise that Lambert thought Mies might have produced for the site. The intensification of the grid at the cross axis would have been as much of a surprise as the building itself. Could Mies have likened in his mind to the discovery of a Neoclassical square that one enters on the side, like arriving at the Altes Museum along Unter den Linden. Ironically, with the setbacks to north and south, it is the Seagram Building rather than the cross-axis that has become prominent. Ezra Stoller's iconic black and white images of the tower depend on the absence of the neighboring building to the north: the empty building site made it possible for the photographer to gain an angle. It is no wonder that later on, hemmed in to the north and south by deeply mediocre gridded buildings, Seagram appeared to be the unwilling progenitor of their flaws. Photography made Seagram's reputation; photography sets the issues around the building.

In a city of right angles, the Seagram Building isn't alone in responding to the grid: that was the whole idea behind selecting the grid two-hundred years ago. But the conversation between the Seagram Building and its neighbors expresses possibilities implicit in the Commissioners' plan. Subsequent changes along Park Avenue have distracted us from Seagram's contextual intentions, overemphasizing the building's abstraction and isolation at the expense of its place within the Neoclassical tradition represented by the grid of New York City.

Bibliographic note

Stanford Anderson, "The Legacy of German Neoclassicism and Biedermeier: Behrens, Tessenow, Loos, and Mies," *Assemblage* 15 (August 1991), pp. 62–87.

Peter Blake, *The Master Builders: Le Corbusier, Mies van der Rohe, Frank Lloyd Wright* (New York, 1996).

Kenneth Frampton, *Studies in Tectonic Culture: The Poetics of Construction in Nineteenth and Twentieth Century Architecture* (Cambridge, 1995).

K. Michael Hays, "Critical Architecture: Between Culture and Form," *Perspecta* 21 (1984), pp. 14–29.

Phyllis Lambert, "How a Building Gets Built," *Vassar Alumnae Magazine* 44, 3 (February 1959), pp. 13–19.

Phyllis Lambert, ed., *Mies in America* (New York, 2001).

Reinhold Martin, *Utopia's Ghost: Architecture and Postmodernism, Again* (Minneapolis, 2010)

Detlef Mertins, ed. *The Presence of Mies* (New York, 1994).

Paul Rudolph, "To Enrich Our Architecture," *Journal of Architectural Education* 13, 1 (Spring, 1958), pp. 9–12.

Franz Schulze, *Mies van der Rohe: A Critical Biography* (Chicago, 1985).

Vincent Scully, "The Death of the Street," *Perspecta* 16 (1980), pp. 91–96.

Mark Taylor, *The Moment of Complexity: Emerging Network Culture* (Chicago, 2001).

Allan Temko, "The Dawn of the "High Modern" *Horizon* 2, 1 (September, 1959), pp. 4–9, 18–20.

Documentary sources:

Canadian Centre for Architecture, Montréal, Papers of Myron Goldsmith, 32-003T-044

Washington, DC, Library of Congress, Papers of Mies van der Rohe, container 21

Essayist Biographies

Mark P. Sarkisian

Mark P. Sarkisian, PE, SE, LEED® AP is the Director of Seismic and Structural Engineering in the San Francisco office of SOM. He received his BS Degree in Civil Engineering from University of Connecticut (1983), where he is a member of the Academy of Distinguished Engineers, and his MS in Structural Engineering from Lehigh University (1985). His career has focused on developing innovative structural engineering solutions for building projects. He has designed over seventy-five major building projects around the world including, the United States Embassy in Beijing; the NBC Tower in Chicago; The Cathedral of Christ the Light in Oakland, CA; Jin Mao Tower in Shanghai, which is currently the seventh tallest building in the world; and the 415-meter-tall Al-Hamra Tower in Kuwait. Mark holds four US Patents for high-performance seismic structural mechanisms designed to protect buildings in areas of high seismic activity and has additional patents pending for seismic and environmentally responsible structural systems. He is licensed to practice civil/structural engineering in sixteen states and has recently written a book entitled *Considering the Tower – Structure as Architecture*.

Nicholas Adams

Nicholas Adams is the Mary Conover Mellon professor in the history of architecture at Vassar College in Poughkeepsie, New York, where he has taught since 1989. He is a member of the editorial board of the Italian architectural magazine *Casabella* and author of *Skidmore, Owings & Merrill: SOM Since 1936* (2007). He has served as editor of the *Journal of the Society of Architectural Historians* and his essays and reviews have appeared in *Architectural Record, Harvard Design Magazine,* and *Arkitektur,* the Swedish review of architecture. He is currently writing a history of Gunnar Asplund's Law Court Extension in Göteborg. He has been a fellow of the American Academy in Rome and the Institute for Advanced Study, Princeton, and has also taught in the architecture schools at Harvard University, Columbia University, and UCLA.

Thomas A. P. van Leeuwen

Thomas A. P. van Leeuwen is a teacher and researcher and was a professor of architectural history, cultural history, and art criticism at Leyden University for many years. He is currently taking part in the Platitudes and Plans research projects at the Berlage Institute. His books include *The Skyward Trend of Thought: Metaphysics of the American Skyscraper* (1988) and *The Springboard in the Pond: An Intimate History of the Swimming Pool* (2000). These studies are part of a tetralogy with each volume centered on the relationship between architecture and one of the classical elements. In preparation are *Columns of Fire: The Un-doing of Architecture* and *The Thinking Foot: A Pedestrian View of Architecture*.

William F. Baker

William F. Baker is the Structural Engineering Partner for SOM. Throughout his distinguished career, Bill has dedicated himself to structural innovation. His best known contribution has been to develop the "buttressed core" structural system for the Burj Khalifa, the world's tallest manmade structure. While widely regarded for his work on super-tall buildings, his expertise also extends to a wide variety of structures like the GM Entry Pavilion (Detroit) and Millennium Park's Jay Pritzker Pavilion and BP Pedestrian Bridge (Chicago). Bill is also known for his work on long-span roof structures, such as the Korean Air Lines Operations Hangar (Seoul) and the Virginia Beach Convention Center, as well as for his collaboration with artists like Jamie Carpenter (Raspberry Island-Schubert Club Band Shell, in St. Paul, MN), Iñigo Manglano-Ovalle *(Gravity is a Force to be Reckoned With,* various locations), and James Turrell (Roden Crater, in Flagstaff, AZ).

In addition to working at SOM, Bill is actively involved with numerous institutions of higher learning, as well as various professional organizations. He is the recipient of a 2011 ASCE Outstanding Projects and Leaders (OPAL) Lifetime Award for Design. Bill is the 2010 recipient of the Gold Medal from the Institution of Structural Engineers (IStructE) and the 2009 recipient and first American to receive the Fritz Leonhardt Preis (Germany). In 2008, the CTBUH awarded him the Fazlur Rahman Khan medal. Bill is a Fellow of both the American Society of Civil Engineers (ASCE) and the IStructE, and frequently lectures on a variety of structural engineering topics within the US and abroad.

Editorial Board Biographies

Kenneth Frampton

Kenneth Frampton was born in the United Kingdom, in 1930, and trained as an architect at the Architectural Association School of Architecture, London. He has worked as an architect and an architectural historian and critic, and is currently the Ware Professor of Architecture at the Graduate School of Architecture, Preservation and Planning, Columbia University, New York.

He has taught at a number of leading institutions in the field including the Royal College of Art, the ETH in Zurich, the EPFL in Lausanne, the Accademia di Architettura in Mendrisio, and the Berlage Institute in The Netherlands. He is the author of numerous essays on modern and contemporary architecture, and has served on many international juries for architectural awards and building commissions. His more recent writings include *Modern Architecture: A Critical History* (2007), *Studies in Tectonic Culture* (1995), *Le Corbusier* (2001), and a collection of essays entitled *Labour, Work & Architecture* (2005).

Juhani Pallasmaa

Juhani Pallasmaa established his Helsinki office, Juhani Pallasmaa Architects, in 1983, after twenty years of collaboration with a number of architects. In addition to architectural design, he has been active in urban, product, and graphic design.

He has taught and lectured widely in Europe, North and South America, Africa, and Asia, and has held positions as Professor and Dean at the Helsinki University of Technology, State Artist Professor, Director of the Museum of Finnish Architecture, and Rector of the Institute of Industrial Arts, Helsinki. He has held visiting professorships at Washington University in St. Louis, the University of Virginia, and Yale University.

Pallasmaa has published books and numerous essays on the philosophy and criticism of architecture and the arts in thirty languages. His books include *Encounters: Architectural Essays 1976–2000* (2004), *Sensuous Minimalism* (2002), *The Architecture of Image: Existential Space in Cinema* (2001), *Alvar Aalto: Villa Mairea* (1998), and *The Eyes of the Skin* (1996 and 2005).

Juror Biographies

Erik L. Olsen, PE

Erik Olsen is a mechanical engineer and an expert in the integration of architectural and low-energy indoor comfort solutions. He leads Transsolar Climate Engineering's New York practice with a rigorous technical approach and focus on high-comfort, low-impact environments. His collaboration with clients, architects, urban planners, and other engineers worldwide focuses on development and validation of low-energy, architecturally integrated indoor and outdoor climate and energy concepts. The scope of these concepts ranges from from the completely passive Raising Malawi Academy for Girls to the groundbreaking Angelos Law Center at the University of Baltimore. Erik has served on the US Green Building Council's Greening the Codes Committee, the US Green Building Council Chicago Chapter board of directors, and as a consulting mechanical engineer and director of the City of Chicago's Green Permit Program. Erik has lectured at numerous conferences and universities including MIT, University of Pennsylvania, and University of California, Berkeley. He is a graduate of MIT and Purdue University, and a licensed professional engineer in Illinois.

Luis Fernández-Galiano

Luis Fernández-Galiano is an architect, a professor at the School of Architecture of Madrid's Universidad Politécnica, and editor of AV/Arquitectura Viva. Between 1993 and 2006 he was in charge of the weekly architecture page of the newspaper El País, where he now writes for the opinion section. A member of the Royal Academy of Doctors, he has been Cullinan Professor at Rice University, Franke Fellow at Yale University, a visiting scholar at the Getty Center of Los Angeles, and a visiting critic at Princeton, Harvard, and the Berlage Institute. President of the jury in the 9th Venice Architecture Biennial and juror for the Mies van der Rohe European Award, he has curated the exhibitions El espacio privado, Extreme Eurasia (in Tokyo and in Madrid) and Bucky Fuller & Spaceship Earth. Among his books are La Quimera Moderna, Fire and Memory, Spain Builds, and Atlas, Global Architecture Circa 2000, a series of five volumes.

Peter MacKeith

Peter MacKeith is Associate Dean and Associate Professor of Architecture at the Sam Fox School of Design and Visual Arts, Washington University in St. Louis. He received his MArch from Yale University and his BA in Literature and International Relations from the University of Virginia. MacKeith directed the international masters program in architecture at the Helsinki University of Technology from 1994 to 1999, and previously taught design and architectural theory at Yale University and the University of Virginia. MacKeith has worked in practices in both the United States and Finland, and has written and lectured extensively in the United States, Finland, and across the Nordic countries. A past editor of Perspecta: The Yale Architectural Journal, he is also the author and/or editor of Encounters: A Selection of Essays by Juhani Pallasmaa, The Dissolving Corporation: Contemporary Architecture and Corporate Identity in Finland, and Archipelago, Essays of Architecture. MacKeith is the recipient of a Fulbright Fellowship, research grants from The Graham Foundation for Advanced Studies in the Visual Arts, and is active in both the ACSA and the EAAE. In 2008, he received a Creative Achievement in Design Education Award from the Association of Collegiate Schools of Architecture (ACSA).

Rita McBride

Rita McBride is an artist living in Italy and Germany, where she is a professor at the Kunstakademie Duesseldorf. In the last decade her work has been the subject of solo exhibitions in Austria, France, Germany, The Netherlands, Lichtenstein, Switzerland, and the US. Recent solo exhibitions include Previously (Kunstmuseum Winterthur), Public Works (Musuem Abteiberg, Moechen Gladbach), Exhibition (The Sculpture Center, Long Island City, NY); Naked Came the Stranger (Kunstmuseum Liechtenstein, Vaduz), Secession Tower (Wiener Secession, Vienna). Group exhibitions include The World as a Stage (Tate Modern, London), Farsites/Sitios Distantes (San Diego Museum of Art and Centro Cultural Tijuana), Living Inside the Grid (New Museum of Contemporary Art, New York). She is an editor of the Ways series published by Arsenal Pulp Press, Printed Matter, and the Whitney Museum of American Art. She has recently completed an innovative carbon public sculpture commissioned by the city of Munich entitled Mae West.

Joan Ockman

Joan Ockman served as Director of the Temple Hoyne Buell Center for the Study of American Architecture at Columbia University from 1994 to 2008, and was a member of the faculty of Columbia's Graduate School of Architecture, Planning and Preservation for more than two decades. She is currently teaching at the University of Pennsylvania and has also taught at Yale, Cornell, the Graduate Center of City University of New York, and the Berlage Institute in Rotterdam. Educated at Harvard and Cooper Union School of Architecture, she began her career at the Institute for Architecture and Urban Studies in New York, where she was an editor of Oppositions journal and was responsible for the Oppositions Books series. Among her numerous publications, her award-winning anthology Architecture Culture 1943–1968 is now in its fifth printing. In 2000 she conceived and curated a major project on Pragmatist philosophy and architecture, which resulted in a conference at the Museum of Modern Art and a book entitled The Pragmatist Imagination: Thinking about Things in the Making. The American Institute of Architects honored her in 2003 with an award for collaborative achievement. She is currently editing a book on the history of architecture education in North America and completing a history of architecture and the Cold War.

Project Credits

Chongqing River Tower
Chongqing, China
Design, 2010

Client
Sunshine 100
Design Partner
Michael Duncan
Managing Partner
Gene Schnair
Senior Designer
Sean Ragasa
Project Manager
Larry Chien
Team Members
Kye Archuleta, Jungmoo Lee, Sheng-Wei Lo, Ben Mickus, Woranol Sattayavinij, Constanza Valenzuela
Structural Consultant
SOM|SF (Mark Sarkisian, Geoffrey Brunn, John Gordon, Zhao-fan Li, Eric Long)
Technical Coordinator
Michael Oerth
Environmental Consultant
SOM|SF (Ruth Kurz, Krista Raines)

John Jay College of Criminal Justice
New York, New York
Design, 2006

Client
City University of New York

Design Partner
Mustafa Abadan
Managing Partner
TJ Gottesdiener
Senior Designer
Chris Cooper
Project Managers
Jeff Young and John Ostlund
Team Members
Mustafa Abadan, TJ Gottesdeiner, Lisa Gould, Lana Touma, Jeff Young, John Ostland, Guy Punzi, Scott Melencon, David Maestres, Sal Raffone, Basil Lee, Lai Mei Chau, Jim Hickerson, Kelly Wallace, Michiko Ashida, Adriana Portela, Suzzanne Schreider, Frank Ruggiero, Julia Murphy, Rui Borges
Structural Consultant
Leslie E. Robertson Associates
Mechanical Consultant
Jaros, Baum & Bolles
Technical Coordinator
Serge Demerjian
Lighting Consultant
Susan Brady Lighting Design
Landscape Architect
Quennel Rothchild
Programming/Planning
Scott Page Architect
Education Planning
Cannon Design
Lab Planning
GPR
AV/IT
Shen Milsom & Wilke

Lotte World 2
Seoul, Korea
Design, 2007

Client
Lotte Moolsan
Design Partner
Mustafa Abadan
Managing Partner
TJ Gottesdiener
Senior Designer
Chris Cooper
Project Manager
Brant Coletta
Team Members
Alan Stevenson, Anthony Sullivan, Basil Lee, Chris Zoog, David Maestres, Eugene Templeton, Donald Marmen, June Hyun, Kat Park, Phillip Luse, Sal Raffone, Jongmin Kim, Sebastian Guerrico, Matt Lewis, Katarzyna Zwierko-Hausbrandt, Lauren Bass, Richard Lam, Rowan Georges, Hyungsup Sim, Lucy Wong, Hsin-Kan Lee, Alexandra Pollock
Structural Consultant
Chuck Besjak, Skidmore, Owings & Merrill LLP
Mechanical Consultant
Flak + Kurtz
Technical Coordinator
Nicholas Holt
Vertical Transportation
Van Deusen Associates
Lighting Consultant
Susan Brady Lighting Design

Project Floyd
Geneva, Switzerland
Design, 2010

Client
JT International SA
Design Director
Kent Jackson
Managing Partner
Jeffrey McCarthy
Senior Designer
Yasemin Kologlu
Project Manager
Julia Skeete
Team Members
Anne Seol, Daniel Silva, Hessam Kazemzadeh, Hyun Jun Kim, Katherine Pink, Korey Kromm, Kris Mainstone, Linnea Isen, Maciej Olczyk, Mark Hogan, Matteo Noto, Nicholas Muir, Paolo Rossi, Pedja Pantovic, Roza Mavromati, Shumin Zheng, Steve John, Ta-Kang Hsu, Yoon Mi Lee
Technical Coordinator
Martin Grinnell, Ania Lill
Structural Consultant
William Baker – SOM
Senior Structural Engineer
Stuart Marsh – SOM
Local Architect
Group 8
Mechanical Consultants
Weinmann-Energies SA and MAB Ingénierie SA
Cost Estimating Consultant
Davis Langdon

PSAC II
The Bronx, New York
Design, 2008–11

Client
NYC Department of Design and Construction (DDC)
Design Partner
Gary Haney AIA
Managing Partner
Peter Magill
Senior Designer
Rob Rothblatt, AIA
Project Manager
Joseph Sacco, AIA
Team Members
Judy Betts, Todd Cossman, Paul Edsall, Joel Hagerty, Justin Huang, Wendy Lam, David Light, John Midgette
Structural Consultant
Weidlinger Associates
Mechanical Consultant
JB&B (Jaros Baum & Bolles)
Technical Coordinator
Jennifer Curtin
Cost Estimating Consultant
Ellana
Environmental Consultant
SOM Sustainable Group

Hundred-Year Vision for the Great Lakes and St. Lawrence River Region
Design, 2009–11

Client
Skidmore, Owings and Merrill LLP
Design Partner
Philip Enquist
Managing Partner
Richard Tomlinson
Senior Designer
Clint Bautz
Team Members
SOM City Design Practice, Jeannine Colaco
Environmental Consultant
David Ullrich, Great Lakes and St Lawrence Cities Initiative; Lynn McClure, National Parks Conservation Association; Rick Findlay, International Joint Commission

High Performance Building Enclosures
Poly Beijing
Design, 2002

Client
China Poly Group Corporation
Design Partner
Brian Lee, FAIA
Managing Partner
Gene Schnair, FAIA
Structural Director
Mark Sarkisian, PE, SE, LEED® AP
Senior Design Architect
Leo Chow, AIA
Project Manager
Larry Chien, AIA
Team Members
Tamara Dinsmore, Angela Wu, Mark Schwettman, Carsten Voecker; Cheng-Yu Ho; Philip Kaefer

Design Architects

Hendra Bong, Stephan Ciulla, Justin Ho, Assoc AIA, Philip Kaefer, AIA, LEED® AP, Mark Schwettmann, AIA, Patricia Tjandrawinata, AIA, Carsten Max Voecker, RIBA, Diplom-Ingenieur Sandra Ventura, AIA, Angela Wu, AIA

Technical Director

C. Keith Boswell, AIA

Senior Technical Coordinator

Maurice Hamilton, AIA

Technical Coordinator

Mathew Staublin, AIA, LEED® AP

Associate Director, Interior Design

Tamara Dinsmore, AIA, IIDA, LEED® AP

Interior Designers

David Loo, AIA, LEED® AP, Virgil Skipton, AIA, IIDA

SOM Structural Engineers

Neville Mathias, PE, SE, LEED® AP, Aaron Mazieka, AIA, LEED® AP, John Gordon, PE, CEng, MIStructE, Cathy Ge

MEP Consultant

WSP Flack + Kurtz

Associate Architect/Engineer

Beijing Special Engineering Design Institute

China World Trade Center

Design, 2001

Client

China World Trade Center Co. Ltd.

Design Partner

Brian Lee, FAIA

Managing Partner

Gene Schnair, FAIA

Senior Designer

Patrick Daly, AIA

Project Manager

Steve Sobel, AIA, Larry Chien, AIA

Technical Director

C. Keith Boswell

Senior Technical Coordinator

Raymond Kuca

Team Members

Mark Borkowski, Stephan Ciulla, Christiana Kyrillou, Hana Maulana Murdan, Anne Poone, Ayumi Sugiyama, Surjanto Surjadji, Carsten Max Voecker, RIBA, Diplom-Ingenieur, Eric R. Keune, AIA, LEED® AP

Structural Consultant

Ove Arup & Partners Ltd.

Mechanical/Electrical/Security/IT Consultant

Parsons Brinkerhoff (Asia) Ltd.

Quantity Surveyor

WT Partnership Ltd.

Hotel Interior Design

Hirsh Bedner Associates

Cost Estimating Consultant

W T Partnership

Environmental Consultant

EMSL

UNC Chapel Hill

Design, 2004

Client

University of North Carolina at Chapel Hill

Design Partner

Peter Ruggiero, AIA

Managing Partner

Richard Tomlinson, FAIA

Senior Designers

Peter Van Vechten, AIA, James Michaels, AIA

Project Managers

Michael Lingertat, SE, Thomas Fromm, AIA, ACHA

Team Members

Joan Suchomel, AIA, ACHA, Kenneth Maruyama, AIA, Iana Gueorguieva, Hyejung Ryoo, AIA, Doojin Cho, Christopher Ciraulo, Issac Persley, Kevin O'Connor, AIA, Dan O'Riley, Nik Haak

Structural Consultant

SOM (William Baker, S.E., C.E, P.E., SECB, FASCE, FIStructE, Bradley Young, SE, PE, Robert Sinn, Arkadiusz Mazurek, CE-CA)

Mechanical Consultant

SOM: Roger Frechette, PE, LEED®AP, Ermenegildo Di Iorio, PE, Michael Ho, PE, LEED® AP, AEI – Affiliated Engineers Incorporated

Technical Coordinator

Anwar Hakim, AIA

Interiors

Jaime Velez, FIIDA, ASID, Jennifer Holstad, Dan Bell, Christine Dumich, LEED® AP

Environmental Consultant

Arvinder Dang, LEED® AP

Laboratory Consultant

RFD – Research Facilities Design

Rolex Tower

Design, 2005

Client

Ahmed Seddiqi & Sons; Dubai Contracting Company LLC

Design Partner

Peter Ruggiero, AIA

Managing Partner

George Efstathiou, FAIA

Senior Designers

Ping Jang, Jo Palma, OAA, MRAIC

Project Manager

Michael Lingertat, SE

Interior Design Principal

Jaime Velez, FIIDA, ASID

Design Team

Eric Zachrison, Jorge Soler, Christine Dumich, LEED® AP, Daniela Dan, Peng-Chien Chang, Tim Kleinert, Arthur Cantwell, Henry Lee, AIA

Structural Consultant

SOM (William Baker, S.E., C.E, P.E., SECB, FASCE, FIStructE, Robert Sinn, Andrew Murray, Rebecca Ulaszek, PE

Mechanical Consultant

Ermenegildo Di Iorio, PE, Riad Jamal, Ernesto Ocampo

Technical Coordinator

Anwar Hakim, AIA

Jinao Tower

Design, 2002

Client

Jiangsu Goldenland Real Estate Development (Group) Co., Ltd.

Design Partner

Brian Lee, FAIA

Managing Partner

Gene Schnair, FAIA

Structural Director

Mark Sarkisian, PE, SE, LEED® AP

Senior Design Architect

Patrick Daly, AIA

Project Manager

Larry Chien, AIA

Technical Director

C. Keith Boswell

Senior Technical Coordinator

Michael Fukutome, RA, LEED® AP

Associate Director, Interior Design: Tamara Dinsmore, AIA, IIDA, LEED® AP

SOM Structural Engineers

Neville Mathias, PE, SE, LEED® AP, Eric Long, PE, SE, LEED® AP, Eric Ho

Design Architects

Stephen Aldrich, RA, Michael Fukutome, RA, LEED® AP, Hana Maulana Murdan, Surjanto Surjadji, George Waters

MEP Consultant

WSP Flack + Kurtz

SOM Research

Design, 2005–ongoing

Team Members

Design Partner

William F. Baker, Partner

Alessandro Beghini, Keith Besserud, Juan Carrion, Josh Cotten, Benton Johnson, Neil Katz, Arkadiusz Mazurek, Bulent Mercan, Justin Nardone, Kat Park, David Pirnia, Alexandra Thewis, Cenk Tort

Academic Collaborators

Glaucio Paulino, Professor at UIUC

Lauren Stromberg, Graduate student at UIUC

Image Credits

pp. 21, 25: © Eduard Hueber, archphoto.com
p. 24: © Tom Arban
pp. 43, 44, 45: © Crystal CG
p. 51: © Jack Pottle
p. 54: © Chris Hoxie
pp. 56, 57: © SWIM
p. 60: © IM Chan Kyung, IMCK
pp. 71, 72, 73 (fig. 20), 74 (figs. 22, 23): © SWIM
pp. 89, 90 (fig. 20), 91: © PHOTONBASE
p. 92: © Google Earth
p. 103: © DBox
p. 106: © Tim Griffith
p. 116: © ESRI
p. 118 (fig. 2): © ESRI, (fig. 4) US Army Corps of Engineers
p. 121: © ESRI; US Indian Atlas of the United States
p. 122 (fig. 6): © Modis Satellite Image, National Oceanic and Atmospheric Administration; (fig. 8) EPA Great Lakes Atlas; (fig. 9) Google Earth
p. 124 (fig. 2): © Steven L. Pierce; (fig. 3) © Google Earth; (fig. 5) © US Dept. of Energy and Environment, Canada; (fig. 6) © ESRI; (fig. 7) © Michael Baker; (fig. 8) © Staci Evans
p. 152: © Bush-Brown, Albert. *Louis Sullivan* (New York: George Braziller, 1960). Fig. 54. Reprinted with the permission of George Braziller, Inc.
p. 153 James Laughlin, from *Poems New and Selected,* © 1938, 1945, 1959, 1965, 1969, 1970, 1978, 1982, 1983, 1984, 1985, 1986, 1987, 1988, 1989, 1990, 1992, 1994, 1995, 1996, James Laughlin. Reprinted by permission of New Directions Publishing Corporation.
p. 163 (all images): © Ian Lambot
p. 165: © 2000–2007 The New York Times Building, Renzo Piano Building Workshop in collaboration with FXFowle Architects, P.C. (New York). Photo: Michel Denancé
p. 192: © 1991 Dover Publications, *New York at the End of the 20th Century,* by James Spero Jr. and Edmund V. Gillon

All other images courtesy of SOM unless otherwise noted.

Every reasonable effort has been made to identify owners of copyright. Errors or omissions should be submitted to SOM and will be corrected in subsequent editions.

Edited by Juhani Pallasmaa

Editorial board:
Juhani Pallasmaa and Kenneth Frampton

Associate editor:
Amy Gill

Copyediting:
Eugenia Bell, Tas Skorupa

Graphic design:
SOM

Typesetting and reproductions:
Weyhing digital, Ostfildern

Production:
Ines Sutter, Hatje Cantz

Typeface:
Arial MT

Paper:
Nopacoat matt, 150 g/m^2

Printing and binding:
fgb freiburger graphische betriebe

© 2011 Hatje Cantz Verlag, Ostfildern; Skidmore, Owings & Merrill, LLP; and authors

Published by
Hatje Cantz Verlag
Zeppelinstrasse 32
73760 Ostfildern
Germany
Tel. +49 711 4405-200
Fax +49 711 4405-220
www.hatjecantz.com

Hatje Cantz books are available internationally at selected bookstores. For more information about our distribution partners, please visit our website at www.hatjecantz.com.

ISBN 978-3-7757-3197-3

Printed in Germany

Acknowledgments:
The Partners of SOM extend their thanks to the Editorial Board, Juhani Pallasmaa, the Jurors, and to all those who have contributed to the represented work. We would also like to thank Scott Duncan, Mersiha Veledar, Carolina Burdo, and the SOM New York IT department in assembling, writing, and coordinating the materials for *Journal* 7.